Distance Learning Online For Dummies®

Cheat Sheet

D0580409

(Study) Rules of the House

To keep the peace in your home as you complete your distance-learning agreement that you and your family can live with, or just use this one:

- ✔ I need you to respect my privacy while I'm studying. I appreciate you keeping voices, the TV, and other noise to a minimum.
- ✔ If I'm in the middle of studying, please don't interrupt me unless it's an emergency. If it is something you consider important, I promise to stop working and respect you by giving you my undivided attention until the situation is resolved.
- ✔ Please don't move my papers and books around. I'll try to keep clutter to a minimum around my work-space if you promise not to reorganize my stuff.
- ✔ If you need to use the computer I use for class, please don't delete files or install software without asking me first. I'll respect your work on the computer with the same courtesy.
- ✔ If I'm ignoring you or being rude to you because of my studies, be honest and tell me so.

Distance-Learning Information Sites

These Web sites list distance-learning providers around the world and supply information about the latest leaders in the distance-education arena. Use these sites to narrow down your search for the right school or training organization.

Site Name	URL
Distance-Educator	distance-educator.com
Distance Education and Training Council	www.detc.org
International Centre for Distance Learning	www-icdl.open.ac.uk/icdl
The World Lecture Hall	utexas.edu/world/lecture

Reference Tools

When you're learning at home, you may need special research tools to help with your studies. Visit these Web sites for just such assistance:

Site Name	URL
Britannica Encyclopedia	britannica.com
New Promise	www.newpromise.com
ResearchPaper	www.researchpaper.com
Roget's Thesaurus	www.thesaurus.com
Infoplease	www.infoplease.com
Merriam Webster Dictionary	www.m-w.com/dictionary

BESTSELLING
BOOK SERIES

Distance Learning Online For Dummies®

Cheat Sheet

School Contacts

Fill out the appropriate contact information for your school and keep this list near your phone.

Registrar's office

Address: _____

Phone number: _____

E-mail: _____

Instructors

Name: _____

Phone number: _____

E-mail: _____

Name: _____

Phone number: _____

E-mail: _____

Academic advisor

Name: _____

Phone number: _____

E-mail: _____

Library

Phone number: _____

Web site (URL): _____

Technical support for Web site problems

Phone number: _____

E-mail: _____

Bookstore

Phone number: _____

Web site: _____

Support staff for the distance-learning division

Name: _____

Phone number: _____

E-mail: _____

Name: _____

Phone number: _____

E-mail: _____

The school teleconferencing bridge

Phone number and code: _____

School login Web site

URL: _____

Financing

If you ever need help paying for a course, one of these resources may be able to offer just the assistance you need.

Site Name	URL
Key Education Resources	www.key.com/educate
Embark	www.embark.com
Estudent Loan	www.estudentloan.com
Lifelong Learning	www.lifelonglearning.com

IDG BOOKS WORLDWIDE

Copyright © 2000 IDG Books Worldwide, Inc. All rights reserved.

Cheat Sheet $2.95 value. Item 0763-X.

For more information about IDG Books, call 1-800-762-2974.

For Dummies®: Bestselling Book Series for Beginners

™

References for the Rest of Us!®

BESTSELLING BOOK SERIES

Are you intimidated and confused by computers? Do you find that traditional manuals are overloaded with technical details you'll never use? Do your friends and family always call you to fix simple problems on their PCs? Then the ...*For Dummies*® computer book series from IDG Books Worldwide is for you.

...*For Dummies* books are written for those frustrated computer users who know they aren't really dumb but find that PC hardware, software, and indeed the unique vocabulary of computing make them feel helpless. ...*For Dummies* books use a lighthearted approach, a down-to-earth style, and even cartoons and humorous icons to dispel computer novices' fears and build their confidence. Lighthearted but not lightweight, these books are a perfect survival guide for anyone forced to use a computer.

> *"I like my copy so much I told friends; now they bought copies."*
>
> — Irene C., Orwell, Ohio

> *"Quick, concise, nontechnical, and humorous."*
>
> — Jay A., Elburn, Illinois

> *"Thanks, I needed this book. Now I can sleep at night."*
>
> — Robin F., British Columbia, Canada

Already, millions of satisfied readers agree. They have made ...*For Dummies* books the #1 introductory level computer book series and have written asking for more. So, if you're looking for the most fun and easy way to learn about computers, look to ...*For Dummies* books to give you a helping hand.

Distance
Learning Online

FOR

DUMMIES®

Distance Learning Online FOR DUMMIES®

by Nancy Stevenson

Foreword by Andrew M. Rosenfield

IDG Books Worldwide, Inc.
An International Data Group Company

Foster City, CA ◆ Chicago, IL ◆ Indianapolis, IN ◆ New York, NY

Distance Learning Online For Dummies®

Published by
IDG Books Worldwide, Inc.
An International Data Group Company
919 E. Hillsdale Blvd.
Suite 400
Foster City, CA 94404
www.idgbooks.com (IDG Books Worldwide Web Site)
www.dummies.com (Dummies Press Web Site)

Library of Congress Control Number: 00-103648

ISBN: 0-7645-0763-X

Printed in the United States of America

10 9 8 7 6 5 4 3 2 1

1O/RS/QZ/QQ/IN

Distributed in the United States by IDG Books Worldwide, Inc.

Distributed by CDG Books Canada Inc. for Canada; by Transworld Publishers Limited in the United Kingdom; by IDG Norge Books for Norway; by IDG Sweden Books for Sweden; by IDG Books Australia Publishing Corporation Pty. Ltd. for Australia and New Zealand; by TransQuest Publishers Pte Ltd. for Singapore, Malaysia, Thailand, Indonesia, and Hong Kong; by Gotop Information Inc. for Taiwan; by ICG Muse, Inc. for Japan; by Intersoft for South Africa; by Eyrolles for France; by International Thomson Publishing for Germany, Austria and Switzerland; by Distribuidora Cuspide for Argentina; by LR International for Brazil; by Galileo Libros for Chile; by Ediciones ZETA S.C.R. Ltda. for Peru; by WS Computer Publishing Corporation, Inc., for the Philippines; by Contemporanea de Ediciones for Venezuela; by Express Computer Distributors for the Caribbean and West Indies; by Micronesia Media Distributor, Inc. for Micronesia; by Chips Computadoras S.A. de C.V. for Mexico; by Editorial Norma de Panama S.A. for Panama; by American Bookshops for Finland.

For general information on IDG Books Worldwide's books in the U.S., please call our Consumer Customer Service department at 800-762-2974. For reseller information, including discounts and premium sales, please call our Reseller Customer Service department at 800-434-3422.

For information on where to purchase IDG Books Worldwide's books outside the U.S., please contact our International Sales department at 317-572-3993 or fax 317-572-4002.

For consumer information on foreign language translations, please contact our Customer Service department at 1-800-434-3422, fax 317-572-4002, or e-mail rights@idgbooks.com.

For information on licensing foreign or domestic rights, please phone +1-650-653-7098.

For sales inquiries and special prices for bulk quantities, please contact our Order Services department at 800-434-3422 or write to the address above.

For information on using IDG Books Worldwide's books in the classroom or for ordering examination copies, please contact our Educational Sales department at 800-434-2086 or fax 317-572-4005.

For press review copies, author interviews, or other publicity information, please contact our Public Relations department at 650-653-7000 or fax 650-653-7500.

For authorization to photocopy items for corporate, personal, or educational use, please contact Copyright Clearance Center, 222 Rosewood Drive, Danvers, MA 01923, or fax 978-750-4470.

About the Author

Nancy Stevenson is an author, instructional designer, and consultant who has written over two dozen books on topics ranging from motivating employees to online search techniques and a variety of software applications. She has taught technical writing at Indiana University/Purdue University at Indianapolis, and holds a certificate in Distance Learning Design from the University of Washington.

In previous positions with software and publishing companies, Nancy has trained Fortune 500 employees in project management technology, and orchestrated the launch of successful technology training products.

ABOUT IDG BOOKS WORLDWIDE

Welcome to the world of IDG Books Worldwide.

IDG Books Worldwide, Inc., is a subsidiary of International Data Group, the world's largest publisher of computer-related information and the leading global provider of information services on information technology. IDG was founded more than 30 years ago by Patrick J. McGovern and now employs more than 9,000 people worldwide. IDG publishes more than 290 computer publications in over 75 countries. More than 90 million people read one or more IDG publications each month.

Launched in 1990, IDG Books Worldwide is today the #1 publisher of best-selling computer books in the United States. We are proud to have received eight awards from the Computer Press Association in recognition of editorial excellence and three from Computer Currents' First Annual Readers' Choice Awards. Our best-selling *...For Dummies®* series has more than 50 million copies in print with translations in 31 languages. IDG Books Worldwide, through a joint venture with IDG's Hi-Tech Beijing, became the first U.S. publisher to publish a computer book in the People's Republic of China. In record time, IDG Books Worldwide has become the first choice for millions of readers around the world who want to learn how to better manage their businesses.

Our mission is simple: Every one of our books is designed to bring extra value and skill-building instructions to the reader. Our books are written by experts who understand and care about our readers. The knowledge base of our editorial staff comes from years of experience in publishing, education, and journalism — experience we use to produce books to carry us into the new millennium. In short, we care about books, so we attract the best people. We devote special attention to details such as audience, interior design, use of icons, and illustrations. And because we use an efficient process of authoring, editing, and desktop publishing our books electronically, we can spend more time ensuring superior content and less time on the technicalities of making books.

You can count on our commitment to deliver high-quality books at competitive prices on topics you want to read about. At IDG Books Worldwide, we continue in the IDG tradition of delivering quality for more than 30 years. You'll find no better book on a subject than one from IDG Books Worldwide.

John Kilcullen
Chairman and CEO
IDG Books Worldwide, Inc.

Eighth Annual Computer Press Awards ➤1992

Ninth Annual Computer Press Awards ➤1993

Tenth Annual Computer Press Awards ➤1994

Eleventh Annual Computer Press Awards ➤1995

Dedication

To all my colleagues working in the area of distance learning, with the hope that the foundation that we are laying now will make greater educational opportunities available to all in the future.

And, as always, to Graham for his constant support.

Author's Acknowledgments

I'd like to thank my two terrific acquisitions editors, David Mayhew and Laura Moss, for their support and help on this project. Editor Shannon Ross has done a diligent and professional job of whipping my material into shape, and my capable tech editor, Camille McCue, ensured that I have been accurate and comprehensive in my coverage of distance learning.

Thanks also to several people in the forefront of distance learning who helped by taking the time to talk with me about their views, including Dr. Nicholas C. Farnes of the International Centre for Distance Learning; Derek Prior, the Director of the Communications Group at The Open University in England; and David Szatmary, Vice President of the University Extension program at the University of Washington. Thanks also to Andrew Rosenfield, the busy and dynamic leader of UNext.com and Cardean University, for taking the time to contribute the foreword for this book.

Finally, I want to express my gratitude to and affection for my friend Laurie Rozakis who helped me get this book going; Laurie, we've just got to write one together one of these days!

Publisher's Acknowledgments

We're proud of this book; please register your comments through our IDG Books Worldwide Online Registration Form located at `http://my2cents.dummies.com`.

Some of the people who helped bring this book to market include the following:

Acquisitions, Editorial, and Media Development

Project Editor: Shannon Ross

Acquisitions Editors: David Mayhew, Laura Moss

Copy Editor: Shannon Ross

Proof Editor: Teresa Artman

Technical Editor: Camille McCue

Permissions Editor: Carmen Krikorian

Editorial Manager: Constance Carlisle

Production

Project Coordinator: Amanda Foxworth

Layout and Graphics: Amy Adrian, Joe Bucki, LeAndra Johnson, Gabriele McCann, Barry Offringa, Tracy K. Oliver, Brian Torwelle, Erin Zeltner

Proofreaders: Corey Bowen, Susan Moritz, York Production Services, Inc.

Indexer: York Production Services, Inc.

General and Administrative

IDG Books Worldwide, Inc.: John Kilcullen, CEO; Bill Barry, President and COO

IDG Books Consumer Reference Group

> **Business:** Kathleen A. Welton, Vice President and Publisher; Kevin Thornton, Acquisitions Manager

> **Cooking/Gardening:** Jennifer Feldman, Associate Vice President and Publisher

> **Education/Reference:** Diane Graves Steele, Vice President and Publisher; Greg Tubach, Publishing Director

> **Lifestyles:** Kathleen Nebenhaus, Vice President and Publisher; Tracy Boggier, Managing Editor

> **Pets:** Dominique De Vito, Associate Vice President and Publisher; Tracy Boggier, Managing Editor

> **Travel:** Michael Spring, Vice President and Publisher; Suzanne Jannetta, Editorial Director; Brice Gosnell, Managing Editor

IDG Books Consumer Editorial Services: Kathleen Nebenhaus, Vice President and Publisher; Kristin A. Cocks, Editorial Director; Cindy Kitchel, Editorial Director

IDG Books Consumer Production: Debbie Stailey, Production Director

IDG Books Packaging: Marc J. Mikulich, Vice President, Brand Strategy and Research

◆

The publisher would like to give special thanks to Patrick J. McGovern, without whom this book would not have been possible.

◆

Contents at a Glance

Foreword xxiii

Introduction 1

Part I: Welcome to School on the Information Superhighway! 9
Chapter 1: Bringing Learning to a Desktop Near You 11
Chapter 2: Researching Your Options 27
Chapter 3: Picking the Perfect Provider 43

Part II: Setting Yourself Up to Learn 67
Chapter 4: A Technical Education: Hardware and Software
  for Distance Learning 69
Chapter 5: Distance Learning for People with Disabilities 91
Chapter 6: Organizing Your Life for Learning 109

Part III: Taking the Plunge 119
Chapter 7: Applying Yourself 121
Chapter 8: Orientation Express 135

Part IV: Communicating in Cyberclass 149
Chapter 9: Ready? It's the First Day of Virtual School 151
Chapter 10: Interacting in a Virtual Classroom 171
Chapter 11: Building Relationships Online 187

Part V: Virtual Study Hall 197
Chapter 12: Online Study Habits 101 199
Chapter 13: No All-Nighters: Taking Tests 215
Chapter 14: You're in Charge with Self-Paced Courses 227

Part VI: Distance Learning in the Real World 239
Chapter 15: Distance Learning at Work 241
Chapter 16: Marketing Your Distance Education 249

Distance Learning Online Directory D-1

Part VII: The Part of Tens 259

Chapter 17: Ten Schools to Watch 261
Chapter 18: Ten Tips for International Students 269
Chapter 19: Ten Ways to Get Along Online 275

Glossary...283

Index 291

Book Registration Information.....................Back of Book

Cartoons at a Glance

By Rich Tennant

"OH YEAH, AND TRY NOT TO ENTER THE WRONG PASSWORD."

page 239

"It still bothers me that I'm paying a lot of REAL dollars to a REAL university so you can get a degree in ARTIFICIAL intelligence."

page 9

"IT WAS ACTUALLY ON THE WEB ONE NIGHT THAT CAPT. AHAB CAUGHT UP WITH HIS OBSESSION."

WHALE CHAT

White? Really? Where can we meet?

page 149

"IT'S AMAZING HOW MUCH MORE SOME PEOPLE CAN GET OUT OF A PC THAN OTHERS."

page D-1

"It happened around the time George signed up for a class online. Taking tests makes him nauseous."

page 197

"Look at that craftsmanship. Notice the patina. It's already three years old. In the computer industry, that makes it a genuine antique."

page 67

WELL, THERE'S YOUR DRAWING SCANNED INTO YOUR BOOK REPORT. I JUST CAN'T FIGURE OUT WHAT THAT GREY FUZZY THING IS ALONG THE EDGE.

page 119

"Ronnie made the body from what he learned in Metal Shop, Sissy and Darlene's Home Ec. class helped them in fixing up the inside, and then all that anti-gravity stuff we picked up off the Web."

page 259

Fax: 978-546-7747
E-mail: richtennant@the5thwave.com
World Wide Web: www.the5thwave.com

Table of Contents

Foreword..*xxiii*

Introduction 1

What's in This Book? 2
Part I: Welcome to School on the Information Superhighway! 2
Part II: Setting Yourself Up to Learn 2
Part III: Taking the Plunge 2
Part IV: Communicating in Cyberclass 2
Part V: Virtual Study Hall 3
Part VI: Distance Learning in the Real World 3
Distance Learning Online Directory 3
Part VII: The Part of Tens 3
Glossary 4
How to Use This Book 4
Never Assume? 5
Conventions Used in This Book 6
Icons Used in This Book 6
Getting to Work on Your Online Education! 7

Part I: Welcome to School on the
Information Superhighway! 9

Chapter 1: Bringing Learning to a Desktop Near You 11

Who's Who in Online Distance Learning 12
Earning your degree 12
Honing your technical skills 14
Getting certified 14
Just for fun 16
Taking a Tour of Distance Learning 17
Technology: Making it all possible 17
Student-driven learning 19
Tools for communicating 19
Is Distance Learning for You? 21
How much time can you spend? 21
How long will this be going on? 22
Will you miss the four walls? 23
Are you a self-directed learner? 23

Chapter 2: Researching Your Options 27

   Finding Information About Distance-Learning Programs .27

      Getting a higher education online 27

      Considering online training companies and technical schools 31

   Doing Your Research 36

      Consulting directories of distance-learning providers 36

      Searching for schools online 37

      Getting the scoop from school sites 40

      Ordering catalogs 41

Chapter 3: Picking the Perfect Provider 43

   Five Questions to Consider 43

      What will it cost? 44

      How long will it take and when can I start? 44

      Do they have the courses I need? 46

      Are their courses any good? 47

      Do they have their distance-learning act together? 47

   Assessing Accreditation 49

      What is accreditation? 50

      Who are these mysterious accreditors? 51

      How can accreditation help me? 53

      Do you need credit for what you do? 54

   Avoiding Fraud 55

      When is a university not a university? 55

      Appraising Joe's Online Training Co. 56

      Checking professional credentials: Who's who? 56

   Setting a Budget 57

      How much will the tuition be? 57

      Application and registration fees 58

      What about all the extras? 59

   Letting Somebody Else Foot the Bill 60

      Will my employer help out? 60

      Should I get a loan? 61

      What about a scholarship or grant? 63

      Is my education tax-deductible? 65

Part II: Setting Yourself Up to Learn 67

**Chapter 4: A Technical Education: Hardware
and Software for Distance Learning** 69

   Back-to-School Shopping! 69

      Do you have the right computer? 70

      Getting all the right Internet connections .73

      Concerning plug-ins, players, and other online utilities 76

      Which software applications will you need? 78

Getting Online 80
    Hooking up with an Internet provider 81
    Who's providing Internet access? 81
    What does it cost? 82
    Browsing for the right browser 83
    The mail game: Setting up for e-mail 85
Do You Need More Stuff? (VCR, Fax, Scanners) 85
Who You Gonna Call? Tech Support for the Distance Learner 87

Chapter 5: Distance Learning for People with Disabilities **91**
Assessing Accessibility 91
Software That Makes It Possible 93
    Setting up Windows' accessibility features 93
    Adjusting the display 97
    Getting your computer to recognize your voice 98
    Using voice output systems 100
    Making print LARGER 101
Hardware to Help 102
    Keyboarding and printing made easy 102
    Tame your mouse 103
    Making a phone call 104
    Magnifying printed text 105
How Your School Can Help 106

Chapter 6: Organizing Your Life for Learning **109**
A Room of One's Own 109
    Finding a place to learn 110
    Establishing a phone monopoly 110
    Seeing and hearing your classes 111
Family Ties: Making Your Learning Fit Your Life 112
    Finding time for it all 113
    Getting support from those you love 113
    Coping with change 114
Occupational Hazards 115
    It's all in the wrist 116
    Avoiding eye strain 116
    I have this little pain in my back 117

Part III: Taking the Plunge *119*

Chapter 7: Applying Yourself **121**
Following the Paper Trail 121
    Taking standardized entrance tests 122
    Accounting for prior education 124
    Do you have any references? 126
    Completing the application form 126

Writing the application essay (Or "How
    I Spent My Summer . . .") 128
Registration, or What Fresh Hell Is This? 129
    Choose your courses and be ready with alternates 129
    The registration game: Adding, dropping, changing 132
Paying the Piper 133
    Deciphering school fees 133
    Paying online: Is it safe? 134
    The customer is always right: Getting refunds 134

Chapter 8: Orientation Express **135**
Getting in Your Face: When It's Not All Online 135
    Getting oriented 136
    Small group get-togethers 136
Getting Your Supplies Together 137
    Information, please 138
    Buying your textbooks 138
    Using special software 141
    Assembling your school contacts 143
    A trip to the online office-supply store 144
At Your Service 145
    Using the library 145
    Taking advantage of student deals 146
    Getting guidance 147

Part IV: Communicating in Cyberclass *149*

Chapter 9: Ready? It's the First Day of Virtual School **151**
Setting Your Expectations 151
College Bound 152
    Logging on 152
    Viewing the class syllabus 155
    Raising Your Hand 156
    Finding the lecture hall 160
    Getting and posting assignments 161
    Looking for your instructor 162
Test Driving a Class 162
    Getting started 163
    Viewing your course material 165
    Getting help and resources 168
    Checking your progress 169

Chapter 10: Interacting in a Virtual Classroom 171

Putting It into Words 171
E-mailing 101 172
Airing your ideas in discussion groups .174
Chatting away in chat rooms 176
You're the Star: Videoconferencing 177
Attending videoconferences 178
Accessing conferences online using desktop
videoconferencing 179
Speaking to the group 181
Videoconferencing etiquette 181
Interacting with Instructors and Advisors 182
Asking questions 182
Getting and giving feedback 183
Planning your long-range education with an advisor 183

Chapter 11: Building Relationships Online .187

Writing Your Way to Success 187
Improving your writing skills 188
Becoming a word mechanic 188
Getting some style 189
Developing a process for writing 190
Finding the Right Approach to Communication 191
Building a Learning Community 193
Becoming a better online citizen 194
Resolving conflict 195
Working with groups online 195

Part V: Virtual Study Hall *197*

Chapter 12: Online Study Habits 101 199

It's a Matter of Time 199
Winning the battle of you versus time 200
Taking it one week at a time 201
"My computer ate my homework" 202
Motivating Yourself 203
Online Research: Your Best Friend 204
Searching for answers 205
Navigating Web waters 208
Downloading files 209
Unzipping: It's a must! 209
Dealing with file formats 213

Chapter 13: No All-Nighters: Taking Tests 215

How Tests Fit into Distance Learning 215
Testing, Testing, 1-2-3 216
What types of tests can I expect? 216
How do online tests get graded? 218
When an online test goes offline: proctored exams 219
Making the Grade 220
Preparing for success 221
Fool-proof test-taking techniques 222
If at first you don't succeed 225

Chapter 14: You're in Charge with Self-Paced Courses 227

Taking a Peek inside Self-Paced Education 227
Getting around 229
Testing your own mettle 231
Talking heads and other multimedia events 234
How do you get to Broadway? Practice, practice, practice! 236
Getting Help with Self-Service Learning 237

Part VI: Distance Learning in the Real World 239

Chapter 15: Distance Learning at Work 241

Exploring the Training Your Employer Provides 241
Making use of your training department 242
Learning at your service: Military distance education 244
Partnering with educational providers 245
Learning in a Cubicle 246
Buddy Up! Studying with a Workgroup 247

Chapter 16: Marketing Your Distance Education 249

Using Your School's Resources to Land a Job 250
Getting Your Records Straight 252
Obtaining transcripts, certificates, and degrees 253
What do you have to recommend you? 254
Tooting Your Distance-Education Horn 254
Spiffing up your resume 254
Publicizing your credentials 256

Distance Learning Online Directory D-1

Part VII: The Part of Tens 259

Chapter 17: Ten Schools to Watch 261

University of California at Berkeley 262
University of Wisconsin 262
Rochester Institute of Technology 263
Charles Sturt University 264
Jones International University 264
UNext/Cardean University 265
University of Washington 266
Indira Gandhi National Open University 266
Penn State 267
University of South Africa 268

Chapter 18: Ten Tips for International Students 269

Watch Your Language 269
Observe Cultural Differences 270
Plan for and Budget an In-Person Visit 271
Find Out What Distance Learning Means Overseas 271
Make Allowances for Time Differences 271
Accreditation Is Not Always Equal 272
Prerequisites Aren't All Alike 272
Being a Student Doesn't Make You a Citizen 273
Look into Credit Transferability 273
Take Advantage of the Experience 274

Chapter 19: Ten Ways to Get Along Online 275

Don't Flame 275
Don't Spam 276
Respect Others' Time 276
Think Before You "Speak" 277
Don't Monopolize the Airwaves 277
Watch Abbreviations 277
Plagiarism: The Dark Side of Cut-and-Paste 278
Don't Cheat 279
Make What You Write Easy to Read 280
Be Patient 281

Glossary 283

Index 291

Book Registration Information ....Back of Book

Foreword

Distance learning makes it now possible to take a course on virtually any subject "anytime and anywhere," giving people all over the world access to educational opportunities literally unimaginable only five years ago. No longer is access to quality education a function of age, location, and financial circumstance.

This revolution in education is both fortunate and fortuitous. Never before has the stock of knowledge and ideas moved so swiftly. Once (maybe only a generation ago) people went to school before they went to work and acquired, in doing so, what many of them viewed as a "lifetime supply" of education. They then drew down on that supply of knowledge throughout their working life and retirement. They acted as though they could "fill up" with education during the early adult years and have enough formal knowledge to coast through life.

Today, this idea is correctly seen as preposterous. No one can hope to acquire all of the knowledge needed for life by, say, their mid-20s, and no one can expect to lead a productive and complete life in a changing and dynamic world drawing solely on the stock of knowledge acquired "in school." To be an informed and productive citizen, one must make a constant commitment to learning. We live in a time of *lifelong* learning.

But beware: Distance learning involves commitment and effort. First, a learner has the obligation to find the right school, program, and course (and this book can help). Second, distance learning — like all learning — works only by doing, not by watching. That is, there is no technology or system (delivered via distance or in person) that causes learning to occur passively or without effort. The programs discussed in this book are not like watching television even if, in some cases, parts of the courses involve video or lecture. People cannot and do not learn just by being told; they learn by doing something themselves. In few other activities is the old adage "you get out what you put in" more appropriate or more accurate.

Distance learning has a complex history. At the beginning of the 20th century, many correspondence courses were available and hundreds of thousands of people in the United States were enrolled in them. Some of the greatest institutions of higher education, The University of Chicago for example, were intensively active in these programs. By the end of the century, little quality distance learning was available. What happened then, and why is distance learning back today?

The widespread availability of traditional facilities-based education, which exploded in the United States in the 20th century, drove out most of the distance-learning programs. This because there is immense power in physically congregating learners. For those who have the time, flexibility, and resources to devote themselves to learning on a full-time basis, there is no doubt that congregated facilities-based learning is the best form of education. The power of people to learn when interacting with one another — when discussing, questioning, debating, and the like — is very great.

The renaissance of distance learning is the result of recent and profound technological change. The Internet finally permits a form of distance learning that is grounded in activity and community. Because the Internet (unlike prior technologies such as television, CD-ROM, video disk, and so on) is an active, community-based medium, learners at a distance can work together (synchronously and across time) and can learn by doing, not by watching.

Many of the programs discussed in this book could not be provided without the new technology of the Internet. The effective programs make students "do" and provide a student-to-student and mentored community that supports learning. By combining anytime anywhere convenience, affordability, and the key features of action and communal learning, distance learning is now able to deliver on its promise.

Welcome to the age of lifelong learning and a world in which effective and active learning opportunities abound.

Andrew M. Rosenfield

Founder and CEO, UNext.com

Introduction

• •

*G*etting an education in which the majority or all of your studies take place at a location that is remote from your school and instructor is called *distance learning*. (It's also called remote learning, open learning, distance education, and a variety of other things.) This approach to education isn't the new kid on the block: It has been around for quite a while — ever since the mid-1800s, in fact, when U.S. colleges began to offer correspondence courses to rural farmers through land-grant programs. At the same time, other countries developed their own distance-learning models.

Today, thanks to the advent of the Internet, millions of people get degrees without ever setting foot in a classroom. This Web-based version of distance learning uses the Internet to distribute course materials; facilitate student and instructor interaction through e-mail, discussion groups, and online chats; and provide multimedia tutorials that a student can complete at his or her own pace (often referred to as *self-paced* tutorials). In addition to the Web component, many distance-learning courses today still use printed materials such as textbooks, as well as video- and audiotaped lectures, technologies such as teleconferencing and videoconferencing, and even the occasional face-to-face meeting. However, at the heart of much of the most cutting-edge distance learning today is an online component. That's why this book focuses on courses that utilize the Internet in a significant and effective way.

The fact that you're reading this book means that you're probably thinking about going back to school. Perhaps you need to take a single class to learn a technical skill for your job. Or you may be even more ambitious; you may be considering getting an undergraduate or even graduate college degree. You've heard the buzz about how technology is making studying from your own home over the Internet as easy as finding sand on a beach.

With all that technology offers, learning online is definitely getting easier, but making the right choices and getting the education you want can still be very confusing. How do you figure out what school is best for you? How do you find the time to fit studying into your busy life? And how do you ask a question when nobody's in the room with you?

That's where this book comes in. With a focus on online distance learning, I've compiled the kind of information and guidance that can save you hours of research and the frustration of making the wrong distance-learning choice. This isn't a directory of distance-learning schools (plenty of those are already out there); rather, this is a guide to making wise choices and being successful when you start down the distance-learning path.

What's in This Book?

This book brings together all the information you need to make the distance-learning choice, find the right school, and be a successful online student. I break this information into several parts.

Part I: Welcome to School on the Information Superhighway!

Part I gives you a glimpse of some of the exciting educational opportunities that technology is making available over the Internet. This is where you begin to analyze your educational needs, get guidance on where to start your research to find just the right school for you, and set a budget for your distance learning.

Part II: Setting Yourself Up to Learn

Just as you can't enter the Indy 500 if you don't have a car, you have to be sure you have the tools to succeed before signing up for an online class. Part II looks at the hardware, software, and workspace needs of the distance-learning student, including special tools to help students with disabilities. This part also includes advice and techniques for learning online while minimizing the disruption to your personal life and family.

Part III: Taking the Plunge

Ready to set foot on the paper trail of applications, registration forms, and transcripts? Part III takes you through the actual process of applying to a school and undergoing (and surviving!) the typical registration and orientation process. This part also includes guidance on buying textbooks and supplies to get you ready for the first day of class. You can even pick up some advice on how to make use of your school's resources, such as library and counseling services.

Part IV: Communicating in Cyberclass

A big factor for success in distance learning is how well you communicate with others in a virtual classroom. Part IV is the place for finding out what goes on in a distance-learning environment, and how to get along with and learn from others you meet there. Here you explore chatting, participating in discussions on virtual bulletin boards, and e-mailing, as well as the communication techniques that make interaction in your online class pleasant and productive.

Part V: Virtual Study Hall

Remember the joys of late-night study sessions? This part is where you get reacquainted with studying and preparing for tests, distance-learning style. See which study habits make you successful in a distance-learning environment, get advice about how to take tests online, and find out how to make the grade in self-paced online classes.

Part VI: Distance Learning in the Real World

Not all distance learning is taking place through universities and training companies. You may find that your own company offers opportunities to learn online from within its own four walls. This part explains how distance learning is exploding into the workplace, and also shows you how to leverage your online educational credentials back at the office to advance your own career.

Distance Learning Online Directory

This useful directory is a grab bag of distance-learning aids, from listings of schools, training providers, and online study tools to contact information for college exam providers and Web sites and publications about distance learning. Here's where you can look up places to buy textbooks, download shareware, and even get more information about assistive technology for overcoming disabilities.

Part VII: The Part of Tens

You could call this the "Part of Three Sets of Ten"! You get three different top-ten lists here, including ten schools to watch for distance learning, ten tips for international distance-learning students, and ten ways to mind your Ps and Qs when learning online.

Glossary

Now, don't think that I'm including a glossary here because this book is full of obscure jargon or ten-dollar words. Throughout the book, I provide information in straightforward terms, defining any new terms you have to know as they come up. But as you explore the great big world of distance learning, you may come across a term or two that puzzles you. That's when the easy-to-understand and easy-to-find definitions in this glossary will come in handy.

How to Use This Book

You don't have the same questions about distance learning as your Aunt Bertha or your nephew Joe. That's why this book is designed so you can jump in at any point and read just the information that's useful to you. Remember, you don't get a degree in a day, so this book should remain a useful companion to you through the weeks, months, or even years of your distance-learning experience. Feel free to jump forward and backward as the need arises!

Here are a couple of suggestions to help you find what you need:

- ✔ **If you have no idea which school you want to attend (and maybe you're even afraid of being fleeced by disreputable online diploma mills):** Start with Chapter 2 and Chapter 3, where you get guidance on researching schools and making that all-important choice of an alma mater. You may also want to read through Chapter 7 to find out how reputable schools deal with things like paying for classes online and issuing refunds if you should withdraw. Finally, look at Chapter 17 and the Online Directory section to see profiles of ten schools that are leading the way in distance education today.

- ✔ **If you know what school you want to take courses from and want to get ready for your first distance-learning class:** Wander over to Chapters 4, 5, and 6 to set up your hardware, software, and workspace layout. Then take a look at Chapter 9 to get an idea of what an online classroom looks and feels like.

- ✔ **If you are concerned about getting all the paperwork done to get accepted for a program:** Mosey on over to Chapters 7 and 8 to get the scoop on applications, registration, paying course fees, and other frankly-boring-but-necessary steps to getting accepted by your school of choice.

✔ **If you're starting classes right away:** Head over to Chapters 12 and 13 to polish your study habits and test-taking skills. Crack open Chapter 14 if you are taking self-paced courses to help you take control of your own learning style. If you're already thinking of how to market your education when you complete your courses, take a peek at Chapter 16.

✔ **If you're considering studying at a school outside of your own country:** Be sure to read through Chapter 18, which offers ten tips for international students. In Chapter 7, you can also find information on taking language-proficiency tests that many schools require of foreign students. And, in Chapters 10 and 11, you can get advice for dealing with language barriers in communicating with classmates and instructors.

Never Assume?

Okay, I have made a few assumptions about you in writing this book:

✔ I assume that your time is valuable. That's why I wrote this book, which gives you the benefit of my hundreds of hours of research on what's available in distance learning today and offers advice from my own distance-learning experiences to keep you from making costly mistakes.

✔ I assume that you're familiar with the basic operations of a computer on some platform (Mac or PC, with any operating system such as Windows, Windows NT, or Linux, for example). Because today's distance learners are using a wide variety of computer software, I don't go into a great deal of how-to-run-a-computer specifics. What I do provide is advice about functioning in the distance-learning classroom environment no matter what operating system you have, and the specifics of using some valuable tools to play media files, handle file formats, and hold synchronous meetings.

✔ I assume that you have an Internet provider, a browser, and an e-mail program and that you understand the basics of how to use each. I don't provide instruction about how to get yourself online, because I think that, if you're considering taking a course online, you're probably somewhat comfortable with the basics of getting around the Internet. If you think you could use a Web tutorial, take a look at *The Internet For Dummies* (published by IDG Books Worldwide), by John R. Levine, Carol Baroudi, and Margaret Levine Young.

✔ Finally, I assume that you are interested in a distance-learning experience that uses the Internet as a key component (rather than a primarily mail-order or audiotape course).

Conventions Used in This Book

This book focuses on education services provided over the World Wide Web. You'll encounter Web-site addresses, known as URLs (Uniform Resource Locators), so that you can find the exact location you need. When I refer to Web sites, I highlight the URL like this:

`www.distance-educator.com`

If the URL appears within a paragraph, it looks like this: `www.idgbooks.com`.

These conventions should help you tell the difference between the name of a Web business, such as TIME.com, and a Web address, such as `www.time.com`.

Note that none of the preceding examples include the `http://` that begins all Web addresses; I omit this prefix because modern browsers don't require you to enter that portion when typing an address.

Icons Used in This Book

In our visual world, what would a book be without little pictures scattered here, there, and everywhere? This book uses these little pictures, called *icons,* to help direct you to special information that provides an extra insight or bit of advice. These icons are

When you see this icon, prepare to get advice about special techniques or approaches to your distance-learning experience that can help you save time, cut costs, or excel at your studies.

This icon is the red alert feature of this book. When you see it, you can be sure I'm cautioning you about a potentially dangerous result, and advising you on how to avoid it.

Just like every other subject in the world, distance learning comes with its own specialized jargon and unrecognizable abbreviations. The definitions attached to these icons are like secret-decoder rings for the uninitiated: Read them to find out what all those distance-learning experts are really talking about.

This icon points to particularly important nuggets of information that are worth a reminder. Anytime you're in need of my own brand of distance-learning insight, or if you're just bored on a Saturday night, you can scan these words of wisdom for a mini refresher course.

Getting to Work on Your Online Education!

Let me reassure you, learning online isn't hard (although, like any worthwhile endeavor, it takes hard work). What can be confusing is finding your way through the plethora of distance-learning providers, navigating the sometimes confusing application and registration processes, and understanding the protocol for how to behave in your online classroom. These are exactly the issues this book endeavors to make simple for you. So relax, think about the real difference additional education can make in your career, your salary, and your personal satisfaction, and dive in!

Part I

Welcome to School on the Information Superhighway!

The 5th Wave   By Rich Tennant

"It still bothers me that I'm paying a lot of REAL dollars to a REAL university so you can get a degree in ARTIFICIAL intelligence."

In this part . . .

When you were a kid, you may have gone to a school on Main Street or Maple Avenue. Perhaps your mom or dad dropped you off, or maybe you hopped on a bus on the corner of your street. When you arrived, your teachers showed you where your classes were.

Well, today your school is not on Maple or Main, it's somewhere on the Information Superhighway called the Internet. And if you want to know how to get there, just think of this part as your personal car pool. This is where you get an overview of what distance learning is, who's doing it, and whether it's the right approach to meeting your educational goals. You also get a roadmap for finding and qualifying potential education providers, and advice on matching their offerings with your needs.

Chapter 1

Bringing Learning to a Desktop Near You

● ●

In This Chapter

▶ Looking at the options available in distance learning today

▶ Exploring the technologies that make distance learning possible

▶ Understanding how people learn online

▶ Analyzing how you fit into a distance-learning setting

● ●

Distance learning is becoming a real buzzword today, right up there with 24/7 and e-commerce. You see it in news stories, you hear about it in the hallway outside your Human Resources department, and you spot ads for study-from-home MBA programs in airline magazines. But just what is this thing called distance learning? Before you take the plunge and sign up for a class, make sure that you understand what distance learning is and what's required of you as a student in a virtual classroom.

Distance learning is simply the process of getting an education when your school and instructor are remote from you. Often, this form of learning involves one or more technologies such as the Internet, videotapes, faxing, videoconferencing, or teleconferencing (but it doesn't have to; in fact, the first distance-learning courses in the 1800s were simply correspondence courses). This book focuses on distance learning that happens primarily online, often using other technologies in addition to computers, such as video or faxing.

Consider this chapter as your introduction to the virtual campus. It provides an overview of who the players are, what technologies are being used (or are waiting in the wings), and just what goes on in an online course. In addition, it provides some guidance about how well you might do in a distance-learning environment, based on your learning style and the time you can devote to your education.

Who's Who in Online Distance Learning

Sometimes it seems as though there are practically as many names for distance learning as there are distance-learning courses. You may hear people refer to *distance education, remote learning, open education, Web-based learning,* and *computer-mediated distance education.* It all comes down to the same thing: You're in one place, and your school is in another.

Whatever you call it, what's going on in distance learning today is similar to what went on in the early days of computing. In other words, things are hopping! People are making all kinds of inroads to using the Internet in education, many new players are popping up, and the technology is changing faster than a politician's stand on issues the day after he's elected.

The perception of courses taken remotely is also improving. Gone are the days of treating graduates with mail-order degrees like second-class citizens; in fact, many employers now view successful distance learners as more self-sufficient than their campus-bound counterparts, due to the less-structured class environment they must navigate.

So where can you go to learn online? A wealth of choices awaits you; in fact, the rush by schools to jump on the online distance-learning bandwagon is akin to a Keystone Cops chase scene. The players in this chase include

- ✔ Ivy-league bastions like Harvard and Yale
- ✔ Mom-and-pop start-up operations
- ✔ Fraudulent diploma mills
- ✔ Several major book publishers
- ✔ Booksellers like `fatbrain.com`
- ✔ Community and junior colleges
- ✔ Training organizations specializing in job-skills training
- ✔ Technical schools
- ✔ Professional associations offering certificates that can lead to licensing

To help you get a handle on all this activity, what follows is an overview of what these education providers have to offer the millions of adults taking distance-learning courses today. For detailed information about what's available in distance learning and how to research various providers, see Chapter 2.

Earning your degree

In the arena of college-level distance learning, which is the focus of much of this book, most major universities around the world have joined the race. In fact, the U.S. Department of Education calculates that the growth of distance learning at the university level measured over 70 percent between 1997 and 1998.

Through distance learning, adult learners are studying with educational organizations located nearby or around the world. One fact that makes international learning possible is that most of the distance-learning programs available today are offered in English, although that fact may change as more and more countries advance their technology, make Internet access less expensive, and put their own stamp on this global educational revolution.

Certain countries have taken a lead:

- England has a strong distance-learning infrastructure through its Open University program, which started back in the 1970s. Though it still bases many courses in TV, video, and audio technologies, to a great extent this national organization is a model for bringing distance learning to the masses. The University of London, whose External Programme home page (www.lon.ac.uk/external) appears in Figure 1-1, is highly respected in the field.

- Australia is another country that has given a great deal of attention to distance learning, perhaps in large measure because of a population that is widely distributed geographically. In a country with rugged terrain and great distances between major cities, the ability to study from remote locations becomes invaluable.

- South Africa, through the University of South Africa, has one of the largest distance-learning operations in the world.

Figure 1-1:
The University of London has an excellent reputation among distance-learning organizations.

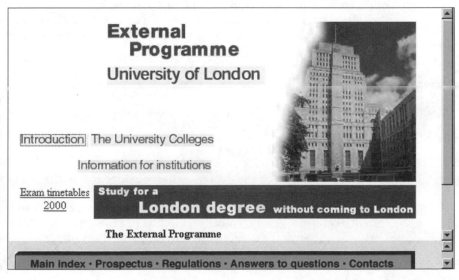

✔ Many of Canada's universities — including Athabasca University and Université du Quebec's Tele-université (the only French-language university in North America) — are strongly focused on distance education.

✔ In the United States, most major colleges (798 in 1999, according to one survey) are involved in distance learning to some extent. Schools such as Penn State, the University of Wisconsin, and the New York Institute of Technology have growing reputations in this area. In some states, such as California, consortia have emerged to link groups of community colleges or state-college campuses into one large online-course clearinghouse. The United States is also home to Jones International University, the first completely virtual university to be recognized by a regional accreditation agency. The only campus this school has is in cyberspace.

Although this book focuses to a great extent on schools in English-speaking countries, almost every country around the globe with a higher-education infrastructure is beginning to speak the language of distance learning.

For a detailed listing of over 200 schools involved in distance learning, take a look at *The Unofficial Guide to Distance Learning* by Shannon Turlington, published by IDG Books Worldwide.

Honing your technical skills

In addition to colleges and universities, many other organizations also offer distance-learning courses online. As you might expect, much of the training available direct to your home computer focuses on computer skills. But many other courses are also available online, including training in such areas as on-the-job safety, human resource topics such as sexual harassment, management skills such as team building, and even the use of specific medical or other equipment.

Online training sites that offer a variety of courses, such as click2learn.com (shown in Figure 1-2), are often called *learning portals* or *learning hubs*.

Getting certified

If you don't want to go the degree route, consider one of the many programs available online through which you can earn a certificate on completion. These programs provide a nice career credential in much less time than a formal degree program (typically 6 months or so, rather than 3 to 6 years). Certificate programs are often offered through extension divisions of colleges, such as the University of Washington's UW Extension, whose Web site (`www.extension.washington.edu/extinfo/certprog.asp`) appears in Figure 1-3.

Figure 1-2:
The e-learning portal at www.click2learn.com offers a variety of professional and technical training.

Don't confuse certification training with certificate programs. *Certification training* prepares you to take a certification exam from a company like Microsoft but, in and of itself, grants no credential. A *certificate* is a credential that a college grants when you complete a course of study.

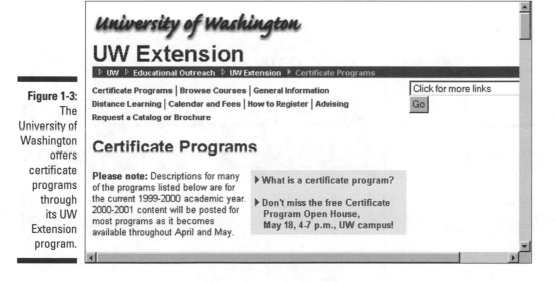

Figure 1-3:
The University of Washington offers certificate programs through its UW Extension program.

Just for fun

Though not the true focus of this book, I can't resist letting you know about some of the classes out there that teach you about fun topics like handwriting analysis and genealogy. Courses on everything from photography to foreign languages, and astrology to oil painting are available online. These courses are typically self-paced and often resemble a book or article posted online. Quite a few of these courses are free or low cost. The following is a tiny sample to give you an idea of the range of topics and prices available:

- ✔ Virtual University (www.vu.org) charges $15 per class term, allowing you to take up to three classes during each term. Courses, as shown in Figure 1-4, break down into four categories: Internet; Writing and the Arts; Mind, Body and Soul; and Explore Your World.

- ✔ FirstFlight (www.firstflight.com) is a virtual flight school with self-paced courses on topics such as preflight checklists (but the site does warn you that this is not a substitute for formal pilot training!).

- ✔ Dear Myrtle (www.dearmyrtle.com/lessons.htm) is a service hosted by AOL that offers free lessons in genealogy, including topics such as the one I reviewed, *Birth Records as Primary Evidence*.

- ✔ MetaStudies University (www.metastudies.com) specializes in the metaphysical. For example, you can take its 30-lesson course in astrology for a fee of $15 per lesson or $400 for all 30. These are self-paced courses; you submit assignments which the MetaStudies staff reviews and returns to you.

Figure 1-4:
Virtual University offers classes on anything from self-awareness to writing a romance novel.

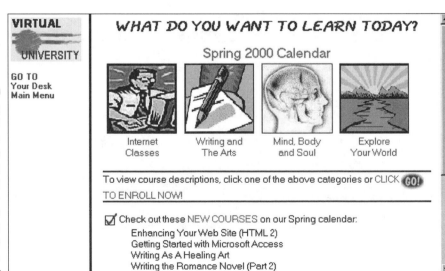

Taking a Tour of Distance Learning

Even when you're smack in the middle of the distance-learning experience, describing your virtual classroom to others can sometimes be difficult. It has no walls and no blackboard or chalk. You can think of the virtual-class experience as being more like a typical workday in an office: You spend some time at your desk, some time online, an hour going to a room and meeting with people, a few minutes here and there on the phone, and some time reading reports or manuals. A virtual classroom shares that mix of various communications technologies. And just as at the office, you make some decisions about what you do and when you do it, while other choices are made for you.

Thinking of a distance-learning class in this way, rather than as a traditional classroom with four walls and an instructor standing at the front of the room, will better prepare you for the experience.

Technology: Making it all possible

Advances in technology have been largely responsible for the recent boom in online distance learning. The computer and Internet have fathered new ways of communicating, as well as storing and disseminating information. Advances in multimedia have also contributed, with high-quality videoconferencing and the use of audio and graphics files and streaming video becoming more commonplace.

In addition, advances that have made high-speed access to the Internet possible have opened the door to new approaches to communication. One form of online interaction, called *synchronous communication,* enables people to communicate in real time as in a chat room; *asynchronous communication,* such as e-mail, typically includes a time gap between sending out a communication and getting a response. Software products such as NetMeeting from Microsoft, whose home page (www.microsoft.com/windows/netmeeting) appears in Figure 1-5, enable several people to meet, communicate through text or audio, and even view video images of each other over the Internet.

Some up-and-coming technologies allow sophisticated synchronous learning, with the instructor observing students' computer screens and making comments on their work as they do an exercise. Students view a video image of the instructor, who gives a lecture or simply guides them through a procedure. This technology creates an environment that's very close to the more traditional classroom, but with added features, such as the ability of each student to ask a question of the teacher privately while class is going on.

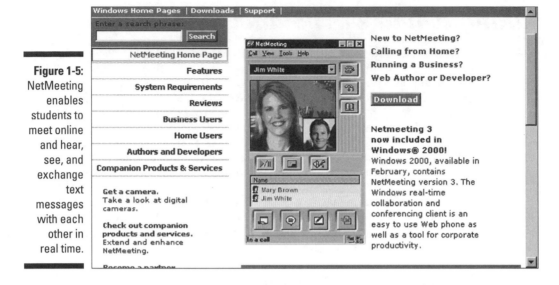

Figure 1-5:
NetMeeting
enables
students to
meet online
and hear,
see, and
exchange
text
messages
with each
other in
real time.

Other technologies that have been around a little longer also add to the richness of the link between remote students and instructors, including

- ✔ Faxing
- ✔ Scanning
- ✔ Teleconferencing
- ✔ Computer-based training via CD-ROM
- ✔ Video and audiotapes

Does distance learning work? Ask Ben Franklin

As with any new way of doing things, some debate exists about the quality of learning online, and many bemoan the loss of face-to-face interaction it involves. These arguments sound strangely familiar — much the same as those common when telephones first appeared in homes and people mourned the death of social interaction.

In reality, studies have shown that learning at a distance is every bit as effective as learning in

person. Researchers find no significant difference between the quality of education you get by dragging yourself to class and the one you get sitting before your computer in your own home.

Want to convince your boss that distance learning works? Mention the fact that both Benjamin Franklin and the two fellas that started Ben & Jerry's ice cream company took distance learning in the form of mail-order courses. And they didn't do so badly for themselves, did they?

See Chapter 4 for more information about the evolving role of the computer in distance learning.

Student-driven learning

One key difference between face-to-face learning and distance learning is the shift in the roles of instructors and students. In an online learning environment, the instructor-as-lecturer model goes away to a great extent. Instead, the instructor disseminates information, facilitates discussion among students, and coaches them on their progress in the course.

This shift in educational theory actually mirrors changes that are going on in the on-campus classroom. Educators are trying many new ways of interacting with students that go beyond the traditional stand-in-front-of-the-class-and-lecture model, including small-group interaction, role playing, and problem solving. Teachers often drive, or are at least involved in, the design of your online course materials, taking their jobs into the realm of both multimedia instructional design and Web design.

As a result of this new instructor role, the distance-learning student's role is different, as well. Students must take more control of their educational experience online. They have to decide when to read the information that their instructors post, when to submit an assignment, and how often to participate in an online discussion. In distance education, you have no class to attend twice a week between 4:15 and 5:30, and nobody stands in the front of the classroom directing your learning. Rather, you must set your own schedule and participate at a level you deem appropriate.

Tools for communicating

One method of participation that distance-learning courses often use is a *discussion board*, like the one shown in Figure 1-6. In this model, someone posts an assignment or comment, and other students are responsible for reading that posting and responding. People come and go, reading and posting messages at times that are most convenient for them.

In place of lectures, instructors usually post a lesson for the week, such as the one shown in Figure 1-7. These lessons often include links to relevant Web sites, as well as information about associated reading assignments, either from a textbook or material provided to students in some other format. Some schools also send out additional materials via regular mail, such as videotapes or even lab materials for a science course. In some countries, course content is also delivered on TV.

Participants may use synchronous communication methods — such as exchanging messages in chat rooms, teleconferencing, or videoconferencing — to interact. In addition, many distance-learning programs require an in-person meeting of the class at least once during the semester. Some institutions that can take advantage of regional study centers may offer a bit more frequent in-person contact along with online lessons. For more about how to communicate in an online setting, see Chapter 10.

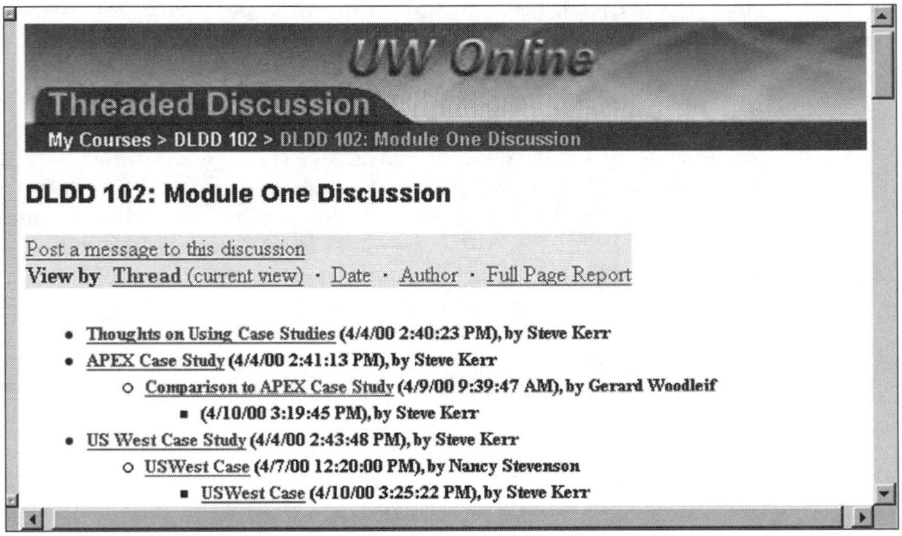

Figure 1-6: This discussion area is for a class leading to a certificate in, of all things, distance-learning design.

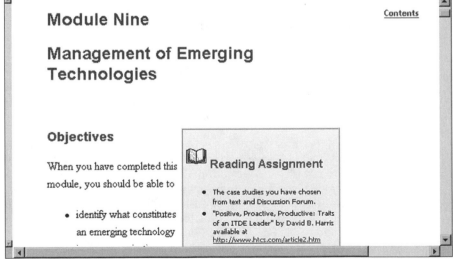

Figure 1-7: Instructors of this course post lectures online, with associated reading assignments available through textbooks or downloadable materials.

Is Distance Learning for You?

Educators have studied what makes a good distance learner, and the results may surprise you:

- ✔ In many cases, people who thrive in face-to-face learning do less well online. People who always raise their hands in class find that the more equal give-and-take required of the entire online class deprives them of the extra attention they've become used to.

- ✔ People who never raise their hands in a four-walled classroom become more assertive and participate more fully when faced with a distance-learning model.

- ✔ Students who think that they'll spend less time taking an online class than a traditional one quite often find that they're mistaken; although they save time by not sitting in a classroom, the demands of controlling one's own learning environment can be great.

After you find out as much as you can about the demands and rewards of distance learning, it's up to you to analyze your own ability to manage your time, make a firm commitment, deal with the isolation of working on your own, and direct your own learning. Only you can decide whether you can be a successful distance learner.

How much time can you spend?

Those taking and administering distance-learning courses estimate that a typical student must spend between 12 and 16 hours a week to handle the reading, online interaction, and communications involved in a typical three-credit college course taken online. In most cases, you can expect to check into your class site almost every day to keep up with messages others have posted. Because you get your information not in the form of a lecture, but rather through reading material or viewing video, online courses typically involve more reading and viewing time than face-to-face classes do.

As an online student, you can expect to encounter the following types of activities in a typical week:

- ✔ Read the instructor's lecture for the week.

- ✔ Locate articles or Web sites to which the instructor provides links and download or print articles or other information from them.

- ✔ Read a textbook assignment.

- ✔ Research and write a weekly assignment and post it to a discussion forum.

- ✔ Return to the forum in a day or two and read any responses to your assignment and respond to them with your own comments.

- ✔ Read other students' assignments and post responses to them.

- ✔ Meet with a small group by phone, e-mail, or in a chat room for a discussion of an assigned topic area.

- ✔ Work through self-paced online materials to problem-solve or practice new skills.

The bottom line: Although the way you organize your time is more flexible in a distance-education setting, you may have to spend more time than you would in a traditional class to participate fully. (For some advice on managing your time, read Chapter 12.)

The flip side of how much time you must spend taking a distance-learning course is how much time you save. You don't have to drive to and from campus as many as three times a week for a typical college course. Even if your commute is only 15 minutes each way, that could add up to an extra hour and a half each week (not to mention savings on the cost of gas, tolls or parking fees, and wear and tear on your car). You save time not listening to questions that you already know the answers to. In a classroom, you have to sit through lecture topics whether you're familiar with that particular information or not; you have to listen to other students' questions, which may or may not be relevant to you. In an online class, you control your learning: You can skip parts of reading assignments that cover topics you already know, and you don't have to read questions in a discussion area about subjects you have down pat.

How long will this be going on?

How long your distance-learning program lasts depends on the type of course you're taking. Most college-level distance-learning classes follow the semester structure of the campus classes, so completing a degree or certificate program online shouldn't take you any longer than if you went to the campus part time to learn. Take an example:

> If you figure that a master's degree program could run about 33 credit hours, you would have to take 11 three-credit classes and complete a thesis to complete the work. If you also have a full-time job, taking two courses a semester, plus perhaps one course in a summer semester, is about the most you could handle. This scenario assumes that you put in about 22 hours of study time every week, or over three hours of study seven days a week! At this breakneck pace of study, you could complete a degree program in as little as two and a half years. But if you opt for a more leisurely pace, you can expect to spend four years or more.

Programs that result in a certificate typically run from six to nine months, and consist of about five or six classes. How long a single course runs varies among institutions: Some schools administer the courses consecutively in five-week sessions; others may take longer for each class, and classes may overlap so that you can take two at a time. Check with any school you're considering to see how it breaks down the timing of its distance-learning courses.

For largely self-administered technical courses (non-college level) and self-improvement courses, you might spend anywhere from a few hours to a few weeks to work through the material, depending on the provider and the structure of the coursework.

Will you miss the four walls?

Online interaction with other students and an instructor is fundamental to the design of most distance learning at the college level, and a useful part of many online training courses, as well. You might even find ways to make personal connections with other online students — for example, by creating an area to post pictures of each other. But when it comes down to it, you're still sitting in a room all by yourself most of the time. Some people are just fine with that; others go a little bit bonkers.

In addition to the loneliness, people who are very extroverted can feel a little frustrated by not being able to be "on" in front of other people. After all, hogging the limelight by posting long, wordy messages may land like a lead balloon in a class of busy people with many postings to read through.

So how do you know whether you can survive in a distance-learning environment? The best advice I can give you is to take one course online before making the plunge to sign onto a full certificate or degree program, and see how you like it.

Are you a self-directed learner?

The type of person who does best in a distance-learning class is someone who is organized, self-reliant, and self-motivated. How do you know whether you can make the grade? Answer Yes or No to the following questions; the more yeses you end up with, the more of a self-directed learner you are:

- ✔ Do you think that you would be comfortable asking questions by e-mail or posting a question in a discussion area if you were unsure of an assignment?
- ✔ Are you willing to learn a new piece of software or new technology?

✔ If no one is around to remind you to, can you make yourself study and meet deadlines?

✔ Are you a good writer, comfortable with communicating via e-mail?

✔ Would you be able to read large chunks of material every week, for weeks or even months on end?

✔ Do you consider yourself to have good time-management skills?

✔ Will you be able to fit a few hours a day of study into your life and still have a life?

Making the choice: A case study

To help you understand why people make the distance-learning choice, look at a typical distance learner. Sue Murphy is an Education Coordinator at Holy Family Hospital in Spokane, Washington. She coordinates life-support certification classes. She works full time and also has many chores to handle outside of work on the family farm. She wanted to take college courses in distance-learning design to enable her to make a shift in her career. Because she lives in a rural area on a small farm, getting to a large university location is difficult. The fact that she works full time and needs flexibility in her study time, coupled with her remote location, made distance learning the logical choice.

Some of Sue's comments reveal her personality as a good fit for distance learning, as well: "I am a fairly independent person," she says. "I enjoy learning and do well completing education on my own once I've decided that it's a topic of importance to me."

Sue's advice to those considering distance learning? "These programs provide a great way to learn and receive feedback. However, quality of instruction varies, so find out if you can sample the course or others from the company or school to see if it meets your needs.

"Effective and responsive support services by the sponsoring institution are key to success," she adds "both for the organization and for the learner. Don't be afraid to speak up when you need something."

Finally, Sue was impressed by the communication in her classes. "Threaded discussion has been the most surprising and misunderstood quality of distance-learning programs. The myth is that online classes cannot compare with face-to-face classes in communicating thoughts and feelings. In fact, the discussions can surpass spoken dialog in that students often think through (and edit) what they want to say. Ideas can be expressed at a deeper level than could be possible in a traditional class, especially considering time limitations."

Another source that can help you decide whether distance learning is right for you is Distance-Educator.com (www.distance-educator.com). On this site, you can take the Distance Learner Quiz, which analyzes, based on a few simple questions, whether your personality fits the distance-learning model.

The truth is, most people can get through a distance-learning experience if they have to, and the advice contained in this book should make your experience as easy as possible. But alternatives to studying online do exist, so why make yourself miserable by choosing the wrong educational format? If you think that the personality traits described in this section apply to anybody but you, think carefully before making the distance-learning choice.

Chapter 2

Researching Your Options

In This Chapter

▶ Exploring colleges and universities

▶ Taking a look at technical training

▶ Researching distance-learning providers

*A*mazing as it seems, computing for the masses has only been around for about 20 years; the Internet as we know it today, with its multimedia-rich World Wide Web interface, is only about half a dozen years old. When you think in those terms, formal distance learning online is a little baby crawling around the virtual floor. When any industry is that new, standards are just beginning to evolve. That makes figuring out who's who and getting information you need a bit complicated. And doing so on the Internet, where nobody's even in charge, can be downright chaotic.

This chapter gives you a good idea of what types of organizations offer distance-learning courses and how you can do your homework to find out what's available in your area of interest, how much it costs, and more.

Finding Information About Distance-Learning Programs

The first step in finding information about distance-learning programs is knowing what types of programs are available. Your choices range from colleges and universities to computer certification programs to courses on leadership and management skills.

Getting a higher education online

You'd be hard put to find an educational institution today that hasn't jumped on the distance-learning bandwagon. From community colleges to the Ivy League, college-level courses are moving online at the speed of light.

Before you go out into the world to gather the details about any particular school's program, take time to find out the kinds of schools that are available and where you can get information on them.

Four-year colleges and universities

Traditional four-year colleges often funnel their distance-learning options through an Extension or Continuing Education division, because distance-learning programs typically serve the adult learner. Some colleges have a dedicated Distance Learning division; for example, some of the schools listed on Distance-Educator.com (`www.distance-educator.com`), shown in Figure 2-1, reflect a trend of naming their distance-learning program the Virtual Campus or Virtual University. These divisions allow students to take degrees part time so that they can continue to work while studying.

Be aware of the length of your commitment if you sign up for an online four-year degree program. A typical four-year degree taken at a part-time pace can take six years or more to complete.

And what are these institutions of higher learning offering online? Everything from individual noncredit courses, to a professionally recognized certificate that carries CEUs (Continuing Education Units), to college-credit granting bachelor's and master's programs. You can find out more about noncredit courses, CEUs, and college credit in Chapter 3.

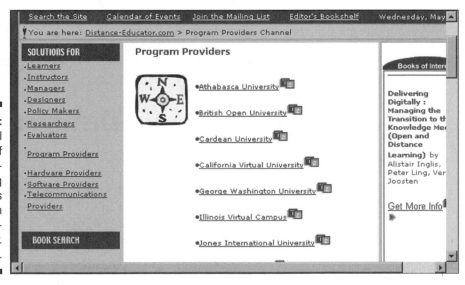

Figure 2-1:
This useful listing of distance-learning providers appears on Distance-Educator.com.

Online courses and degree programs typically cost the same as their on-campus equivalents. Getting accepted to an online degree program usually involves the same process of application and acceptance as campus-based students face. Also, in terms of the quality and content of your education, your virtual degree is no different than any other degree.

Community colleges

Community colleges traditionally offer two-year associate's degrees or certificate programs to non-resident students who live near the school (hence the name *community college*). Some of these students study full time, but many are part-time students and hold jobs while studying.

With the advent of distance learning, community colleges are extending their reach beyond the local community. This is especially good news for people in remote areas who want a lower-priced higher-education opportunity, but have no community college to attend.

Those who opt for a community-college education often use the experience as a springboard to studying at a four-year university. Others use community college courses to get professional certificates or ongoing training in their profession. Community colleges enable you to attain a degree in a shorter period of time, usually taking a couple of years to complete the 60 hours needed for an associate's degree, versus four years to earn a bachelor's degree.

In addition, community colleges are much less expensive than four-year colleges, with tuition running as low as $35 a credit hour, versus $350 or more at a university.

Some community colleges — such as Ulster County Community College, whose home page is shown in Figure 2-2 — are part of a statewide system of colleges. In many cases, within that state school structure, distance-learning students registered at any one school in the system have access to courses from all the other schools around the state. In some states, such as California and Colorado, community colleges have banded together as distance-learning consortia, again offering the combined strength of all their programs to online students through a single entity.

When researching schools that are part of a statewide or consortia organization, you can look for information on any one institution on the collective Web site or by searching for an individual college online. Directories are available to aid in your search, such as *Peterson's 2-Year Colleges 2000*. But if you're considering a community college, a trip to your local college to ask questions about this option might be the easiest and most helpful course to pursue.

Figure 2-2:
Part of the State University of New York system, Ulster County Community College offers online education to students beyond its own community.

International schools

In a sense, distance learning itself is making every school an international school. Even community colleges, once dedicated to students in a defined geographic area, are taking on foreign students through their distance-learning programs. Opening up your perspective on the world by taking courses from a school in another country has a certain lure. In some cases, the best program in your area of specialty may come from across the border or across the sea. For example, if you major in French, perhaps a school in France would be ideal. Or, if your area is international politics or law, maybe a school in London or Geneva would suit your needs better than one in Cleveland. If that's the case, why not take advantage of distance learning to study abroad from your own living room?

To research what's available in another country's university system in your area of study, you can

✔ Look to professional associations in your discipline who might maintain lists of degree granters in your field.

✔ Search the Web by typing keywords such as "U.K. distance learning" or "Asia distance learning" into a search engine.

✔ Get information from associations such as the European Association for Distance Learning, or its U.S. counterpart, the Distance Education and Training Council, both of which you can access from detc.org.

✔ Look up information in an extensive database of global distance-education providers through the International Centre for Distance Learning at www-icdl.open.ac.uk.

Be aware that online distance-education programs differ from country to country, based on a country's educational traditions, technological infrastructure, and attitudes towards distance learning. For example, in some countries where Internet access is charged by the minute, rather than sold for a monthly fee for unlimited use, online distance learning still takes a backseat to more traditional forms of remote education, such as television or video instruction.

For more about studying outside of your own country, see Chapter 18.

Considering online training companies and technical schools

The connection between online learning and computer technology is a logical one, so you can find many organizations offering computer courses online. These range from simple self-paced tutorials on word processing to lengthier courses that qualify you to take exams for professional certification in topics like networking. But computers aren't the only area of study you can pursue through online training companies or technical colleges. You can find courses on everything from management skills to industry safety standards.

Technical schools

Technical schools can be state or government-sponsored, with a goal of providing an alternative to traditional colleges. The courses of study at technical schools lend themselves to technical careers, which can mean anything from auto mechanics to cooking to nursing to computer science. Many are fully accredited by the same organizations that grant accreditation to four-year universities.

Technical schools are moving into distance learning a little more slowly than their university counterparts, perhaps because much of what they offer is of a hands-on nature, requiring special equipment and shop or laboratory work. However, some technical schools, such as Ivy Tech State College in Indiana, are placing courses like computer studies online, and adding an online study element to some of their campus-bound courses. (The Ivy Tech Distance Education Web site, www.ivy.tec.in.us/distance, appears in Figure 2-3).

Technical schools aren't necessarily organized by state the way community colleges are. You can get some information on locating technical education providers by visiting the Technology Student Association Web site at www.tsawww.org. Because some technical schools, such as ITT Technical Institute (www.itt-tech.edu) are chains just like K-mart or McDonalds, you can go to their centralized Web site and find a school in your area.

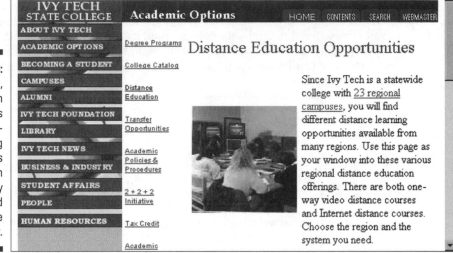

Figure 2-3:
In Indiana,
Ivy Tech
offers
distance-
learning
courses
through
one-way
video and
over the
Internet.

Online training companies

Online training from organizations other than technical colleges or traditional higher education institutions offer courses that cost anywhere from $20 to $700, with the bulk of them priced in the $50 to $200 range. Some professional associations also offer courses in their field online. Some use a subscription model that allows you to access one or more courses for a given time period, such as six months. A subscription-pricing plan has the benefit of allowing you to go through a course several times or go back and check a particular lesson to reinforce your learning.

Many online training sites, such as Headlight.com (www.headlight.com) and Hungry Minds (www.hungryminds.com), are simply clearinghouses for a variety of online-course publishers, so some unevenness in the quality and style of the training is inevitable. Other sites, like learn2.com (www.click2learn.com), work with staff and partners to develop and deliver courses, like the computer hardware course shown in Figure 2-4.

Online training organizations vary not just in quality, but also in the structure of their courses:

- ✔ Some offer instructor-led courses where you can interact with and get feedback from an actual teacher. In these types of courses, you can usually participate with other students in a discussion group or chat area and submit assignments to instructors who will grade and return them.

- ✔ Some offer strictly self-paced tutorials, with students reading through material and taking short tutorials and self-administered tests to evaluate their progress. For more information about self-paced courses take a look at Chapter 14.

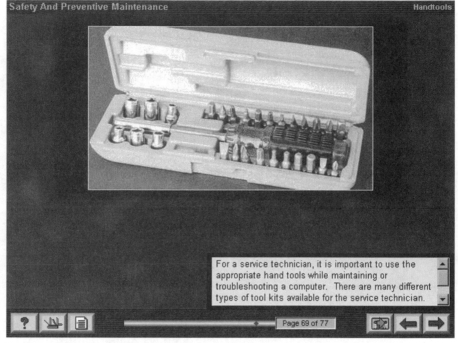

Figure 2-4:
A combination of audio, text, and photos walk you through computer repair in this course from learn2.com.

Online training organizations vary not just in quality, but also in the structure of their courses:

- Some offer instructor-led courses where you can interact with and get feedback from an actual teacher. In these types of courses, you can usually participate with other students in a discussion group or chat area and submit assignments to instructors who will grade and return them.

- Some offer strictly self-paced tutorials, with students reading through material and taking short tutorials and self-administered tests to evaluate their progress. For more information about self-paced courses take a look at Chapter 14.

Certification programs

Certification has become a popular career credential for the technology professional, and is often required by employers for IT (information technology) professionals. Many certification courses are available to train you in topics that can lead to a credential such as MCSE (Microsoft Certified Systems Engineer). However, *certification program* is a bit of a misnomer: These courses don't result in any kind of certification. Instead, they prepare you to take certification exams offered by companies like Microsoft and Oracle.

Online training: Everybody's doing it

Many online training providers are focused on topics other than technical skills like computer programming. The following list shows a sample of other providers to give you an idea of the range of training courses available online:

✔ Dow Jones University (www.dju.com) offers courses in financial planning and investing.

✔ CECity.com (www.cecity.com) hosts courses for the medical profession, including courses for pharmacists.

✔ University.com (www.university.com) provides courses on real estate, law, accounting, financial services, and healthcare.

✔ The American Institute for Paralegal Studies (www.aips.com) offers fully accredited online classes for becoming a paralegal.

✔ Digital University (www.digitaledu.com) specializes in courses on graphic design and multimedia.

✔ Emind.com (emind.com) specializes in training in accounting, IT, and securities.

Many people are offering training on certification topics, and figuring out who's who as you research these offerings can be a little tricky. One place to start is to look for an authorized training company. These providers are authorized by the technology vendors that grant the certification, such as the Novell Education program, whose home page appears in Figure 2-5. These technology companies quite often work through a partnership with third-party training companies who have gone through a process to be qualified as authorized providers. Yes, you still have to take the exam to actually become certified, but you have the comfort of knowing that you're taking training for the exams from a company whose training has been approved by the certification grantor. Look for these companies by going to the granting company's Web site and locating a link to authorized training providers.

Check out a recently launched Web site, exampractice.com, for free practice tests for technical certification topics. Taking a practice test can give you a better idea of whether or not you need a training course before taking the official certification exam.

Testing companies such as Virtual University Enterprises, shown in Figure 2-6, are designated exam givers; some of these testing companies also offer training, so don't forget to click the link to authorized testing centers when you're on the technology company Web site to find them. Keep in mind that, whomever you take training from, you have to pay for taking the exam as well as for the training. Getting the best training you can is important (and probably worth a little extra money).

Figure 2-5:
You can find a networking course from an authorized provider at education. novell. com.

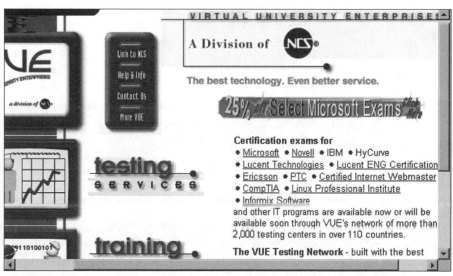

Figure 2-6:
Testing companies like Virtual University Enterprises (www.vue. com) deliver tests and ensure that your scores are conveyed to the company who grants the certification.

Doing Your Research

People like me have spent a lot of time online to help you understand what distance learning is and what you can expect of the online learning experience. But at some point, you're going to have to get out there and collect your own information about specific schools and make your own choice. Several good sources of information are out there just waiting for you.

Consulting directories of distance-learning providers

Over the years, companies like Barron's and Peterson's have published several excellent (if hefty) directories of schools. Those same companies, and a few others, have begun publishing equally hefty distance-learning-specific directories, priced at about $20 on average.

If you want the nuts-and-bolts information about a particular school, including contact information, programs offered, tuition, and accreditation, consider turning to one of these books, all of which provide directories of colleges offering distance learning:

- *The Unofficial Guide to Distance Learning* by Shannon Turlington, published by Arco.
- *The Best Distance Learning Graduate Schools* by Vicky Phillips and Cindy Yager published by The Princeton Review.
- *Barron's Guide to Distance Learning* by Pat Criscito, published by Barron's Educational Series, Inc.
- *College Degrees by Mail & Internet* by John Bear, Ph.D and Mariah Bear, M.A., published by Ten Speed Press.
- *Peterson's Guide to Distance Learning Programs 2000,* compiled and published by Peterson's.

Several of the books in the preceding list include other useful information, such as the teaching methods used (online, TV, audio, and so forth) and the requirements for on-campus time.

Some of these directories are updated yearly, others aren't. Always make sure that you're buying a directory published in the current year. School information, especially concerning what they offer in the way of distance learning, changes very quickly.

If you are looking for online technical training, check with your company's human resources professionals. These folks have probably spent a lot of time researching good providers of technical courses, and are in a good position to make some recommendations for you.

Searching for schools online

Where do you begin your search for the handful of schools that may fit your particular distance-learning needs? Luckily, a great many distance-learning sites are out there, offering information about various kinds of providers, search engines to find the school that offers courses in your field, and links to other useful sites. Some include links to articles about recent activities in the distance-learning arena at various schools. These articles can help you spot the schools that really seem to be at the forefront of distance learning.

Be careful: Some of these distance-learning advice sites are actually run by consultants or training clearinghouses trying to sell you their product or service under the guise of offering objective information on distance learning. Check the About Us section of the site to see who runs it and why.

Some helpful sites to visit are:

✔ Peterson's, the publisher of directories and guides for college-bound students, maintains a Web site at `www.petersons.com/dlearn`. Here, you can search for the right college in Peterson's extensive online directory of school information.

✔ CollegeQuest (`www.collegequest.com`), shown in Figure 2-7, is another site run by Peterson's that helps you search for schools by various criteria.

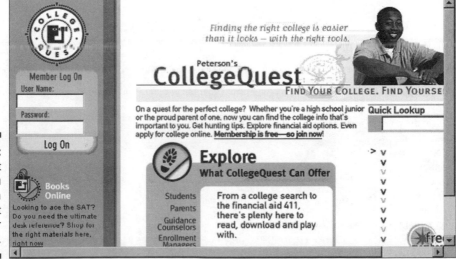

Figure 2-7: CollegeQuest helps you search for a school that fits your needs.

✔ geteducated.com (`www.geteducated.com`) offers a free e-mail news-letter on distance learning, as well as listings of distance learning providers. All listings have links to school sites, so this is a great one-stop place to get information and to get to the school itself, without having to search for their sites individually.

✔ The Adult Distance Education Internet Surf Shack (see Figure 2-8) (`www.edsurf.net/edshack`) is an oddly named but worthwhile place to visit to get the lowdown on virtual universities, as well as online training providers.

✔ The Digital Education Network (`www.edunet.com`) is one place to visit if you're looking for an education from a provider in another country. You can search by dozens of types of providers, such as training organizations, technical schools, language schools, art and media schools, and so on in many countries around the world.

✔ NewsDirectory.com's section on college newspapers may be of help in understanding the student population and environment of the school you're considering. Go to `newsdirectory.com/college/press` to explore school newspapers from around the United States.

✔ `R1edu.org` is a site that acts as a portal to 28 institutions of higher education, all with appropriate accreditation, and described as the best in the United States. All schools are rated as Research Universities I by the Carnegie Foundation for the Advancement of Teaching, creator of this well-recognized classification system for institutions of higher learning.

✔ If you go online through a service provider such as AOL or MSN, look for an area devoted to education (see Figure 2-9). This section often presents an organized way to get information on many kinds of schools from one handy location.

Figure 2-8: This Surf Shack makes finding centralized information about all kinds of distance-learning providers easy.

Figure 2-9:
CompuServe's
College
Planning
page, part
of its
Research &
Education
section,
offers
information
on schools,
testing, and
financing.

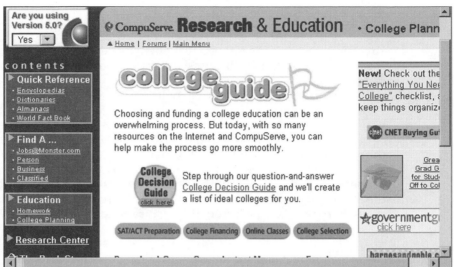

Don't forget to look online for professional organizations that focus on the
discipline you're interested in studying. You can narrow your search for such
groups by entering the keywords "distance learning" (in quotation marks) in
combination with a word like *psychology* into your search engine of choice
(such as Yahoo!, Lycos, or AltaVista). An example of the results you may get
is the Social Psychology Network page on Distance Learning in Psychology
(www.socialpsychology.org), shown in Figure 2-10.

Figure 2-10:
Extensive
links to
schools
and advice
about
distance
learning
for those
studying
psychology
are all
centralized
on this web
page.

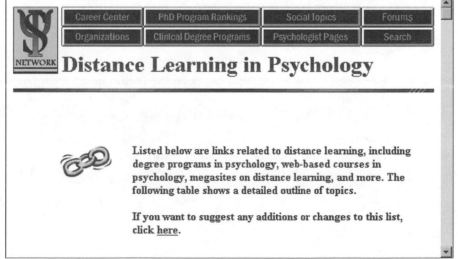

Getting the scoop from school sites

You can expect any organization that offers distance-learning courses over the Internet to have an online presence. After you determine that a school may be of interest, why not go right to their own Web site for up-to-the-minute information on courses and policies.

When you find the site for a school you're interested in (either by using one of the directories mentioned in the previous section or by simply entering the school name in a search engine), look for an area dedicated to distance-learning programs. This is where you can expect to find an explanation of delivery methods and approach — some schools even provide a demo of their distance-learning offerings on their Web sites. But don't limit your research to this area; look around the entire college or university Web site for these important features:

- An online catalog of courses
- An academic calendar with important dates for class registration and testing
- Information about student support services
- Information on the school application process, including any previous education or tests (such as the GRE) required to enter a degree program
- Information on the school's accreditation
- Details on degree and certificate programs available

Online training providers also offer a wealth of information about themselves on their own Web sites, including

- Course listings, often with a detailed course syllabus
- Demo courses so that you can see what their training looks like
- Self-administered pre-assessment tests that help you determine the appropriate level of class with which to start
- Information on pricing and the school's refund policy
- Information on faculty qualifications, course development partners, and any authorized training center status they might enjoy

Ordering catalogs

If you're like me, you love to get catalogs. Although college catalogs aren't as colorful as The Sharper Image catalog or as exciting as Victoria's Secret, they are jam-packed with all you ever wanted to know about a school and what it has to offer. Printed catalogs have the advantage over online catalogs in that you can browse through them while waiting at the dentist's office or sitting in front of the TV.

You can order school catalogs by mail, by phone, or by sending a request via e-mail through the school's Web site. You can also find sites like CollegeSource Online (www.collegesource.org), shown in Figure 2-11, that are clearing-houses for ordering multiple catalogs online.

Other sites provide access to catalogs from distance-learning institutions, such as EdSurf, shown in Figure 2-12. You can use this particular site to order catalogs not only from universities but also from online training companies and technical colleges.

Figure 2-11: CollegeSource Online offers 13,000 catalogs through one Web site.

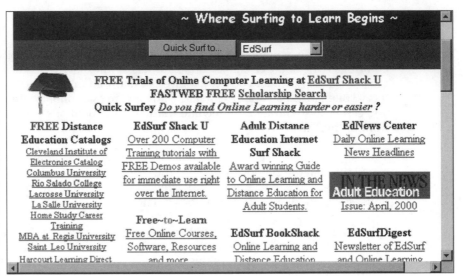

Chapter 3

Picking the Perfect Provider

● ●

In This Chapter

▶ What should I look for in a distance-learning school?

▶ What can accreditation do for me?

▶ How much will a distance education cost?

▶ How can I get financing?

● ●

You're probably familiar with a TV game show where the host gives the answer and you have to come up with the question. Well, in this chapter, I'm going to play the game in reverse. I try to walk through all the questions you should ask before committing to an online distance-learning provider, along with some advice about what kinds of answers you might come up with. And because everything comes down to money (well, most things, anyway), I offer some valuable information about funding your online education.

Five Questions to Consider

In some ways, choosing the wrong school can be as disastrous as choosing the wrong spouse. Considering that studying for a degree can take as much as six years (which is longer than a lot of marriages last), you'll want to make this choice carefully.

Whether you're interested in taking a single course from an online training company or earning a master's degree from an Ivy League university, certain basic criteria can help guide your choice.

What will it cost?

Every school has its own pricing policy that you must look into carefully. Be aware, though, that you do make certain trade-offs when you opt for a cheaper education. Only you can determine what is important to you and your career, and what you're willing to pay for.

The following variables affect the cost of your education:

- ✔ **School accreditation:** A degree that is not recognized by any professional organization as having value may be cheaper, but is a degree with no value of value to you? (See more about accreditation in "Assessing Accreditation," later in this chapter.)

- ✔ **School reputation:** Sometimes you pay for a name. That's true with designer jeans, and it's also true with elite universities. However, right or wrong, a degree with an impressive name attached can pay off in career advancement down the road.

- ✔ **Type of school:** Community colleges don't cost as much as four-year colleges, and online training companies may offer courses for less than technical schools. Look into all the options.

- ✔ **Government support:** In the United States, for example, state universities cost less than private schools, but often carry residency requirements.

See the "Setting a Budget" and "Letting Someone Else Foot the Bill" sections, later in this chapter, for more on budgeting and financing your education.

How long will it take and when can I start?

You can find ways to get through your education more quickly and fit it into your schedule more easily. Check the academic calendar of schools you are considering to see whether they run on a traditional college academic calendar (see Figure 3-1) or on a modular calendar with shorter sessions that start up on a more frequent basis (see Figure 3-2). By choosing a school that lets you begin a course within a week of signing up, you can get started more quickly.

Many online training providers allow you to start a course anytime you want, because their courses are largely self-paced. (See Chapter 14 for more on self-paced learning.)

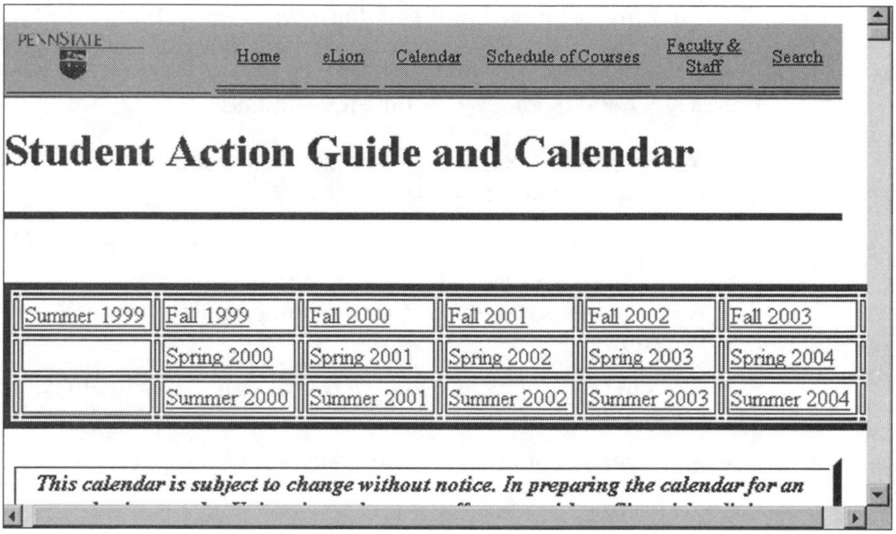

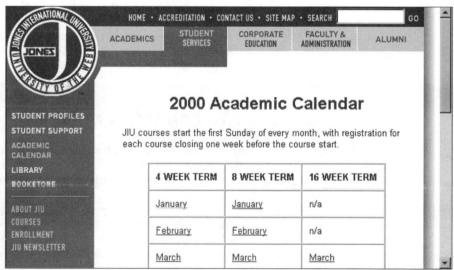

Figure 3-1: Look for an academic calendar for schools with a traditional semester structure, such as this calendar for Penn State (www.psu. edu/ registrar).

Figure 3-2: Some schools, such as Jones International University (www. jones interna tional. edu/ student_ services), offer students the opportunity to start courses at frequent intervals.

The other major impact on the timing of your education is the type of education you choose and how many courses you can juggle at one time. Choose the type of education that fits with both your timeframe and career goals. Here's a general guide to your time investment:

- ✔ A single course can take two hours from an online training company or five weeks from a university.

- ✔ A certificate program from a university usually takes from five to nine months.

- ✔ An associate's degree from a community college is usually a two-year program.

- ✔ A bachelor's degree is a four-year program; when taken part-time, it can stretch out to as much as six years.

- ✔ A master's degree can be earned in two years, but on a part-time basis, plan on three or more.

If you plan to earn a degree online, look for a school that may give you credit for what you already know. If you take tests, such as those offered through the College Level Examination Program (CLEP), some schools will consider your scores and grant credit for your knowledge. I took the CLEP tests when I got my undergraduate degree and was instantly awarded 18 college credits for my scores. That's nine classes I didn't have to sit through, and my parents didn't have to pay for! Many schools will also consider work experience as a way to bypass some course requirements. For more information about CLEP, go to www.collegeboard.org/clep.

Do they have the courses I need?

This one seems somewhat obvious: If you want a degree in education and a school doesn't offer an education major, cross that school off your list. However, even if all the schools you're considering offer the concentration you want, not all programs or courses are equal.

When you're calculating which courses you need to take to meet your degree requirement, remember that a school with more breadth of course offerings provides more flexibility. If you want to take a technical course of study and the school in question doesn't offer courses in the most cutting-edge technology, it may not be the right school for you. Take the time to compare the specific course listings among schools that offer programs in your area of interest. The number and variety of courses offered might make the difference in the school you choose.

As you roam around a school's catalog or Web site looking at courses, make sure that all the courses you need are offered online. Even if a school has a distance-learning program, some of its courses may still be campus-based only. Also be aware that some courses are only offered every other semester.

Are their courses any good?

This is a tough one: How do you know how good a school's courses are until you take one? Here are some ways to check:

✔ Online training companies often offer a demo of a course for free. Step through the free one before you sign up for the one that will cost you cash.

Universities are also beginning to offer simulated classes for the prospective student to explore.

✔ Check credentials. Ask for the following information about the faculty in the school you're interested in: the level of degree instructors hold, the real-world experience they bring to the course, and their years of teaching experience. Check prospective schools' accreditation by various agencies. (See more about accreditation in "Assessing Accreditation," later in this chapter.)

✔ Find out how online courses have been developed. If a lone Web designer has slapped existing notes from a course up on a Web site in HTML format, stay away. Ask questions to make sure that you're getting the equivalent course quality and content in the distance learning version.

If you're really concerned about committing to a whole program before you try a real (as opposed to a demo) class, go ahead and take a low-cost, non-credit course from the school before going to the trouble and expense of committing yourself to a full degree program.

Do they have their distance-learning act together?

Distance learning is something everybody's doing because it's hot, but not everybody is doing it well. Some are just testing the waters, others have committed to it wholeheartedly. Finding a school that really understands what makes good distance learning tick is very important.

As you consider various schools, take a look at the following tip-offs:

- ✓ **Their course development process:** Do they have on-staff distance-learning designers, or do they buy distance learning course content from third parties or farm out course development to freelancers who may or may not be qualified? One look at the content partners for a school like Unext.com's Cardean University, shown in Figure 3-3, for example, gives you a warm and fuzzy feeling about their courses.

- ✓ **The infrastructure they've created to support students:** Do they have advisors to help students when questions come up? Do they offer distance-learning students access to student services such as work-placement programs and a library? Do they offer technical support to distance learners? Just by visiting the distance-education Web page for a school such as Penn State (www.outreach.psu.edu/DE), you can get some idea of how robust and organized its distance-learning efforts are (see Figure 3-4).

- ✓ **The breadth of courses they offer via distance learning:** If a school only has a few courses available, it's in start-up mode — and you may not want to be part of its breaking-in period. If a school has several degrees, certificates, and individual courses available online, it has already gone through its own training period and gained the experience necessary to make your learning endeavor successful.

Figure 3-3: Cardean University (www.cardean.com) partners with the best: Columbia, Stanford, and The London School of Economics, to name a few.

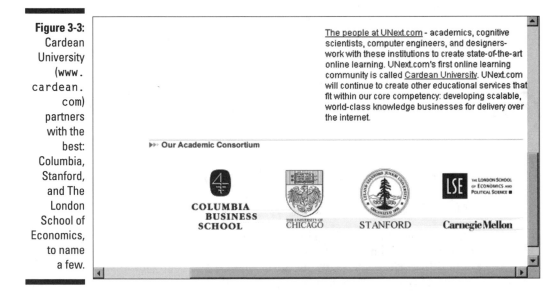

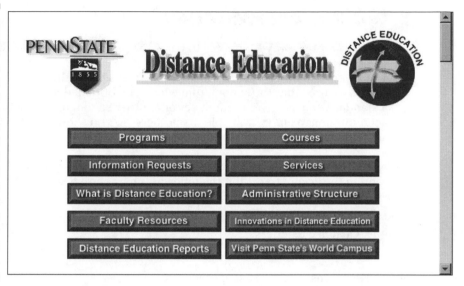

Keep in mind that the quality and level of technology that schools use to support distance learning varies and may not always be consistent with a school's traditional-classroom reputation. Setting up a distance-learning program can range from converting some lecture material to online material, to investing in million-dollar plus multimedia facilities. Although a school may be accredited and have a good history in traditional education formats, be sure to get specifics about how well it supports its distance-learning initiative before applying.

Assessing Accreditation

Sure, some people may take classes because of their love of learning, but most of us endure the long hours of study and stress of assignment deadlines for something more concrete. We're looking for a credential, something that can get us a job, a promotion, or a brand-new career. In order for you to get the greatest edge from your learning, however, the institution you take your classes from should be accredited by some recognized authority. For an online training company, this authority might be Microsoft authorizing the company to teach courses on its products. In a university setting, accreditation comes from formal accrediting agencies.

What is accreditation?

Accreditation is a way for people to know that an educational organization meets certain standards. When you take a course from an accredited school, employers and other schools who approve transfer of educational credits can be assured that the school from which you obtained your education met a standard of quality. Your employer or another school may view some accreditations as more valuable than others, so you should understand something about the different forms accreditation takes.

A variety of agencies grant accreditation to schools, but most typically require the school to exhibit the following characteristics:

- Fiscal responsibility
- Qualified teachers
- Good facilities for students
- Responsible advertising practices
- Approved admission policies
- Acceptable quality of course content

Who accredits the accreditors? Each country has its own body that approves accrediting organizations. For example, in the United States, it's the Council for Higher Education Accreditation (see Figure 3-5), and in Canada, it's the Association of Universities and Colleges of Canada. These organizations put schools through a rigorous application process for accreditation, which can sometimes take years to complete.

Figure 3-5: The Council for Higher Education Accreditation (www.chea. org) is a U.S. government agency involved in setting standards for accreditation.

Who are these mysterious accreditors?

Accreditation can come from different bodies, each of whom may specialize in a different area. The Distance Education and Training Council (DETC), a private, non-profit organization started in 1926 by the Carnegie Foundation and the New York Better Business Bureau. The DETC (originally called the Home Study Council) grants accreditation to distance learning schools. The DETC Web site, at www.detc.org, has a link called Directory of Accredited Institutions (see Figure 3-6) that you can click on to search through the institutions that the DETC has accredited.

The European Association for Distance Learning (EADL) is a sister organization to the DETC that accredits schools in 15 European countries. This organization was founded in 1985 as the Association of European Correspondence Schools. You can find similar organizations for countries and regions throughout the world.

Another organization that recognizes adult education, including distance-learning providers, is the International Association for Continuing Education and Training, which approves institutions granting Continuing Education Units (CEUs) rather than university degree credit hours.

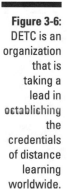

Figure 3-6: DETC is an organization that is taking a lead in establishing the credentials of distance learning worldwide.

THE DISTANCE EDUCATION AND TRAINING COUNCIL

Bringing Learning Opportunities To Millions.

What is the DETC?
What does Accreditation Mean?
Directory of Accredited Institutions
Subjects Taught
High School Programs
Degree Programs
Publications of Interest
Frequently Asked Questions
Upcoming Meetings
DETC's Honor Society
Useful Resources
How to Contact the DETC
DETC Online Seminar (Members Only)
European Association

Web Site Last updated 4-04-00

DIRECTORY OF ACCREDITED INSTITUTIONS

The two dates shown after the dated founded indicate when the institution was first accredited and the next scheduled re-accreditation review. For more information about any of the courses offered by these institutions, please contact the institution directly.

1. American Academy of Nutrition, College of Nutrition
1204 Kenesaw, Knoxville, TN 37919 (Send inquiries to: 3408 Sausalito Drive, Corona Del Mar, CA 92625-1638; Phone: 1-800-290-4226; Fax: 949-760-1788; E-mail: info@nutritioneducation.com; Web Site: http://www.nutritioneducation.com). Founded 1985 (1989/2000). Individual courses, diploma program in Comprehensive Nutrition

The United States has six regional accrediting agencies for colleges and universities, such as the Western Association of Schools and Colleges, whose Web page is appears in Figure 3-7. If you're studying with an American college, an accreditation from one of these agencies is probably most important credential for the school you select to have, both for employers considering your qualifications and for other U.S. colleges assessing transfer of credit from another college. Why? This set of accrediting agencies is simply more established and recognized by human-resource departments and college admissions offices than a more modern or specialized association such as the DETC. All these agencies have coordinated their accrediting policies so that credit earned at an institution accredited by one agency is recognized by a school accredited by another.

Figure 3-7: Accrediting agencies such as the Western Association of Schools and Colleges provide different types of accreditation for different types of schools.

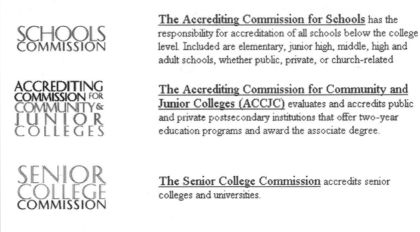

SCHOOLS COMMISSION

The Accrediting Commission for Schools has the responsibility for accreditation of all schools below the college level. Included are elementary, junior high, middle, high and adult schools, whether public, private, or church-related

ACCREDITING COMMISSION FOR **COMMUNITY** & **JUNIOR COLLEGES**

The Accrediting Commission for Community and Junior Colleges (ACCJC) evaluates and accredits public and private postsecondary institutions that offer two-year education programs and award the associate degree.

SENIOR COLLEGE COMMISSION

The Senior College Commission accredits senior colleges and universities.

The six regional U.S. accrediting agencies for colleges and universities are

Middle States Association of Colleges and Schools	www.msache.org
New England Association of Schools and Colleges	www.neasc.org
North Central Association of Colleges and Schools	www.ncacihe.org
Northwest Association of Schools and Colleges	www.cocnasc.org
Southern Association of Colleges and Schools	www.sacscoc.org
Western Association of Schools and Colleges	www.wascweb.org

In addition to distance-learning, continuing-education, and university accreditors, you can also find professional accreditation organizations that recognize schools for their courses in specific topic areas, such as psychology. Keep in mind that a school can be accredited by one of the regional associations as meeting certain educational standards, but not have the professional accreditation for a particular department. For example, a college might be accredited by its regional agency for overall educational quality, but to confirm the quality of its nursing courses, you should also make sure that its school of nursing is accredited by the appropriate professional association.

How can accreditation help me?

The value of accreditation is in the eye of the beholder. Your employer or another school must recognize the accreditation of the school you attend as being of value. Not all schools will allow you to transfer credits from a school that is only approved by the DETC, for example. Schools in another country might not recognize your country's accreditation system. Your best bet is to check with the institution you are planning to take a course from and ask what organization they are accredited by; then ask potential employers or other schools about how they view that accreditation. You can also get some general information on accreditation from the Web sites of accrediting agencies, such as the one shown in Figure 3-8 for the North Central Association of Colleges and Schools (www.ncacihe.org).

Figure 3-8: The North Central Association of Colleges and Schools is just one of six regional accrediting agencies in the United States.

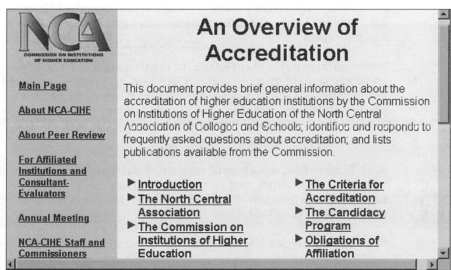

The benefit of accreditation finally comes down to impressing people. If employers or other schools recognize your school's accreditation, they are in

The benefit of accreditation finally comes down to impressing people. If employers or other schools recognize your school's accreditation, they are in essence acknowledging the quality of your educational credential. Degree credentials from an unaccredited institution may not carry much, or any, weight.

Some professions, such as accounting and nursing, require that you take accredited courses on a regular basis to retain your professional status. If that is your concern, be very careful to check your chosen school's accreditation before signing up for a course.

Do you need credit for what you do?

The terms *credit* and *accreditation* may sound similar, but they're not the same thing. *Accreditation* is recognition that the quality of education at an institution meets certain agreed upon standards. *Credit* is what a college (whether accredited or not) grants you on completion of a course.

The two basic options when dealing with credit at the college level are

- ✔ **College-level credit hours:** These are what you receive when you take (and pass!) a for-credit college-level course.

- ✔ **Continuing Education Units (CEUs):** This a system recognized in the United States for earning and transferring continuing education received through noncredit college-level courses. Although CEUs cannot count towards a college degree, professional agencies and employers do recognize them.

When you research a course, look for the designation *credit* or *noncredit* to know which of the two categories it falls into. Employers recognize both credit and noncredit coursework to varying degrees, depending on the job you're applying for and the institution you attended. A computer software company may value your CEU certificate in networking over a Harvard degree in English literature, for example.

Keep in mind that, even if a course carries no formal credit, most employers will appreciate training that you take to improve skills, such as taking a course in Excel from a training school. Taking the training shows your eagerness to add to your skill set.

Recognition of credit becomes less subjective when you want to transfer credit gained at one educational institution to another. Typically, if a school recognizes the institution from which you received your credit hours or CEUs, you will be able to transfer credit. That recognition of another institution hinges on the school's accreditation.

Although getting a degree at a community college is a good choice for many people, remember that an associate's degree is not comparable to a bachelor's degree, although it can count towards the completion of a more advanced degree if you eventually decide to pursue one. If you think further study is a possibility, be sure to ascertain the transferability of credit received at a community college to a four-year college before you sign up.

In addition to college credit, you may be considering getting a professional certification granted by a company like Oracle. Professional certifications don't directly transfer into credits that you can use towards a college degree; however, some schools do take special consideration of that kind of work in waiving certain course requirements for a degree.

Avoiding Fraud

Education as a commodity isn't all that well regulated. I know this because I have visited at least 20 sites that state that they are *the* leading provider of online training in the world today. Well, I'm not stupid: Somebody has to be lying, and no official body is overseeing the field to point it out.

In areas where no professional standards exist, as with online technical training, just about anybody can confer a form of degree. A company can set itself up to give you its own certification in surfing or brain surgery, but all you'll have when you get your certificate is a piece of paper that says that you met the standards of that organization. Depending on the organization, that certificate may carry some weight with your employer . . . or it may not.

When is a university not a university?

A key point to keep in mind is that the use of the term *university* is not governed by any regulation in the United States, and the same is true of many other countries. You could hang out a shingle today and call yourself Hole in the Wall University, and nobody could do a thing about it.

If you're considering attending a university, community college, or technical college, your best bet is to look at its accreditation and reputation in campus-bound education. Look through some college directories, such as *Peterson's Guide to Distance Learning Programs* or the *Unofficial Guide to Distance Learning* (published by IDG Books Worldwide), to find out how long the school has been around and who accredits it.

Appraising Joe's Online Training Co.

In the world of online training companies, many of which are only a few years or months old, judging quality can be tricky. Consider these tips to help avoid the fly-by-night operation:

- **Look for free sample courses or demos:** You're better off buying from a company that isn't afraid to let you look at its product before you buy.

- **Guarantees are good:** The company that offers a no-strings-attached guarantee of satisfaction is probably your best bet.

- **Ask questions:** Who designs courses, who teaches them, and so on. If the company guarantees that all instructors hold the certification they're preparing students to take, or that they hold MAs or PhDs in the topic they're teaching, it's a good sign.

- **Check out any connection to a reputable parent company:** Some training sites are run by established, face-to-face training companies that have a lengthy track record in the training world. Other good bets are sites run by companies, such as publishing houses, that have very stable business histories.

- **Sample a cheaper class:** When all is said and done, you can't know what your educational experience will be like until you go through it. Find a low-priced course (something at about $25 to 50) from a couple of providers who look good, and take only that class before signing up for the whole program. Fifty bucks isn't too much to be out to be sure that you've chosen the right school for a $500 certification class.

Checking professional credentials: Who's who?

In some fields of study, for example information technology or accounting, you can gain professional certification. If you know that an employer or another school you're interested in won't recognize your distance-learning program unless it has such professional credentials, you have to do your homework to be sure that your online-learning efforts aren't in vain. Here are some tips to checking credentials of professional certification programs:

- Contact a professional organization in the field, such as the Association of Veterinary Technician Educators (www.br.cc.va.w/avte), to find out what standards that profession requires a distance-learning provider to meet for professional certification, and make sure that your provider meets those standards.

✔ Check to see whether your prospective school is an authorized training provider, where such a distinction exists. This is especially important in computer technology training, where the company that designs the software or hardware provides authorized status only to those who meet its standards.

Some training organizations have been known to stick a company's logo on their Web sites, implying that they are authorized providers of training for that company when they're not. The best place to find out whether a training company enjoys authorized status is on the Web site of the organization granting authorization. To find out if a training company is an authorized Microsoft trainer, for example, look on Microsoft's Web site (www.Microsoft.com) rather than relying on the claims of the training company.

✔ Be sure to find out whether certificate programs through universities confer college credit hours or CEUs (Continuing Education Units) for the work you do. College credit hours count towards a degree program; CEUs, in most cases, do not.

Setting a Budget

It would be nice if I could tell you to ignore money as a criterion for picking the right school and to just go out and get the best darn education you can, regardless of cost. But that advice is unrealistic for most people. The fact is that money may be the key determinant of which school and what type of education you can access. So bite the bullet and get ready to create your educational budget!

How much will the tuition be?

Tuition is almost always the same whether you're attending classes on campus or from your home office. And tuition is the biggest hit in any educational budget.

Why not just get this over with and tackle the tough numbers first. If you want to study at Harvard, you can expect to pay $574 per credit hour this year, which means over $1,700 per course. If you need ten courses, you'll have to find a spare $17,000 somewhere. But that's the top end, and you have many options to explore on the way down:

✔ You can expect a typical state university to charge $200 to $350 a credit hour.

✔ Community colleges typically charge about $40 for a credit hour.

✔ An online training company might charge anywhere from fifty dollars to hundreds of dollars for a set of courses to prepare you for professional certification. Remember, though, that you also have to pay the exam fee. For most technical certification, that's only about $100, but for some, such as SAP (Systems, Applications, and Products in Data Processing), the fee for taking the exam might be thousands of dollars.

If you have a list of schools you're considering, do your research to find out what each one's tuition costs are. If the numbers don't work, consider the option of a community or technical college.

Many directories of distance-learning schools — such as *The Unofficial Guide to Distance Learning* by Shannon Turlington, published by Arco — include tuition information for schools in their listings.

Application and registration fees

Colleges typically charge some form of an application fee, which can be minimal for a single course (perhaps $15) and hefty for a degree program ($100 or more). This fee is nonrefundable, even if you're not accepted. Fees for registration are also included in tuition (perhaps around $20 a semester); if you withdraw from a course, you won't get the registration fee back. Also, you may be assessed a yearly student fee that goes towards paying for student support services.

Can I save money by giving up credit?

Whether or not you can save money by taking noncredit courses is a tricky question. Certainly courses that award CEUs rather than credits charge lower tuition. But do they really get you what you need in the way of a credential? And will the quality of education be as good?

As with anything in life, you get what you pay for. CEUs can still impress an employer because they mark you as an ambitious, lifelong learner, but they never culminate in a degree which some companies require for certain positions. If getting that degree is important to you, but

you're strapped for cash, consider these options before resorting to a noncredit program:

✔ Take for-credit courses from a technical college instead of a university.

✔ Look at a state university rather than a private one.

✔ Consider taking just some credit courses now, but not the full degree. You can always go for the degree later, when your finances are in better shape or your employer agrees to underwrite some of the tuition.

Online training companies don't have an add-on fee structure like universities. Typically, what they charge you for the course (your tuition) is all you have to pay.

What about all the extras?

After you do your homework about tuition and application/registration fees for the program you're considering, you can go ahead and fill in all the extras in your budget. Search the school catalog or Web site for information about extras like fees for materials or postage (see Figure 3-9). Estimate what you might spend on computer equipment or phone calls for the course. Think about whether you will need to set up a second phone line because of your increased online activity. Consider whether you will have to, or want to, visit the school in person at least once during your studies and estimate the cost of travel.

Now you're ready to create your own budget. Table 3-1 shows a sample educational budget. It covers all the costs involved in taking a five-course online certificate program from a university several hundred miles away. The sample budget assumes that you take the five courses over two semesters, and so you incur some fees or costs two times. The first three lines cover tuition and fees; the rest of the table lists the type of extra costs you should consider in creating your own budget.

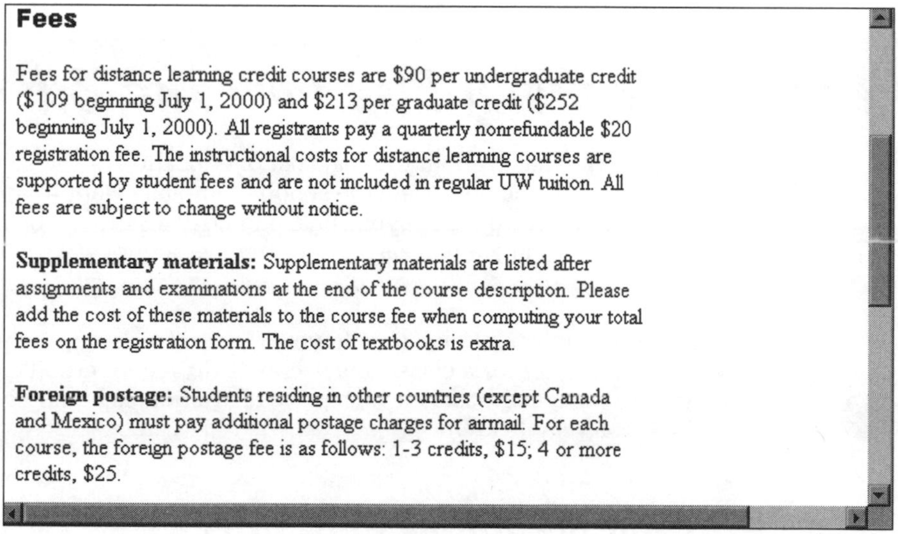

Figure 3-9:
Look for
information
about
non-tuition
costs,
such as
postage and
supple-
mentary
materials,
on your
school's
Web site.

Fees

Fees for distance learning credit courses are $90 per undergraduate credit ($109 beginning July 1, 2000) and $213 per graduate credit ($252 beginning July 1, 2000). All registrants pay a quarterly nonrefundable $20 registration fee. The instructional costs for distance learning courses are supported by student fees and are not included in regular UW tuition. All fees are subject to change without notice.

Supplementary materials: Supplementary materials are listed after assignments and examinations at the end of the course description. Please add the cost of these materials to the course fee when computing your total fees on the registration form. The cost of textbooks is extra.

Foreign postage: Students residing in other countries (except Canada and Mexico) must pay additional postage charges for airmail. For each course, the foreign postage fee is as follows: 1-3 credits, $15; 4 or more credits, $25.

Table 3-1	A Student Distance-Learning Budget		
Item	*Cost*	*Quantity*	*Total*
Tuition per course	$445	5	$2,225
Application fee	$40	1	$40
Student fees	$20	2 (1 per semester)	$40
Textbooks	$30	10	$300
Lab materials	$25	2 (1 per semester)	$50
Lab fees	$20	2 (1 per semester)	$40
Long-distance phone calls	$100	n/a	$100
Shipping	$50	n/a	$50
Computer equipment and software	$500	n/a	$500
Trip to school	$500	1	$500
Total Educational Budget			$3,845

By creating a budget like the one in Table 3-1, taking all costs into account over the life of your program, you can begin to see what schools you can afford and whether you might need a little help paying for your education.

Letting Somebody Else Foot the Bill

After you face the music about the real cost of education at the schools you're considering, you might feel the school you really want to apply to is too expensive. Before you make your final choice of a school, consider whether a little help might make a more expensive school work within your budget.

Don't count on a payment plan to help you. Most schools require payment in full when you register for a class. Some schools do accept credit cards, but using them on a regular basis for high-price-tag tuition can land you in serious debt, if you're not careful.

Will my employer help out?

Training that keeps employees on top of changes in their industry and prepares people to take on new or more complex roles in an organization is one of the hottest trends in the business world today. Employers know that retaining good people means challenging and promoting them; to do so, employers are stepping up to the plate at an impressive rate to support employee education. They are also recognizing the value and quality of distance education, which allows their employees to get a great education while continuing to work full time.

Ask your human resources department about your organization's tuition reimbursement policy. Many companies will help to support your education if the program or degree is related to your job duties, or would make you viable in a more responsible position in your company. Expect your company to ask for particulars about the school you want to attend and its accreditations.

Tuition reimbursement programs are, as the name suggests, set up on a reimbursement basis. You are required to pay for your own education, and if you get a certain grade in a class, your employer reimburses you.

Many unions negotiate for educational benefits when they work out a new contract. If you belong to a union, ask the union business manager about this provision.

What will an employer reimburse you for? Policies vary, but many cover

- ✔ Tuition, or a percentage of your tuition

- ✔ Books, lab fees, and materials

- ✔ Travel to and from school (not quite as relevant for distance learning, but even if you have to make just one in-person visit, this could be a significant amount)

If you're interested in taking a distance-learning program, see whether you can negotiate with your employer to also cover monthly fees for an Internet service provider for the duration of the course, extra software or hardware you must purchase, and long-distance phone calls.

Teachers in public schools are often eligible to have tuition reimbursed by their school district for courses carrying college credit. Check with your union or school administrator to research the district's policy.

Should I get a loan?

Getting a loan for your education is always an option if you have good credit and you think that you can manage the monthly payments and interest. You should consider how additional education will reward you in the way of career advancement or a higher salary down the road; however, banking on that advancement by taking on more debt can be stressful and can backfire on you if advancement never comes.

If you do decide a loan is the right option for you, you can find many lending institutions that offer educational loans, with new ones appearing every day. When you're ready to commit to your distance education, you have to do your homework to find the best lending institution and the best loan program. Because you're planning to take courses online, why not begin your bank search online, too?

✔ **Online banks and lenders:** Many banks and lending institutions maintain Web sites where you can find out about any special programs they may offer. For example, Key Bank (www.key.com), shown in Figure 3-10, offers a loan called Key CareerLoan that is specifically designed for part-time students studying through distance learning.

✔ **EstudentLoan:** This online loan company has a program called LoanFinder on its Web site (www.estudentloan.com) that gives you comparisons of up to 12 loan programs from different lenders.

✔ **Embark.com:** To get a full range of financing options, from government aid to personal loans, go to Embark.com (www.embark.com) and look for their four-step approach to finding the right financing option, as shown in Figure 3-11.

✔ **National, state, or provincial sites:** You can also explore loans through Web sites run by countries, such as the Canada Student Loans program site (www.hrdc-drhc.gc.ca/student_loans), or through provinces or states, such as the Rhode Island Student Loan Authority site shown in Figure 3-12 (www.risla.com). Open your favorite search engine and enter the keywords "student loans" (including the quotes) to see a list of loan programs for various locations. To further refine your search, you can add your state or country to the keyword string.

Figure 3-10: Online banks and lending institutions, such as Key Bank, make applying for a loan easy. (Paying it back is the hard part!)

Figure 3-11:
This handy table of financing options is accompanied by a four-step process to find and apply for a loan online.

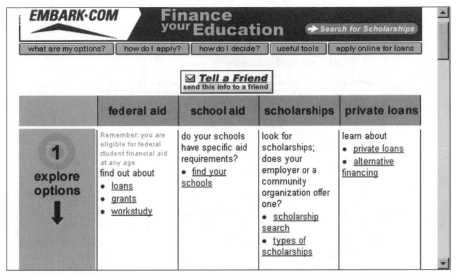

Figure 3-12:
Your state, province, or region might maintain information about educational financing, as do Rhode Island, New Mexico, and Oklahoma, to name a few.

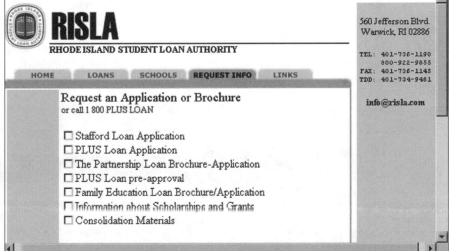

What about a scholarship or grant?

Scholarships and grants share one important trait: You don't have to repay them . . . ever. An award may be a few hundred dollars or thousands of dollars towards your education. The variety of scholarships and grants available out there is astounding, and usually it doesn't matter whether you're taking courses in person or from the Arctic when qualifying for one. Keep in mind, however, that some do require you to be a full-time student.

Here are some of the more common criteria for a scholarship or grant award:

- ✔ Financial need
- ✔ Academic performance
- ✔ Parent's place of employment (more typically for younger students, but it doesn't hurt to ask!)
- ✔ Athletic prowess
- ✔ Artistic ability
- ✔ Ethnic or racial origins

Because so many scholarships and grant programs are available, be sure to perform a thorough search to find one that is a match. Try visiting FastWeb (www.fastweb.com) to run a search for scholarships for which you may qualify (see Figure 3-13). Also, ask your school's financial aid office for information about scholarships and grants. They may have information on awards from religious groups, alumni groups, community organizations, major corporations, foundations, or arts organizations.

Work-study programs can be useful if you're not currently employed and you want to take classes online. Under these programs, you work in a job related to your field of study. In the United States, payment is mandated to be at least the current minimum wage, but you may get a bit more. Some of these jobs are located on campus, but not all are. You may even be able to get some academic credit for your work. Check with school's career-counseling or financial aid office for more specifics.

Figure 3-13:
Perhaps you qualify for a scholarship? Check 100s of scholarships through FastWeb. com.

You can find out more about how scholarships, grants, and other programs work at Embark.com (www.embark.com).

Is my education tax-deductible?

Every country differs, but many countries offer a tax break for people investing in their educations. England offers help through the Education Maintenance Allowance. Australia has the Higher Education Contribution Scheme (HECS). In the United States, you can claim a tax credit of up to $1,000 under a tax regulation called the Lifetime Learning Credit. You can tally up to $1,000 of credit by claiming 20 percent of the first $5,000 you spend on qualified tuition. Related expenses may also be included in this credit. (IRS Publication 3064, titled Notice 97-60, Education Tax Incentive, provides details on educational tax credits.)

Tax laws change all the time, so be sure to check with your tax adviser when you're ready to claim an educational tax credit for the latest relevant regulations.

Part II
Setting Yourself Up to Learn

The 5th Wave By Rich Tennant

"Look at that craftsmanship. Notice the patina. It's already three years old. In the computer industry, that makes it a genuine antique."

In this part . . .

You can figure out what 2 + 2 is by entering a formula into a spreadsheet program, or by counting on your fingers. The finger approach takes little in the way of specialized equipment. Taking classes by distance learning, on the other hand, is more like the spreadsheet method. In other words, you have to line up the right computer hardware, software, and space to spread them all out before you can even walk through your virtual classroom door.

In these chapters, you discover what you need in the way of hardware and software to learn online. You get advice about setting up your workspace and your life so that you can handle the time commitment of studying on the Web. And, if you have a disability, you can find ways that distance learning and assistive technology are making continued education accessible to everyone.

Chapter 4

A Technical Education:
Hardware and Software
for Distance Learning

In This Chapter

▶ Checking whether your computer is up to speed

▶ Connecting to phone or cable lines for fast Internet access

▶ Gathering plug-ins to run multimedia files

▶ Getting online and browsing

▶ Using VCRs, faxes, and scanners

▶ Finding technical support

*W*henever I have a crisis and call on the plumber, auto mechanic, or electrician to rescue me, I'm always struck with the same thought as they fix my pipes/car/lights with aplomb: With the right tool, anything is possible. Well, as it is in life, so it is in distance learning. Learning online challenges your time management, study skills, and concentration, but it all starts with the simple act of gathering the right tools to communicate and perform research.

In this chapter, I give you a checklist of technical necessities you must consider in preparing for your online distance-learning experience, from computers to fax machines, and from phone lines to browsers. Along the way, I also point out ways that your school might help you with your technology homework.

Back-to-School Shopping!

Chances are you wouldn't even be considering taking a course over the Internet if you didn't already have a computer of some kind lying around the house. But does that computer have what it takes to meet the technical requirements of distance learning? If you're not wired for the latest high-speed phone technology, are you ready to connect with an online class?

You'll be glad to hear that most schools consider the average learner with average technology when designing their programs. They realize that aiming their course towards the computer user with dozens of gigabytes of memory and super-duper, high-speed Internet access seriously limits their potential student body. That said, there are some technology basics you simply must have.

Do you have the right computer?

Computers seem to get smaller, faster, and better every other day or so. Given this frenzied pace of change, how can you be sure that your computer will make the grade in online learning? Your first step is to check your school's Web site for specific recommendations for hardware and software required to take its online courses. Figure 4-1 shows one such system requirement document for Learn2.com.

Don't let the ever-changing nature of home computing stress you out too much. Because course design, and therefore delivery technology, tend to be set for at least one or two semesters, the requirements at the start of a school year will probably get you through 12 months without much change. And schools are notoriously behind the times compared to the average corporation.

Figure 4-1:
This program's Web site lists its minimum requirements for such techie tools as hardware, browser, and operating systems.

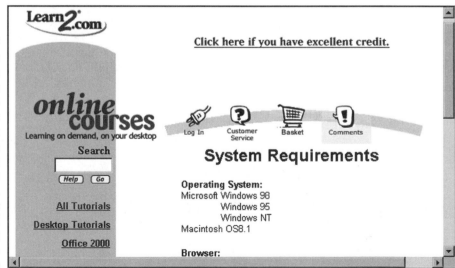

Before taking on an Internet-based distance-learning course, check for the following requirements:

- ✔ **Operating system:** This is the underlying software that contains systems files that make your computer and other software run. Windows, Mac OS, and Linux are examples of operating systems. New computers come with an operating system already installed and configured. You may, however, need to upgrade that operating system periodically when a new version is released.

- ✔ **Processor speed:** Your computer processor is contained on a microchip, and determines the speed at which your computer performs its many chores.

    Different operating systems measure speed differently. Windows processor speed used to jump in logical increments (286, 386, 486), but around 586, the terminology switched to Pentium-speak (Pentium I, Pentium II, and so on). To really understand your computer's speed, check the number of megahertz (MHz) listed for the processor. Each *megahertz* represents one million cycles per second. A 486 typically ran at 50 MHz, but Pentiums can burn up the road at speeds around 800 MHz.

- ✔ **Memory:** Memory is basically storage. Computer memory comes in two forms:

    - RAM, or *Random Access Memory,* is like your computer's workbench. The more RAM, the more space your computer has to spread out programs on the bench so they're available when you need them. If you have less RAM, your computer must store away one program before it can get at another, which can slow down or even crash your system.

    - ROM, or *Read Only Memory,* is the space available to store data and instructions on your computer. When you save the newsletter you've just written to the PTA, this is where it goes.

- ✔ **Modem:** A computer modem connects your computer to the phone and converts your computer digital data into audio *(analog)* impulses that can move over phone lines. Different modems transmit this data at different speeds, measured in bits per second (bps), kilobits per second (Kbps), or megabits (Mbps). The speed with which data moves over phone lines is impacted not only by a particular modem's speed but also by the type of phone line you have and the kind of connection it is able to make at any point in time, based on Internet traffic.

    Note that new modem technology includes cable and satellite modems. These don't use phone lines to transmit data, but instead use the same connection your cable TV uses, or a satellite transmission, respectively.

✔ **Browser:** Browser software is what enables you to find, load, and read information on Web sites. Browsers can also enable you to play audio and graphics files on multimedia Web sites, and some include features such as chat areas and videoconferencing. Internet Explorer and Netscape Navigator are two popular browsers. Internet services such as AOL and Prodigy also incorporate a browser into their interface.

✔ **Video cards:** Video cards convert any graphic or video images that your computer plays into signals that display on your monitor. A video card controls the resolution, refresh rate, and colors displayed on-screen. Advancements in video cards provide for video output to a TV, and enable you to use your computer for desktop video editing.

The most common types of video cards are PCI or ISA; which one you get relates to your motherboard and number of free slots in the guts of your computer. PCI offers faster processing of the two, if your computer can use PCI. Whatever card you buy, make sure that it's accelerated. An accelerated card can speed up the way your computer handles video even more than a processor upgrade.

✔ **CD/DVD-ROM drive:** A CD-ROM (Compact Disk Read Only Memory) or DVD-ROM (Digital Video Disc Read-Only Memory) is a storage medium for computer data that can hold much more data than your 3.5-inch computer disk. DVD is the more recent technology, and stores as much as 16 times more data than a CD-ROM. To read the data stored on a CD, your computer has to have a CD-ROM or DVD-ROM drive. Some computers have built-in drives, but you can also buy an external CD/DVD-ROM drive, if your computer doesn't have one. If your course includes CD-based material, you have to have a CD or DVD drive.

✔ **Sound card:** Most computers come with a sound card installed, but if you want to upgrade, make sure that the card you buy can handle 15-bit sound at a minimum (32-bit is better). It should also have technical bells and whistles like FM synthesis and wavetable sound. Note that, even if you have a sound card, you won't hear a thing unless you also have speakers or a headphone. You can also use a sound card to input sound into your computer by connecting a microphone.

Table 4-1 provides my recommendations for the technology you should have on hand before embarking on your distance education, along with the least you can probably get away with.

Because things do change quickly in the world of technology, use the information noted here as a guideline only; your safest bet is to check your school's requirements to get up-to-the minute information when you sign on for a course.

Table 4-1	Computer System Requirements for Online Learning	
Item	*Recommended*	*Minimum*
Monitor display	19 inch	15 inch
Operating system	Windows 98 or Windows 2000, or Macintosh System OS 8.5	Windows 95, or Mac OS 7.6
Processor speed	Intel Pentium 500 MHz (Windows), or Macintosh PowerPC	Intel Pentium 133 MHz, or Power Macintosh
Memory	Windows 128 MB RAM, or Macintosh 32 MB RAM	Windows 16 MB RAM or Macintosh16 MB RAM
Hard drive	6 gigabytes	2 gigabytes
Modem speed	56 Kbps or faster	28.8 Kbps
Browser	Netscape Navigator 4.5 or Internet Explorer 5	Netscape Navigator 4.5 or Internet Explorer 5
Sound card	USB (Universal Serial Bus) or PCI (Peripheral Component Interconnect)	ISA (Industry Standard Architecture)
Video card	Support for True Color and 3-D	Support for16-bit color
Storage drives	3.5-inch floppy-disk drive, and writeable CD or Zip drive	3.5-inch floppy-disk drive
Media peripherals	DVD-ROM drive	CD-ROM drive

Getting all the right Internet connections

When it comes to phones and your distance-learning experience, the two real questions are how many lines should you have, and what technology should they use?

First, remember that, with a standard one-line phone connection, if you're online, your family can't use the phone. Period. If you think that you'll spend enough time online to send your family into telephone withdrawal while taking a degree program that could last for a few years, a second phone line may be a good idea. If you think that others in your house can stand the silence for an hour or so a day, I recommend you save the money and stick with one line.

Mac or PC? Or . . .

Does it matter whether you have a Macintosh or a Windows-based PC? Not really. Both platforms support most major software packages, with graphics packages being especially robust in the Mac arena. Both operating systems access the Internet in the same way, as far as the user is concerned.

The main issue here is whether you can handle converting files from one format to another. If your teacher sends out materials in PC format, and you are a Mac user, most mainstream programs like Microsoft Word can handle the conversion automatically. But if you use some less mainstream programs, you may want to look into getting software such as Soft PC, which emulates a Windows environment so that you can more easily run Windows-based software.

And what about Linux? Linux is a free operating system developed by a global community of programmers who contributed lines of code. Linux works like Windows in many ways, but was developed as a free alternative to Microsoft's ubiquitous operating system. Several companies have started offering up their own flavor of Linux, so you can buy a specific product and have a company standing behind it to help you out.

More and more software is being developed on the Linux platform, but not all software available on Windows machines is available in Linux yet. In addition, installing Linux can be a bit of a challenge. Many manufacturers are now coming out with new computers that have Linux already installed, so if you like the idea of never having to pay for an operating-system upgrade again, you may want to check into Linux.

However, your answer to the second question — what kind of technology to use — might make the concern about having an additional phone line moot. For example, with a DSL (digital subscriber line) or a cable modem connection, your Internet connection won't tie up your phone line. With these technologies, your family can watch TV, surf the Net, and even make an old-fashioned phone call all at the same time. DSL brings data across your copper telephone wires, whereas a cable modem uses the lines that bring programs to your TV. Both of these technologies provide much speedier access to the Internet than your standard phone line, making surfing and downloading faster.

These technologies aren't available everywhere, but the phone and cable companies are working on it. If you can obtain this kind of connection, expect to pay anywhere from $30 to $60 a month, plus the cost of installation.

ISDN (Integrated Services Digital Network) is another common Internet-connection buzzword; however, ISDN is no longer cutting edge; it's being replaced by its successor, DSL. Unlike DSL or cable, if you experience a power outage with ISDN, your phone line won't work at all.

The following table compares the access speeds of the different options that are available.

Access type	Access speed
Computer modem	Various speeds, such as 28.8, 33.6, 56 Kbps
ISDN	64 Kbps to 128 Kbps
Cable modem	1 Mbps to 3 Mbps
DSL	1.5 Mbps to 9 Mbps

Many new homes being built today are already wired for high-speed Internet access. If you're about to build a home, ask about the cost of pre-wiring. If you're moving into a recently built home, ask whether the home is pre-wired. You'll still have to pay a monthly fee, but you won't have any installation charges.

So how do you decide whether you should stick to one phone line, add a second line, or upgrade your technology? It's all a matter of budget and whether you expect to get long-term benefits from either the new technology or the second line. You have to consider the inconvenience to others living with you if you're online a great deal, and how frustrated you get when slower connections to the Internet cause content to load slowly or files to download at the speed of a weary snail. Start by visiting your local phone company's Web site (such as Ameritech's site, shown in Figure 4-2) to see what's available to you, and at what price.

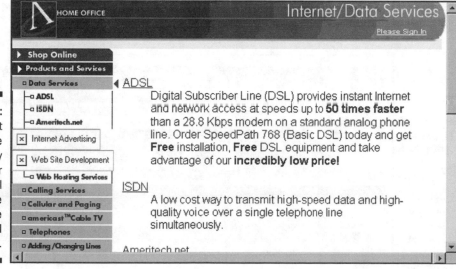

Figure 4-2: Check what your phone company can offer you; not all services are available to all customers.

Concerning plug-ins, players, and other online utilities

In the world of computer hardware, you may plug in speakers to your monitor and plug in a printer to your computer. *Software plug-ins* — utilities that add some kind of functionality to another software program — work in a similar way.

Plug-ins exist for many functions, but the ones you're most likely to use in your distance learning are those that enable you to read files or play multimedia. During the course of a typical class, your instructor may ask you to visit Web sites that have audio, video, or animation files you can only play by using a plug-in. In addition to plug-ins, you may also need to acquire freestanding players for multimedia files and software products, such as NetMeeting, for holding meetings online.

Plug-ins, players, and even some meeting software are often free, or at least inexpensive. The free versions may be less robust than the full package, but they'll probably do for most students. These products are available for downloads from a few different places:

✔ The manufacturer's Web site, such as the Netscape site, where you can download plug-ins for your Navigator Web browser (`home.netscape.com/plugins`)

✔ Centralized download sites, such as the CNET site shown in Figure 4-3, where several free plug-ins are available in one spot

✔ Links provided on the Web pages that require the plug-in in the first place (If a Web site contains files that you can't view without a particular plug-in, it usually provides a link to another site where you can download that plug-in.)

Figure 4-3: The CNET download page at `download.cnet.com` is a good place to get many utilities from one location.

The following list includes some common utilities you may want to locate and load onto your computer in preparation for your distance-learning class:

- RealPlayer, from Real Networks plays both audio and video files. (Look for RealPlayer at `www.real.com`, shown in Figure 4-4.)

- Apple QuickTime is set of Macintosh extensions that plays video, audio, and animation files. (Look for it at `www.apple.com/quicktime`.)

- Adobe Acrobat Reader enables you to exchange all sorts of documents with all sorts of people. Traditionally, to view a file (such as an Excel spreadsheet), you had to have the program in which the file was created (such as Excel) loaded on your computer. But if you have Acrobat Reader, you can view an Excel file (or any other file) that has been saved in Acrobat format, regardless of whether you have Excel on your computer. (Look for Adobe Acrobat Reader at `www.adobe.com`.)

- Windows Media Player, which Microsoft supplies in its Windows operating system, can play both audio and video files. (You can also download Media Player from `www.microsoft.com/windows/mediaplayer`.)

- Shockwave is a multimedia file player often used with online computer games. (Look for Shockwave at `www.macromedia.com`.)

- Flash from Macromedia plays files created with Flash, a 3-D animation program that can create sophisticated multimedia events which you display through your browser. (Look for Flash at `www.macromedia.com/software/flash`.)

- NetMeeting is a program from Microsoft which allows you to interact in live videoconferencing sessions, where you can both hear and see other participants. (Look for NetMeeting at `www.netmeeting.com`.)

Figure 4-4:
Real.com makes audio and video player plug-ins available for download through its Web site.

Your school may have licenses to some of these plug-ins, which allow students to download them from the school site. Check your school's computer-services department or ask your instructor about this possibility.

Which software applications will you need?

Your school may supply you with special software for accessing your class, you may also download some plug-ins or players to view multimedia files, and you're likely to have a good browser for surfing the Net already. But what about plain old-fashioned productivity software like word processors and spreadsheet programs? Nobody's going to give these to you for free, they aren't cheap, and you're likely to need at least a few of them ready and waiting on your computer the day your class starts.

If you think you'll need more than one of these programs, consider a full-blown office suite. A suite of productivity applications such as Microsoft Office 2000 or Lotus SmartSuite Millennium can run you about $500 to $700, but typically includes full-featured word processor, spreadsheet, database, presentation, desktop-design, and Web-page-design software.

Word processing

The most obvious software you will need for just about any class is a word-processing package. Word processors are pretty full-featured these days, allowing you to create documents and even save them as Web pages. With a modern word processor, you can manipulate text, photographs, drawings, and even video and sound files. You'll need such a program to type your assignments, and perhaps even to design Web pages. The three major word processing products are Word from Microsoft, WordPro from Lotus, and WordPerfect from Corel. They all share pretty much the same functionality, with a few variations, and at a similar price (about $275 to $300).

Several lower-end word processors are also available, and come built into productivity suites like Works and ClarisWorks, which often come already loaded on a new computer. These programs have perfectly acceptable features for all but the power document designer. To give you an idea of the difference between these two levels of word processor, Figures 4-5 and 4-6 show the main screen from Word for Windows and the word processor element of Works.

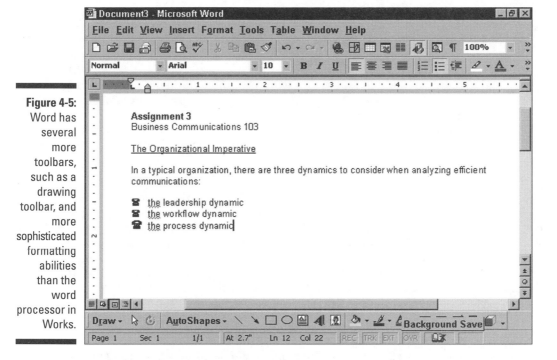

Figure 4-5:
Word has several more toolbars, such as a drawing toolbar, and more sophisticated formatting abilities than the word processor in Works.

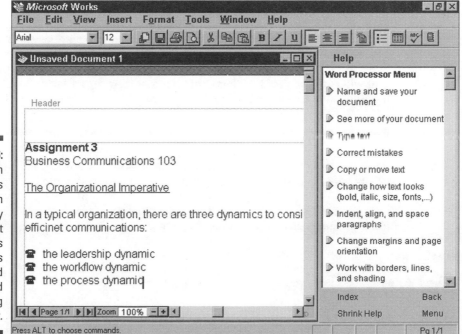

Figure 4-6:
Although Works has enough functionality for most users, it is Microsoft's simplified word processing product.

I don't recommend trying to make do with a basic text-editing program like WordPad, an accessory built into Windows (or Notepad, the standard Macintosh text editor), for your class work. The functionality of this type of program is frustratingly basic.

Because you're likely to use a word processor for many things, I don't recommend that you buy one just because it's the program your instructor has. Buy a software product for the features you prefer. As long as it's a reasonably mainstream product such as the ones mentioned here, your instructor will be able to read your assignments, which you typically submit as an attachment to an e-mail or forum posting, from his or her word processor.

Spreadsheets

A spreadsheet program is the numbers-cruncher of the computing world. Programs like Excel and Lotus 1-2-3 offer a ledger-like interface where you can enter numbers and perform calculations on those numbers with formulas and functions. If you're taking a math or accounting course, you might need a spreadsheet program, which will run you around $300. Alternately, the spreadsheet programs built into more basic suites like Works are usually fine for most folks.

Databases

A database is a place to store and manipulate data such as client contact information, information for product catalogs, and research data for term papers. The power of a database comes from its ability to sort through and view data in different ways. Although your school isn't likely to require that you have a database program (unless you're taking a database-design course), these programs are very useful for organizing all the information you may gather over the course of your studies. Well-known database products that will run you about $300 include Microsoft Access, ClarisWorks' database module, and Corel Quattro Pro.

Presentation

If you think that your instructor will require you to develop slide presentations for your class (perhaps you're taking a business communications course?), you're likely to need a presentation package. Although I could list a few options here, I won't. I'll simply recommend PowerPoint from Microsoft; this robust program has become a standard because of its great features and easy-to-use functionality. It costs about $340 if you buy it as a stand-alone program.

Getting Online

How hard is it to get connected the Internet nowadays? First, plug in your computer. Then, turn it on.

With Internet access software and browsers built into new computers, hooking up to the Internet really is just about that easy. And if you don't have a brand-new computer, all you have to do is obtain an Internet Service Provider's software, which usually steps you through all you have to do to get connected within minutes.

Hooking up with an Internet provider

To connect to the Internet you need to open an account with an Internet Service Provider (ISP). This service is your onramp to the Internet.

Without getting down into the keystrokes involved in signing up with a specific ISP, I'll sketch out the basic steps involved in getting online:

1. **Pick a provider, such as America Online (AOL), EarthLink, or your local ISP equivalent.**

   See the following sections for advice on finding the perfect Internet provider for your needs.

2. **Get the provider's software.**

   Free AOL sign-up disks are hard to avoid: They are available for the taking in banks, office-supply stores, and probably your dentist's office. You may find access software for a variety of online services — such as AOL, MSN, Prodigy, and CompuServe — loaded right onto your new computer's hard drive. If all else fails, pick up the phone, call a provider company, and have them mail you the software.

3. **Put the provider's CD in your CD-ROM drive and follow the directions.**

   During installation, be prepared to provide credit card information to pay for any access charges, to choose an account name, and to pick a local phone number that your computer dials to access the Internet.

If you have a modem and a phone or cable line connected to your computer, you're now in business.

Who's providing Internet access?

Companies that provide accounts that you use to access the Internet are called Internet Service Providers, or ISPs for short. Although ISPs come in all shapes and sizes, in general they fall into one of three categories:

- **Local companies:** These small businesses exist just to connect a few thousand users through their servers to the Internet.

✔ **National and international Internet access companies:** These companies, such as EarthLink and AT&T WorldNet Service, focus mainly on Internet access, but on a much larger scale than local providers.

✔ **Huge online service corporations:** These giants — such as America Online (AOL), Microsoft Network (MSN), CompuServe, and Prodigy — don't just offer access: They are big sales machines with online stores and a whole slate of member services.

You can think of the differences between your local provider, national or international access companies, and full-boat Internet services as being similar to the difference between your hometown fair, a large-scale amusement park, and Disneyland. The differences lie in their size, number of services, and price.

Services such as AOL or MSN, and even some access providers like EarthLink, organize areas of information and services like shopping malls and reference libraries that can be useful. They also police their user community a bit more, so if you have kids using your Internet connection, an online service like one of these may be a good choice. Another benefit to these services is the more business-like infrastructure. They make getting and installing the software simpler in most cases, and have dependable customer service and tech support.

One other category of provider exists: the kind that offers access for free, such as freeXDSL. A few of these companies set limits on the number of hours you can spend online each month, but not all do. The hook here is that they make their money from advertisements that run the whole time you're online. The ads can be distracting, and they also slow down your browser in accessing sites.

What does it cost?

Internet access companies charge about $20 for unlimited access. However, most services offer alternative plans that include a flat fee for a certain number of hours, plus an additional charge per hour. Some services, such as EarthLink, also have a $25 sign-up fee, but you can often find some promotion going on that waives the sign-up fee.

If you really want to go all out, you can use an online service such as AOL or MSN, which typically charge you about $20 to $22 a month for unlimited Internet access. Some of these services will knock a little off your monthly fee if you prepay for a year of service.

If you're searching for the best deal on Internet service access with a provider such as AOL or Prodigy, look for special offers with as much as 500 free hours when you sign up for a new account, but beware that you're often required to use those 500 hours in your first month of use. Or, if you're in the market for a new computer, look for rebates of about $400 on your purchase if you sign up for a few years of Internet access with a given provider.

Not every country in the world has unlimited access; in some countries, you can only get an account with *measured access,* which means you pay as you go for the minutes you spend online. If you do have the option of an unlimited access pricing plan, it's worth paying for — at least for the duration of your distance-learning program.

Browsing for the right browser

A *browser* is a software program that enables you to move around the Internet and read information on Web pages. Browsers use one or more search engines to help you locate information online. Browsing software also offers a home page with links to useful sites and summaries of information like the latest headlines, your horoscope, or the results of today's soccer game.

Many ISPs and all online services include a browser in their connection software, but that browser may not be the one you want to use. Because most browsers are essentially free, you might as well use the best one you can find. Look for additional browsers choices preinstalled on your computer, available for download from the maker's Web site, or on discs available at stores or through promotions.

Be aware that all browsers are not created equal when it comes to being able to read a Web page. For various reasons that involve technical things like Java and frames, which I won't bore you with, not all browsers display a Web page exactly as the designer of the page intended. Schools are likely to design their Web sites to work with one of the two most popular browsers: Netscape Navigator (see Figure 4-7) and Microsoft Internet Explorer (see Figure 4-8).

What a Web page looks like is not the only thing that can be affected by which browser you use. At one university where I took some courses, something about their Web site crashed my computer whenever I tried to enter discussion areas with CompuServe's browser. The school flat out said that they didn't have the time to support any browsers but Internet Explorer and Netscape Navigator, so I switched browsers.

Figure 4-7:
The
Netscape
Netcenter
(home.
netscape.
com) is the
home page
for the
Netscape
Navigator
browser.

Figure 4-8:
Microsoft
offers
Internet
Explorer as
part of the
Windows
operating
system or
for free
download
from this
site: www.
Microsoft.
com/
windows/
ie/
default.
htm.

The mail game: Setting up for e-mail

Many online services include an e-mail client in their software so that you can send, receive, and file away e-mail messages, along with any attachments. Other sources of e-mail software are products like these:

✔ **Microsoft Outlook:** Available as part of Office 2000, in a "lite" version called Outlook Express included with the Internet Explorer browser, or sold separately

✔ **Netscape Messenger:** A part of the Netscape Communicator package, which also includes the Navigator browser

✔ **Lotus cc:mail:** Part of SmartSuite Millennium or sold separately

If you buy a new computer, an e-mail program such as Outlook is usually included.

Many search sites such as Yahoo! and WebCrawler also make e-mail available for free. Other sites with free e-mail include Hotmail and WebMail. However, be forewarned that these sites have had some controversy lately over the security of their users' messages.

If you have need of a couple of e-mail addresses, find out whether your provider offers more than one mailbox to users, or use one mailbox in your ISP account and one or more mailboxes from a free provider.

Do You Need More Stuff? (VCR, Fax, Scanners)

Although our lives may revolve around computers more than we like to think these days, computers are not the only piece of hardware you may need for distance learning. Three other pieces of equipment might come in handy:

✔ **A fax machine to send and receive hardcopy content such as a newspaper clipping:** Fax machines come in a few forms: a simple fax machine; a combination fax/phone; or a multipurpose machine that can fax, scan, copy, and even act as a printer.

Most computers have faxing software and a fax modem built in so that you can take a document from a program like a word processor and send that file to a fax machine directly. If you have this software installed on your computer, you can also receive faxes directly to your printer. One such faxing software that is often built into computers is WinFax Pro from Symantec.

As an alternative to buying fax equipment, you can also receive faxes by signing up with an online faxing service, which is usually free. These services assign you a phone number, which may or may not be local to you (I live in Indiana, and my fax number is in Washington State!). You tell people to fax you at that number, and your faxing service sends you an e-mail when a fax arrives. Using software that the faxing service provides, you can open up, save, and print these faxes. One such provider is efax.com, shown in Figure 4-9.

✔ **A scanner to scan hardcopy documents into electronic form:** Scanning essentially saves the image as a computer file that you can then manipulate or e-mail. For example, if you want to send a photograph of a specimen to your instructor for a science course, you can scan the image, reduce it, add callouts to it, crop it to remove some non-essential background images, and send the file on its way.

Scanners come in two basic types: *Flat-bed scanners* allow you to place a page on a flat surface to be scanned, making them perfect for things like books and magazines; *paper-fed scanners* work best when you have separate sheets of paper you can feed through. Flat-bed scanners do tend to be pricier.

✔ **A VCR (and of course, a TV to go with it) to play videotaped lectures or other course material:** If you haven't figured out how to use your VCR yet (and I know you're out there), now's the time to crack open that owners manual! And if your VCR looks like a relic from the cold war, consider upgrading to one with a remote control, freeze-frame pause, and auto head-cleaning features.

Figure 4-9:
efax.com offers online faxing and voicemail that won't cost you a penny.

The world of videoconferencing

Videoconferencing is the technology that enables two or more people in different locations to see and hear each other. You can use products such as NetMeeting to hold online videoconferences, but you may also encounter videoconference technology that doesn't take place on your desktop. With this kind of videoconferencing equipment, you can upload images from any location to a satellite and download them to remote sites.

Videoconference facilities that you can use for a fee are located in a variety of places; for example, many major copy-store chains, conference centers, or large hotels have such facilities. Some companies and schools have their own videoconferencing setup. Your instructor may arrange for remote students to be part of an on-campus meeting by having them go to a local videoconference site.

Although low-cost videoconference systems are available, no continuing education school requires you to have your own videoconferencing set up. You might, however, be asked to go to a local videoconferencing location (or participate in the audio portion of an online meeting that includes one-way video through software such as NetMeeting).

For more information about the evolving role of videoconferencing in education, visit `www.kn.pacbell.com/wired/vidconf/home.html`.

Who You Gonna Call? Tech Support for the Distance Learner

When you're a distance-learning student, you don't have a handy network guy named Tony in that closet-sized room down the hall to call when your computer crashes . . . or do you? True, you don't have an actual person around to help you recover a lost file or install software, but distance-learning organizations are realizing that, to make the online learning experience successful, they do have to provide a certain level of technical support and information to students.

Whether you're taking classes from an online training company or a major university, you will probably have a technical support group to help you. Tech support can come in a few forms:

✔ The school may have a help desk you can e-mail or call with a question.

✔ The school Web site may offer a FAQ (Frequently Asked Questions) database or documents about common technical concerns that you can read online or print out (see Figure 4-10).

✔ Your class Web site may have a discussion forum dedicated to technical questions and issues. Here, you may get an answer from another student, or your instructor may forward some questions to the school computer-support division for a response.

Figure 4-10:
This Australian university provides information and support through CSU Online (www.csu.edu.au/CSU online).

The types of questions you can expect answers to are those that deal with accessing the school's site, browser problems when using the site, and any questions relating to special software the school may have provided to access its course materials.

In addition to answers to your questions, your school may also provide free software and software upgrades. For example, the site shown in Figure 4-11, from the University of Washington, offers students free upgrades to two popular Web browsers.

Figure 4-11:
In addition to technical support, your school may provide easy ways to upgrade your software.

Keep in mind that your school may not give you a response quite as quickly as a corporate tech support department; it may take a day or two (or three) to hear from somebody. But look at it this way: Telling your teacher you couldn't get your homework done on time because you couldn't access the school server is a great excuse for being late!

If you get a message that your school's server is down or offline, do not bother the tech support people with a phone or e-mail message. The problem in that case is on their end, not yours; believe me, they know all about their problem and they're dancing as fast as they can to solve it.

Chapter 5

Distance Learning for People with Disabilities

In This Chapter

▶ Understanding how online accessibility standards are evolving

▶ Finding out about software that makes online learning possible

▶ Using hardware to make the online experience easier

▶ Getting support from your school

*P*erhaps you are considering distance learning but are concerned about the amount of computer use involved because you have a disability that makes using the computer difficult. Good news: In most cases, distance learning can be even more accessible to people with disabilities than in-person classrooms.

People who are visually challenged can take advantage of software that reads what's on their computer screens to them or software that displays text in large print. People with impaired hearing can read their lectures on-screen and participate in live written discussions through chat technology. People who have mobility or dexterity challenges don't have to get to a classroom to learn anymore; they can participate fully in a learning experience without having to leave their homes by taking advantage of several alternative input devices.

If you have a disability and want to understand how you can take courses online, this chapter introduces you to some remarkable possibilities.

Assessing Accessibility

According to recent estimates, as many as 500 million people in the world today have disabilities. Microsoft, which supports an active accessibility initiative, estimates that, in the United States, as many as 20 percent of the population has a disability that could interfere with their use of a computer.

As the Internet has evolved, discussions about accessibility standards have become more ubiquitous. Several organizations are involved in these discussions, including many computer hardware and software companies, and groups such as the World Wide Web Consortium (www.w3.org), whose home page is shown in Figure 5-1. What all these folks are trying to do is to provide access to the world of computing to people with various kinds of disabilities by creating standards in the industry.

Many software and hardware tools exist to support computer users with disabilities. However, not all efforts towards accessibility are in the hands of users; groups that set standards for online design and use, such as the World Wide Web Consortium, are modifying the very architecture underlying the Internet over time to be more user-friendly. In addition, a great deal of Web content and the browsers that access that content are being designed these days with disabilities in mind.

Evolving accessibility standards and technology can help people with

- ✔ Visual impairments
- ✔ Color blindness
- ✔ Hearing and speech impairments
- ✔ Cognitive and language impairments (such as dyslexia)
- ✔ Mobility impairments (such as hand and limb injuries, or arthritis)
- ✔ Seizure disorders

Figure 5-1:
The World Wide Web Consortium was created in 1994; part of its mission is the creation of accessibility standards.

W3C WORLD WIDE WEB *consortium*®

Leading the Web to its Full Potential...

W3C Issues First Public Working Draft of XForms

W3C announces the first public Working Draft of XForms Data Model. XForms architecture separates purpose from presentation, and paves the way for forms that deliver the power of XML with the ease of HTML, to a wider range of devices. (Press Release, Testimonials.)

User Interface Domain
 Document Object Model: DOM
 Graphics: SVG, WebCGM
 HTML
 Internationalization
 Math: MathML
 Mobile Access
 Style Sheets: CSS, XSL
 Synchronized Multimedia: SMIL
 Television and the Web
 Voice Browser
Technology and Society Domain
 Metadata: RDF, PICS
 Micropayments
 Privacy: P3P
 XML Signature
Architecture Domain
 HTTP

Although computer accessibility is helping people learn online, remember that many distance-learning programs still rely on other delivery methods such as print, video, or audio, some of which may not be appropriate for you. Look carefully at the mix of technologies used by any school you're considering and find out whether the school offers alternative formats.

Software That Makes It Possible

The terms _adaptive technology, accessibility aides_ and _assistive technology_ are being bandied about more and more these days, and distance-learning organizations have taken note. These terms all refer to any technology that makes computing more accessible to the entire population. Here are just a few of the technologies that exist:

- Screen enlargers to magnify on-screen text

- Screen readers that use synthesized speech to read what's on-screen to the computer user

- Voice input (also called speech recognition) programs that enable people to enter commands or text into a computer through the spoken word, rather than by using a mouse or keyboard

- Keyboard technology, including on-screen keyboards that allow people to point to a key to enter data, larger keyboards that make keyboarding easier, and even sip-and-puff systems that let users provide input with their breathing

- Controls for adjusting screen contrast and color scheme, as well as for enlarging text size

- Visual signals to display sounds and voice commands on-screen for the hearing impaired

- Features that measure the reading level of material for people with learning disabilities

- Captioning for video programs

- Keyboard enhancement features in software that make up for keyboarding irregularities such as tremors or delayed response

- Word prediction features (offered by some software, such as word processors) that guess what word or phrase you're entering before you finish typing it and complete it for you

Setting up Windows' accessibility features

In Microsoft's continuing effort to have every computer user in the entire world in its pocket, the Windows operating system has several accessibility features built in to support users with disabilities. These features began to appear in Windows 95 and later.

You can set up most accessibility features by following these steps:

1. **From the Windows desktop, choose Start⇨Settings⇨Control Panel.**

   The Control Panel window opens.

2. **Double-click on the Accessibility Options icon.**

   The Accessibility Properties dialog box, shown in Figure 5-2, appears.

Figure 5-2: You can control several accessibility options from one place by accessing the Accessibility Properties dialog box through the Control Panel.

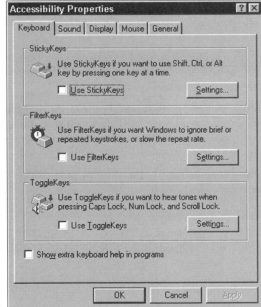

3. **Click on the tab for the type of options you want to adjust to display those options.**

   Your choices are Keyboard, Sound, Display, Mouse, and General. (See the bulleted list after these steps for more information about the options on each tab.)

4. **Click the checkbox for each setting you want to activate, or click the Settings button next to each option to reveal more possibilities.**

   To find out what each setting does, click on the question mark in the upper right corner of the dialog box and then click on the setting you want to know more about.

5. **After you make changes to the settings, click OK to save your changes and exit the dialog box.**

The Accessibility Properties dialog box is chock-full of options to make your computer easier for you to see, hear, and manipulate:

✔ On the Keyboard tab of the Accessibility Properties dialog box (refer to Figure 5-2), you can make any of four selections to modify keyboard functionality:

   • **Use StickyKeys:** This feature allows you to use keyboard shortcuts without having to press two keys at once; with StickyKeys, you can use a command such as Ctrl+V (the paste shortcut) by hitting each key sequentially — first the Control key and then the letter V.

   • **Use FilterKeys:** This feature compensates for imprecise keyboarding. With this setting, you can tell Windows to ignore brief or repeated keystrokes. By adjusting the repeat rate, this option lets you tap a single key briefly without the command registering, or hit a key twice in quick succession and have only a single stroke register. From the Settings button, you can also adjust how long you can hold a key down before Windows begins repeating that character over and over again.

   • **Use ToggleKeys:** This feature sounds a tone when you engage a key that turns on a *toggle* feature (a feature that can be turned on or off from the same key, such as the Caps Lock key).

   • **Show extra keyboard help in programs:** This feature causes various Windows programs to display additional advice on the use of keyboards for input.

✔ On the Sound tab, shown in Figure 5-3, you can make two audio adjustments:

   • **Use SoundSentry:** This feature activates visual signals that appear when a system sound occurs.

   • **Use ShowSounds:** This feature generates captions that appear when a program makes sounds or generates speech.

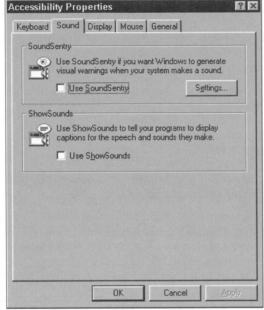

Figure 5-3:
You can set
up Windows
to give you
visual clues
when
system
sounds
occur.

✔ The Display tab has one setting, Use High Contrast; when you check this item, Windows displays colors and fonts in a format that is easy to read.

✔ The Mouse tab has a setting to Use MouseKeys. MouseKeys is a feature that lets you control your cursor movement with the numeric keypad rather that the mouse.

✔ The General tab has settings that enable you to have Windows automatically turn accessibility settings on and off after a certain period of time, or alert you with sounds or messages when these settings turn off or on. You also get an option to Support SerialKey devices, which sets the port you want to use to connect alternative input devices.

Windows also offers another method of changing accessibility options, which may be easier for some people. From the Windows desktop, choose Start⇨ Programs⇨Accessibility⇨Accessibility Wizard, and let Windows walk you through a series of statements, like the ones shown in the dialog box in Figure 5-4. When you check a statement such as "I am deaf or have difficulty hearing sounds from the computer," Windows automatically makes adjustments to settings that would be useful to you.

Check out the Microsoft Accessibility Web site (www.Microsoft.com/enable) for more about how Microsoft products such as Windows and the Office suite of products are addressing accessibility issues.

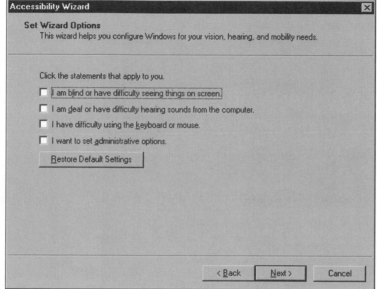

Figure 5-4:
With the
Accessibility
Wizard, you
check the
areas
in which
you have
difficulty,
and
Windows
changes the
appropriate
settings
for you.

Adjusting the display

In addition to the Accessibility Options, you can use the Display settings in the Control Panel to control on-screen color schemes and text size in Windows screens. To change the appearance of your screen, follow these steps:

1. **From the Windows desktop choose Start⇨Settings⇨Control Panel.**

2. **Double-click the Display icon to open the Display Properties dialog box.**

3. **Click on the Appearance tab to display the options shown in Figure 5-5.**

4. **Click on the arrow next to the Scheme drop-down list and select a color scheme.**

   When you make a selection, a preview of the scheme appears in the dialog box. Generally speaking, schemes with the term High Contrast in the title are the easiest to read. Several of these schemes also offer the choice of large or extra large text. This setting controls the size of text that appears in Windows features such as title bars, menus, and messages.

5. **When you find a Scheme that works well for you, click OK to apply the setting and close the dialog box.**

Similar accessibility options are available for operating systems other than Windows, such as Macintosh. Check your computer's help system or documentation to find out exactly what's available to the non-Windows user.

Figure 5-5:
Some color schemes, such as the one shown here, use black and white to make images as clear as possible to those with color blindness or other visual impairments.

Getting your computer to recognize your voice

Imagine this: You sit down at your computer, chat away for a few minutes, and your computer copies down every word, producing a document with no carpal tunnel aggravation and no typos. This isn't a sci-fi dream: Speech recognition makes this scenario possible. *Speech recognition software* uses a technology that converts the spoken word into text in a document. Although many professionals use speech recognition software to make their jobs easier (for example, lawyers may use it to dictate briefs and writers may use it to write novels), the technology can also be a very useful input device for people with disabilities. For example, people who have hand injuries, those who experience tremors or loss of control of their hands, or paraplegics can use speech recognition software to input information into a computer.

When it first appeared on the scene, speech recognition technology was about as useful to effective communication with your computer as two empty soup cans attached with a bit of string. You had to go through a lengthy process to help the software memorize your voice patterns, and then spend half your time correcting errors when the software incorrectly recognized a word like "buzzword" as "bizarre." The good news is that that voice recognition software has improved significantly in the last couple of years, and you can now use this technology for reasonably painless data entry.

Using speech recognition software involves a few steps:

1. **Connect a headset microphone to your computer (the headset usually comes with the software).**

2. **Install the software according to the manufacturer's instructions.**

   During the installation, the program asks you to read some on-screen text into your headphone to help the software learn your inflections and accent. If you skip this step during installation, you do it later, but you must go through this reading session to acquaint the software with your pronunciation.

3. **You can now begin to use the program from within a number of other software programs such as Word for Windows, Internet Explorer, or PowerPoint.** Open a document, activate the software, and speak. Your words will appear on-screen as text in a document.

4. **Be sure that you or someone else reviews the text and, if you find any transcription errors, select the incorrect words and correct them.**

   Each correction you make helps the software to refine its ability to understand your speech. In essence, as you continue to use the software, it will become more accurate. Although these products take some investment up front (in time and money), with use, speech recognition software can become far easier to use than a keyboard.

If speech recognition sounds like a solution you want to explore, take a look at some popular programs, such as

- ✔ **ViaVoice from IBM** (www-4.ibm.com/software/speech): ViaVoice was one of the first speech recognition programs to come out and is actually built into some versions of a few popular software products like Corel WordPerfect. This program is available in Windows, Linux, and Mac format, for around $90.

- ✔ **Dragon NaturallySpeaking from Dragon Systems, Inc.** (www.dragonsys.com): This product, shown in Figure 5-6, is one of the most popular speech recognition programs, and comes in several editions. The Preferred Edition retails for about $199; a Professional Edition with a hefty price tag of $695 includes DragonDictate and a slew of customization features and macro support.

- ✔ **VoiceXpress Professional from Lernout & Hauspie** (www.lhs.com): This program features plug-in vocabularies and mobile dictation. Several specialized versions are available for legal and medical professionals. The suggested retail price is $149.

Lernout & Hauspie acquired Dragon Systems only a few days before I wrote this chapter, so it remains to be seen whether both sets of products will continue to be available long term. Check the Lernout & Hauspie Web site at www.lhs.com for updates on its product line.

Figure 5-6:
Dragon
Systems
offered one
of the first
speech
recognition
products,
and it is still
the most
popular.

Using voice output systems

Whereas speech recognition programs convert what you say into text, screen-reader programs convert text into the spoken word. For blind or visually impaired computer users or those who have difficulty reading text, screen readers make a world of information available. You can use this software with some of the most popular Web browsers.

To use a screen reader, a computer user relies on combinations of keystroke shortcuts or use of the numeric keypad on a keyboard. In addition, Braille viewers are available, such as JFW Braille Viewer from Henter-Joyce (www. hj.com), which allows the user to operate the software with a Braille toolbar.

A couple of popular screen reader programs for Windows are

✔ **Home Page Reader from IBM, priced at $149:** This product focuses on online access, and uses the IBM ViaVoice Outlook synthesizer to help you navigate. The reader speaks not only text, but also information about frames and images displayed on-screen.

✔ **JAWS for Windows Screen Reader from Henter-Joyce:** This company focuses its efforts on the blind and visually impaired community. JAWS retails for about $1,000, but includes special features for the blind or visually impaired such as the JFW Braille reader. The product has also been translated into Spanish, Danish, Dutch, German, French, Italian, Norwegian, and Swedish.

Henter-Joyce also offers a line of audiotape tutorials to help you learn how to use a screen reader with various browsers to get around the Web. The tutorials are priced at about $75.

If you're a Mac user, check into Mac Access Writer and Mac eReader from CAST (cast.org). Mac Access Writer is a word-processing environment that supports word prediction, on-screen keyboards, and text-to-speech features. Mac eReader is a screen-reader program.

Making print LARGER

For low-vision computer users, simply making the text on-screen larger some-times makes the information contained there readable. Your operating system has certain settings to make on-screen text slightly larger (see "Setting up Windows accessibility features," earlier in this chapter). However, if those adjustments don't do the trick, magnification software for use with on-screen text may be what you need.

Magnification software typically supports both black-and-white and color formats, and offers a range of magnification choices. This type of software, which can magnify text and images as much as 32 times their original size, also smoothes enlarged text to remove jagged edges and enables the user to pan around the screen easily. You can also print magnified versions of text.

Some magnification software products to consider are

- **LP-Deluxe Magnification** (www.keyalt.com)**:** This software, which includes a screen reader function in addition to magnification, offers a highlight feature that synchronizes an on-screen highlight with audio readout of the text, making it useful for those with dyslexia or other reading disabilities, as well as for those with vision problems. The software sells for $595 as is available.

- **ZoomText Xtra from AiSquared** (www.aisquared.com)**:** You can buy this software in two versions; Level 1 (priced at $395) is a screen magnifier, and Level 2 (priced at $595) is both a screen magnifier and screen reader. You control magnification through an easy-to-use toolbar, shown in Figure 5-7.

- **MAGic from Henter-Joyce** (www.hj.com)**:** MAGic is a magnification software that offers list boxes that make working with Microsoft Office products easier, as well as support for high and true color, up to 32-bit. You can use MAGic in conjunction with Henter-Joyce's screen reader, JAWS (see "Using voice output systems," earlier in this chapter). This software is priced at $295 for Windows 95 and 98, and $395 for Windows 2000 and NT.

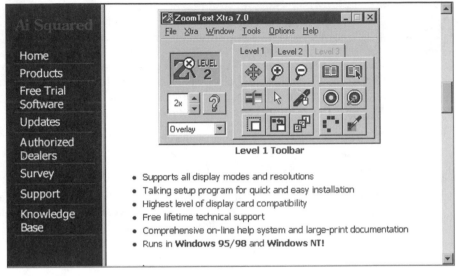

Figure 5-7:
The
ZoomText
Xtra 7.0
toolbar
provides
control over
zoom,
panning,
and image
quality.

Hardware to Help

Several kinds of hardware are available to support the disabled computer user. Special keyboards and mouse devices may help those who have difficulty mastering standard input devices because of an injury, birth defect, or coordination problem. In addition, a range of equipment makes the use of telephones possible for deaf and hearing-impaired students.

Keyboarding and printing made easy

Distance-learning students may spend more time with their keyboards than with their kids or friends, so the quality of the keyboarding experience is important. Alternative keyboards offer modified formats or functionality to help make efficient data input possible for everybody.

Keyboards with large print, like the one shown in Figure 5-8, help visually challenged users to locate the right key at all times.

Other keyboards provide Braille on the keys to assist blind users with data entry, or alternative key arrangements to help avoid wrist and hand strain. Membrane keyboards, such as IntelliKeys from IntelliTools (www.intellitools.com), are designed to allow students to enter data with a head wand. Infrared head pointing is another technology that eases input for those challenged by standard keyboard entry.

Figure 5-8:
The Big
Keys
Keyboard
from Keyalt
(www.
keyalt.
com) comes
in a colored-
keys version
and offers
the
alphabetical
alternative
to the
Qwerty
layout that
many
consider
more
efficient.

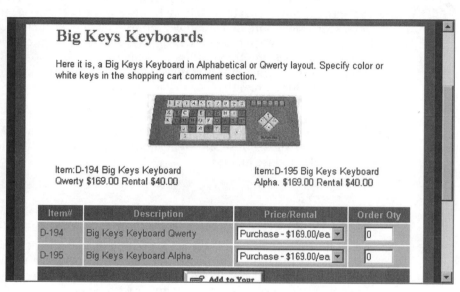

Big Keys Keyboards

Here it is, a Big Keys Keyboard in Alphabetical or Qwerty layout. Specify color or white keys in the shopping cart comment section.

Item:D-194 Big Keys Keyboard   Item:D-195 Big Keys Keyboard
Qwerty $169.00 Rental $40.00   Alpha. $169.00 Rental $40.00

Item#	Description	Price/Rental	Order Qty
D-194	Big Keys Keyboard Qwerty	Purchase - $169.00/ea	0
D-195	Big Keys Keyboard Alpha.	Purchase - $169.00/ea	0

Add to Your

Braille printers are also available, and can emboss about 40 Braille characters a second. Combined with a Braille keyboard and screen-reader software, these printers offer great options for interacting with a computer.

One online store for alternative software and hardware that you might want to visit is Keyalt (www.keyalt.com). There, you can find a large selection of pointing devices, keyboards, Braille displays, and Braille printers.

Tame your mouse

These days, much of what you do on a computer, especially online, takes place with the click of a mouse. If you've visited a computer store recently, you know that mice have been cloned into a wide variety of shapes and sizes, from trackballs to touchpads, and everything in between. Many of these alternatives, such as trackballs, are designed to lessen strain on a user's wrists and hands. There is some debate as to how well they accomplish that goal (the extra strain that a trackball puts on the thumb, for example, is a concern). The best advice is to try out a few types and see what works best for you.

Every mouse is controlled by software that comes with it. (In some cases, this software is already part of your operating system, and so your mouse works without you having to install anything, but the software is still in the driver's seat.) Make sure that whatever mouse you choose includes settings in its software for adding drag lock. *Drag lock* is a setting that enables you to click and drag items on-screen without having to hold the button down while dragging; this feature minimizes static strain (strain from holding your hand in one position for a time) that can cause tendon problems.

Beyond finding the right style of mouse for comfortable computing, you can also get alternatives to a mouse that don't require any involvement of hands, such as the No Hands Mouse shown in Figure 5-9. These devices allow foot-pedal control of mouse functions.

Making a phone call

If you are taking a class online, the odds are that at some point you'll be making contact with your instructor or fellow students by phone. If you have a serious hearing problem and are unable to use the telephone without some assistance, you're probably already familiar with technologies such as TTY (TeleTYpewriter, also known as TDD or Telecommunications Device for the Deaf). A TTY system consists of a keyboard with about 30 character keys, a display, and a special modem. Letters that you type become electrical impulses that are sent over a phone line. On the other end of the call, another TTY setup converts the letters to an on-screen display.

Figure 5-9:
Keyalt,
at www.
keyalt.
com, is the
place to
find this
foot-pedal
controlled
mouse.

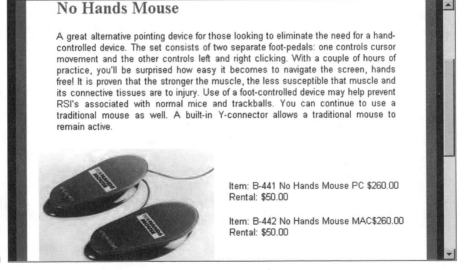

No Hands Mouse

A great alternative pointing device for those looking to eliminate the need for a hand-controlled device. The set consists of two separate foot-pedals: one controls cursor movement and the other controls left and right clicking. With a couple of hours of practice, you'll be surprised how easy it becomes to navigate the screen, hands free! It is proven that the stronger the muscle, the less susceptible that muscle and its connective tissues are to injury. Use of a foot-controlled device may help prevent RSI's associated with normal mice and trackballs. You can continue to use a traditional mouse as well. A built-in Y-connector allows a traditional mouse to remain active.

Item: B-441 No Hands Mouse PC $260.00
Rental: $50.00

Item: B-442 No Hands Mouse MAC$260.00
Rental: $50.00

Most colleges have a TTY phone line set up, and you may be able to use this line to communicate with your instructor. If you want to communicate with someone who doesn't have a TTY — for example, a fellow student — you can use the telephone company's relay service. In this scenario, you type your message and a phone company employee reads your message from his TTY setup for the person on the other end of the phone. You can find out more about TTY and other products at The Disability Mall, www.disabilitystore. com/hearing.

If you are slightly hard of hearing and concerned about phone interactions required by your class, other technologies can help. You can participate in telephone conversations by using volume-control phones that enable you to adjust the volume, or amplified phones that improve sound quality for those who use a hearing aide. You can be alerted to incoming calls by using ring signalers that let you know when a call is coming in with a flashing light, or tactile ring signalers that buzz you on a wristband when a call is coming in.

Magnifying printed text

If reading printed text is a challenge, you can also find a hardware system that includes a scanner and magnifying monitor, such as the one shown in Figure 5-10 from Telesensory.

Figure 5-10:
Products
such as
Telesensory's
Model NX-1
(www.tele
sensory.
com)
combine a
scanner and
monitor with
special
magnifi-
cation
settings for
ease of
reading.

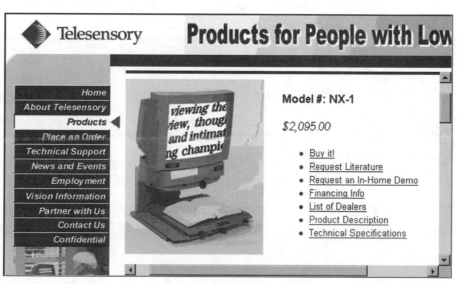

You use these systems by placing printed matter, such a textbook page, under the scanner. The text is then displayed on the special monitor at a magnification factor you set.

Because these systems aren't inexpensive, consider asking a dealer for a free demonstration; many dealers will bring the system right to your home.

How Your School Can Help

Every major university and most training organizations that offer courses online have some form of support for students with disabilities. Any school that counts on government funding is typically required to offer such support, because most governments have some form of disability anti-discrimination legislation.

Exactly what a school offers in the way of support for disabled students can vary, but services can include

- ✔ Special counseling or advising options
- ✔ Audiotaped lectures of printed materials
- ✔ Transcripts of audio lectures
- ✔ Accessibility technology such as screen readers and magnifiers
- ✔ Talking calculators
- ✔ Text telephones or TTY line access
- ✔ Special formats for tests such as Braille, audiotape, or large print
- ✔ Loan programs for specialized hardware

Search your school or training organization's Web site for specific information about how it supports disabled students, or call or write to your school for more information.

The DO-IT program

The potential of the Internet as a way to bring people with disabilities together in a learning environment is just beginning to be explored. One interesting example is a program called DO-IT (Disabilities, Opportunities, Internetworking, and Technology), sponsored by the University of Washington in Seattle. DO-IT is an online support program for students with disabilities started in the early 1990s. The program has won both the National Information Infrastructure Award in Education and the President's Award for Mentoring, and is partially funded by the National Science Foundation and the U.S. Department of Education.

This program uses a *mentor model,* wherein students, faculty, and professionals with disabilities mentor high-school students with disabilities to make their transition to college more successful. Although this program requires a short face-to-face meeting during the summer, all other interactions take place online or by phone. DO-IT lends computers and assistive technology to these students, and representatives go to student homes to set up the technology.

Students involved in this program benefit from communication with other students who have disabilities. The DO-IT community shares information and opinions about issues related to disability accommodations, career options, and educational opportunities. Although most of the DO-IT students go on to attend school on-campus, they are able to do so largely because this distance-learning program educates them in how to be successful in college. Most students involved with DO-IT have gone on to become mentors in the program themselves.

If you want more information, you can contact DO-IT at doit@u.washington.edu, or by phone at (206) 221-4171.

Chapter 6

Organizing Your Life for Learning

• •

In This Chapter

▶ Setting up your home for online study

▶ Helping your family and friends cope with your schedule

▶ Avoiding occupational hazards: eye, back, and hand strain

• •

I'm going to put on your wise Aunt Martha's hat now and give you two pieces of advice about tackling distance learning. First, be realistic about the time commitment; second, don't underestimate the impact your studies can have on your home life. Making a commitment to earning an entire degree online, or even taking a single course that goes on for a few months, is a big deal. It can affect your living space, your loved ones, and your physical well-being.

This chapter provides some tips for setting up your home so that you can study online and make your family comfortable with your new lifestyle. It also includes some advice on how you can stay healthy while hunched over a computer for hours on end (Rule #1, stop hunching!).

A Room of One's Own

It would be nice if everyone had a paneled study in which to set up a home computer and a sophisticated multimedia center for viewing videotaped lessons and listening to audiotapes in Surround Sound. The reality of setting up your home for distance learning is typically far less convenient and some-times involves commandeering your kitchen table as a computer workstation.

Before you even apply to a school, take a stroll around your house and see what challenges you will have to overcome in setting up your own personal classroom.

Finding a place to learn

The most obvious issue in studying at home is finding the space to accommodate your computer, books, notebooks, paper, and pencils, not to mention other hardware you may need, such as a printer, fax machine, or scanner. And that space must afford you some privacy so that you can concentrate and your family can continue to have a life while you learn.

Good quality small printers are available for less than $200 these days. But if you don't want to spend the money or don't have space for a printer, consider saving files you need to print to a disk and taking the disk to a local copy store. They can print the files for you for just pennies a page.

Ideally, you should find a space that's dedicated to your work; however, this doesn't mean that you have to set aside a whole room in the service of your education. Here are some solutions that might work for you:

- ✔ Find a niche under the stairs and install a small desk.

- ✔ Put a card table up at one end of the basement playroom and make that room off limits during study time.

- ✔ Purchase one of those desks-in-a-cabinet that allows you to close the doors when the desk is not in use and keeps clutter out of view.

- ✔ If you can't close the door on noise from elsewhere in the house, consider earplugs, or even a headset and small CD player to cover the noise with less distracting music.

- ✔ If you must set up the computer in a living space that's not exclusively devoted to study, consider putting the computer on a cart with rollers (you can usually find them at reasonable prices at office supply stores) so that you can move the whole thing easily from the closet to the kitchen (or whatever room you choose to study in) each day. You can store your books and papers inside the cart, too.

If all else fails, consider using your desk at work for study after hours or on weekends, as long as your boss has no issue with this use of work equipment.

Establishing a phone monopoly

When you're studying online, you may tie up the phone for hours. Cutting off phone access for that long can be a hardship on anybody's family and friends. One solution is to get a second phone line, dedicated to Internet access and faxing. Check with your phone company to see how much such a line would cost (you may be surprised to find that it's only about $10 or so more a month, but watch those installation costs, which can get pretty high).

Be sure to avoid fancy add-ons like call waiting or caller ID, because you probably don't need them simply to connect to the Internet. See Chapter 4 for more about high-speed phone access.

Keep an eye on changes in telephone technology and associated costs. DSL lines, cable modems, and other high-speed access options can make your connection to the Internet much faster, and make downloading files for your class much easier. However, they come at a cost; if you don't need this fancy technology, don't pay for it.

If the cost of a second phone line is out of the question, consider one of these options to make your online time easier on your family:

- The phone company offers voicemail that picks up calls and records messages even if the line is busy.

- Buy a phone that displays a blinking light when a voicemail message is waiting, so you can disconnect from the Internet and check for messages only when you know that a message is there.

  If you do decide to buy a new phone unit, consider getting a speaker phone with a mute button. These features make hands-free teleconference participation possible. When you're on the phone for an hour or more, hands-free is definitely the way to go! Another great option is an inexpensive headset.

- Cut down on the time you spend online by downloading e-mail and files and then reading them offline.

- Compose your responses to e-mail and even discussion questions offline; then cut and paste the text into an e-mail or discussion-board forum.

- Take a break or two as you work and let your family know they have a 15- or 20-minute window for calls.

  It's easy to feel that your studying is more important than your family's personal calls, but that's not always the case. Remember, they have extracurricular activities that are just as important to them as your classes are to you.

Seeing and hearing your classes

In addition to its online component, your distance-learning course may also include the use of technologies such as videotapes and audiotapes. At England's Open University, for example, a student spends an average of 30 minutes a week watching videos or listening to audiotapes.

Commandeering the family VCR or stereo for 30 minutes each week is usually not all that difficult, but you may have to do so after the kids have gone to bed or early in the morning. If you commute to work, consider using the tape player in your car to listen to audiotapes (but remember, you can't take notes and drive!). If you jog or go to a gym, consider bringing along a tape player so you can learn while you burn.

Because videotapes are often the more entertaining pieces of your study material, you might try asking your family to view the tapes with you each week. Pop popcorn, snuggle in a comfy chair, and share your learning with your family. Depending on how interesting your course topic is, they may actually enjoy it, learn something, and be better able to understand what it is you're doing with all that time they can no longer lay claim to.

Family Ties: Making Your Learning Fit Your Life

A typical distance-learning program can take about 14 hours a week. If you take four or five classes that run about six weeks each, over the course of a year, that's about 450 hours of your time. When's the last time you found a spare 450 hours lying around under the Christmas tree? Don't kid yourself: Taking even a single course can have a significant impact on you and the people in your life.

Before you begin your class, visit your school's Web site to see whether they offer any advice about organizing yourself for the work ahead, as the Open University in England does on its Web site (www.open.ac.uk/ learners-guide), shown in Figure 6-1.

Figure 6-1: You can get help in organizing yourself, managing your time, and getting back into the swing of studying at this Web site.

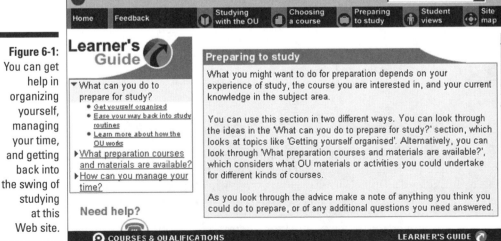

Finding time for it all

I can give you advice till the cows come home, but I can't give you more time. Time is finite, and in taking on a distance-learning commitment you have to face the fact that some serious reshuffling of priorities and the way you usually spend your time will have to take place.

Try making a time budget before you begin your studies to determine exactly how many courses you can handle at any one time. Here's how a time budget for a typical day might look:

Activity	*Time Allotted*
Sleep	8 hours
Work	8 hours
Family	2 hours
Chores (shopping, laundry, cooking)	1 hour
Meals	1 hour
Entertainment (TV, a movie, playing with the dog)	1 hour
Commuting	1 hour
Study	2 hours
Total	24 hours

This is not a leisurely day. What if you work an hour late? Or you want to watch a two-hour movie on TV? Now you're definitely stretching things with 26-hour days. What can you do? Perhaps you can take big chunks out of weekend days to study, but I bet if you do a time budget for a weekend day, you'll find your time every bit as tightly packed as a weekday. You may have to negotiate with your family about that chore time; maybe you can't help out with some of the routine chores for a while. You may want to ask your boss if you can work at home one or two days a week to save on that commuting time. Do not make cuts in meal times or family time: Gulping fast food and becoming a stranger in your own home are not healthy solutions.

If you take a realistic look at what you're committing to in studying online, you'll be able to make the adjustments necessary to maintain a life and avoid burnout.

Getting support from those you love

To paraphrase John Donne: No student is an island. To be successful in your distance learning, you need help from your friends and family. Beyond their tolerance of the hours you'll be spending away from them, you'll need their cooperation to help you focus when you're studying. It might be wise to create an agreement that you and your family can live with, like the following one, and post it near your study station.

✔ I need you to respect my privacy while I'm studying. I appreciate you keeping voices, the TV, and other noise to a minimum.

✔ If I'm in the middle of studying, please don't interrupt me unless it's an emergency. If it is something you consider important, I promise to stop working and respect you by giving you my undivided attention until the situation is resolved.

✔ Please don't move my papers and books around. I'll try to keep clutter to a minimum around my workspace if you promise not to reorganize my stuff.

✔ If you need to use the same computer I use for class, please don't delete files or install software without asking me first. I'll respect your work on the computer with the same courtesy.

✔ If I'm ignoring you or being rude to you because of my studies, be honest and tell me so.

Coping with change

There's a great movie from a few decades ago called *Educating Rita,* about a hairdresser in England who takes a degree program at a distance university. Her studies in literature open her eyes to a world she's never known, a world of ideas and intellectual stimulation that her working-class family simply can't understand. Her desire to improve herself by getting a degree eventually breaks up her marriage and alienates former friends. (Yes, it's a comedy.)

Now, the odds are really good that a distance-learning class won't end up in you getting a divorce, but you do have to realize that, by studying new things, you're trying to change your life to some degree. Changes might include moving into a new career path, becoming more highly paid, or becoming involved with a new set of people with similar interests. If you change yourself and your spouse or friends don't change themselves, you have to appreciate the impact that discrepancy could have.

Keep these things in mind when making the commitment to a significant learning endeavor:

✔ Make sure that your family understands why you're studying, and confirm that they support the changes you're seeking.

✔ Be supportive of changes they may want to make in their lives at the same time, so that you're not monopolizing all the positive-change energy in the family.

✔ Be aware that your studies might change you, and address those changes honestly and sensitively.

✔ Keep lines of communication with your friends and family open. You're putting aside quiet time to study each week; put aside time to talk with your loved ones, as well. Then if a problem is arising, you can be aware of it early on.

✔ Find ways to involve your family in your studies. If you're taking courses in astronomy, make family outings to the planetarium. If you're studying marketing, create a family Web site and use it to create a family brand identity.

✔ Make sure that your significant other isn't threatened by relationships you're building online. Stories about Internet romances are frequent, and who could blame someone whose spouse is exchanging e-mails with members of the opposite sex for hours each night for getting suspicious.

Occupational Hazards

In the 14 or so hours a week you spend taking an online course, you might be typing on a keyboard or reading from a computer monitor for half that time. That's seven additional hours or so a week of computer interaction at the end of busy workdays; this additional work time can cause physical strain. Be sure to follow some of the basic rules of *ergonomics* (the study of how behavior patterns can cause physical strain) to avoid injury.

Your own school may also offer advice, such as the information about computer-workstation ergonomics provided by the University of California at Berkeley Health Services (www.uhs.Berkeley.edu/Facstaff/Ergonomics), shown in Figure 6-2.

Figure 6-2: A healthy student is a happy student: Many universities offer tips, like the ones on this site created by Berkeley, about healthy computing for students.

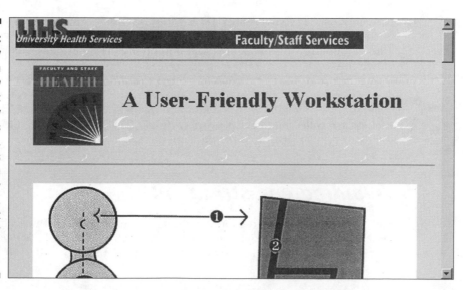

It's all in the wrist

The wrists are especially sensitive to the repetitive motion of computer keyboarding, resulting in Cumulative Trauma Disorders, or CTD. Conditions such as carpal tunnel syndrome and inflammation of tendons can be painful and, in some cases, lead to surgery. If you're spending hours at a keyboard for your class on top of an eight-hour workday that also involves a keyboard, you just may be adding insult to injury.

Problems with the wrists and hands can result not only from repetitive movements like keyboarding, but also from holding a single position for a length of time (for example, gripping your mouse tightly for minutes on end while reading something on screen) or holding a part of the body in an awkward position. Other causes are exertion, such as pounding on a keyboard too forcefully, or constant vibration.

Try these tips for avoiding damage to your hands and wrists:

- ✔ If you have to do a lot of typing or other repetitious work, take frequent breaks and use your hands for different types of activity for a while.

- ✔ Don't grasp things too tightly for any length of time. Just relax: If you're tense, you're more likely to unconsciously grip with more force than necessary.

- ✔ Make smooth motions. Don't jerk your wrists when typing or using a mouse.

- ✔ Stay warm! Cold temperatures can cause discomfort in your hands and wrists.

The greatest key to avoiding CTD is variation. Don't repeat the same motion without break; don't hold the same position without change. Vary your routine to help prevent discomfort and potentially more serious consequences down the road.

If you're having trouble pinpointing the causes of wrist discomfort, consider consulting a specialist who is adept at diagnosing CTD problems. These specialists are called *physiatrists* or *specialists in physical medicine,* and you can ask your regular doctor to recommend one to you.

Avoiding eye strain

Eye strain can be caused by several things: glare, too much or too little light, how readable the material being viewed is, or the variation between the brightness of what you're viewing and your surroundings. When working on a computer, especially in the evening when you are likely to do much of your classroom work by artificial light, take great care in setting up your workspace. Here are some things to pay attention to:

- ✔ Avoid glare. If you've got glare on your computer screen or a light source that's shining in your eyes, get rid of it by moving your computer, closing the curtains, or getting an anti-glare screen for your monitor. Also keep in mind that monitors with flat screens can be easier on your eyes.

- ✔ Take breaks. Staring at anything for a long time causes strain. Look up every now and then and focus your eyes in the distance, rather than on something as close as your monitor. (If you try this at work, explain to your boss that you are not staring out the window daydreaming, you are practicing good employee health).

- ✔ If you have a bright light source right behind your monitor, such as a window or lamp, the contrast between that bright light and your dimmer monitor can cause problems. Move the light, or turn it off.

- ✔ Place your monitor farther away from your eyes. Looking at things close up causes more eyestrain than viewing things at a distance. Put your monitor as far from you as you can while still being able to read what's on it easily.

- ✔ Adjust your monitor height so the top edge of it is at eye level, so that you are looking down at the screen. This keeps your eyelids over your eyes, helping you to avoid dryness, which can result in irritation.

I have this little pain in my back . . .

Some medical sources claim that 90 percent of people will have a disabling back problem at some time in their lives. Not great odds, and just one of many reasons why you should take good care of your back and neck when setting up your home office. Your back and neck can take quite a beating just from sitting in the wrong chair or working on your computer in the wrong position.

If you don't have a comfortable desk chair in your home, it might be a worthwhile investment. The wrong chair can cause damage to your upper and lower back and neck. A good chair doesn't have to cost an arm and a leg. I invested in a $700 desk chair that I used now and then to write checks while sitting at my desk. When I began working at home full time and sat in that ergonomically designed chair day in and day out, I found after a short time that I could hardly walk. I went back to the stores and contemplated $1,500 chairs. Then I went to an office supply store, spent an hour trying out different chairs there, adjusting them in every way they would adjust, and ended up buying a chair for about $199. No more pain. We're all built differently: What's important is to find a chair that's comfortable for you.

A good chair allows you to adjust several things, including

- The height of the seat from the floor
- The tilt of the chair (tilting forward removes stress on hip joints)
- How close the seat of the chair is to the backrest
- The position of the armrests. (Ideally, you want to be able to move your armrests up and down, or in and out. Armrests help to support some of your weight, taking strain off of your back.)

Getting up and moving around occasionally is an excellent idea because it not only eases tension on muscles but also improves the flow of fluid among your vertebrae to keep your discs healthy.

Part III
Taking the Plunge

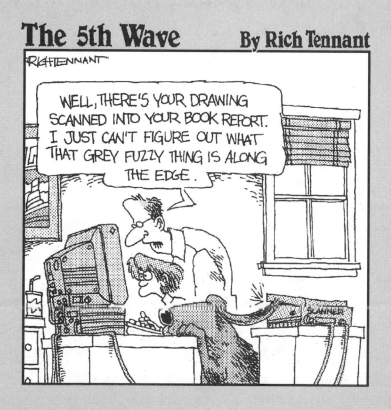

In this part . . .

On the first day of classes at college, people don't just wake up, say to themselves, "Oh gosh, I guess I start school today. Think I'll just wander over to the campus and see what's shaking." Students have to go through quite a few hoops before they ever set foot in a classroom. The same legwork is part of getting ready for a distance-learning course, too — except you do the legwork online.

This part reveals the ins and outs of applying to the school of your choice and registering for college-level classes. You get some advice about buying all the books and supplies you need to study and getting the most out of the support your school offers to all its distance-learning students. So, when your class bell rings, you can be sure that your name is on the roster and you're ready to learn.

Chapter 7

Applying Yourself

In This Chapter

▶ Coordinating the various elements of your application

▶ Registering for classes

▶ Paying for what you learn

epending on what organization you're applying to, getting into a distance-learning course or program can be as easy as taking a minute to fill out a form online and paying with a credit card, or as cumbersome as the process of applying to Harvard Graduate School with all the associated forms, references, and test scores. Your admission might be guaranteed, or you might have to watch the mail anxiously every day looking for that acceptance letter from the office of admissions.

With a focus on the more rigorous admissions process for university-level degree programs, this chapter gives you an overview of what's involved in applying to a distance-learning program, the ins and outs of registering for classes, and payment methods for your education.

If you went through this process once already for an undergraduate college degree, you probably remember what fun it was and appreciate the walk down memory lane. If you've never applied to a college, review this chapter to set your expectations of what's involved to make the whole experience a little less painful.

Following the Paper Trail

Don't make the mistake of thinking that getting into a degree program where courses are delivered online is easier than getting into a campus-based program; it isn't. You're getting the same level of education recognized by the same accrediting body as the in-person student, and you have to prove your ability to pass muster. So prepare yourself for the same pile of paperwork you'd have to go through for any college application.

Be forewarned: Rumor has it that paper was *invented* by a dean of admissions at a college — and that he holds a royalty on every sheet that we use. Of course, admissions applications are posted online in this e-learning age, but I guarantee you, somebody, somewhere prints out all those forms, creating a paper trail that would make the Great Wall of China seem short in comparison. This paper trail starts with standardized testing, meanders through a field of transcripts and letters of recommendation, and winds up with a written essay and a ten-page application form.

Taking standardized entrance tests

Most university continuing-education programs — which is the division that distance learning often falls under the auspices of — don't require testing if you're only going to take a single course, or for a program that results in a certificate or CEU (continuing education unit) credit. However, if you are applying to a college or university to enter a degree program, you're likely to have to take one or more entrance tests to qualify for admission. Entrance exams test your general aptitude for handling college-level work, or your knowledge in a specific area such as math or English.

For undergraduate programs, you are likely to need the scores from standardized tests such as SAT or ACT that you took in high school. You can usually request score reports online. You can obtain SAT scores from the College Board SAT Program, 609-771-7600 (www.collegeboard.org). You can order ACT score reports from ACT Records, 319-337-1313 (www.act.org/aap). For more detailed information on testing services see the Online Directory in this book.

Many schools require the Graduate Record Examination (GRE) for admission to their graduate programs. GRE tests include a General Aptitude Test and Subject Tests that focus on specific areas of study. Check the GRE Web site, run by the Educational Testing Service and shown in Figure 7-1 (www.gre.org), for information about taking the GRE. Note that the GRE now offers a computerized version of its test, and it provides a demo version of the test online.

The Graduate Management Aptitude Test (GMAT) is the entrance exam typically required by MBA programs. This test is also administered by the Educational Testing Service; you can find the GMAT Web site (see Figure 7-2) at www.gmat.org.

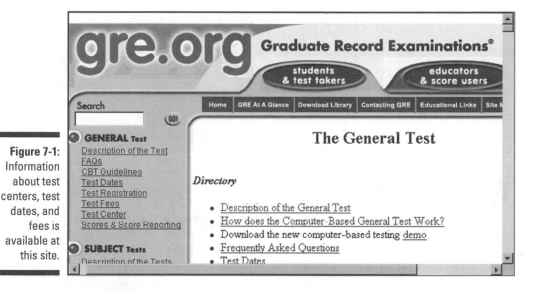

Figure 7-1: Information about test centers, test dates, and fees is available at this site.

Figure 7-2: If an MBA is in your future, so is the GMAT exam.

If you're a foreign student applying to study in the United States, you may be required to prove your English-language competency by taking the TOEFL (Test of English as a Foreign Language). Visit the TOEFL Web site (www. ets.org) to find out about testing sites and dates worldwide.

Accounting for prior education

Before an admissions board will consider you for college entrance, you have to prove yourself. For an undergraduate college program, you must prove that you have a high-school diploma or its equivalent. For a graduate program, you must prove that you have an undergraduate degree. If you are transferring credits earned at another institution, you have to provide proof of those credits in a transcript.

If you're studying in a country outside of the United States, verify prior-degree requirements. In England and Canada, for example, you can often get into a master's degree program without holding a bachelor's degree.

You have to contact the school where you received your diploma or took courses to request that it send transcripts to the school you're applying to. You may have to request a transcript in writing or by phone, although some schools are now set up so that you can order transcripts online. Schools usually charge a nominal fee (perhaps $5) per transcript.

One great idea for dealing with all the hassle of rounding up your previous records is to go through an organization such as the Regents College Credit Bank, whose Web page (regents.edu) appears in Figure 7-3. Two other services of this type are the Thomas Edison State College Credit Bank (www.tesc.edu) and Charter Oak State College Credit Banking (cosc.edu). These are all services that enable you to record all your college credits and examinations towards college credit (such as the College Level Examination Program, or CLEP) in a single report. Obtaining such a report now will make your life easier if you later switch schools or go on to additional study.

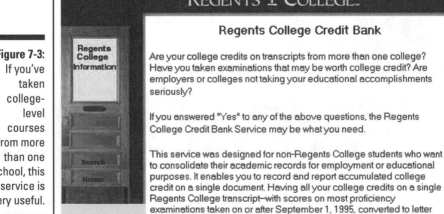

Figure 7-3:
If you've taken college-level courses from more than one school, this service is very useful.

REGENTS COLLEGE.

Regents College Credit Bank

Are your college credits on transcripts from more than one college? Have you taken examinations that may be worth college credit? Are employers or colleges not taking your educational accomplishments seriously?

If you answered "Yes" to any of the above questions, the Regents College Credit Bank Service may be what you need.

This service was designed for non-Regents College students who want to consolidate their academic records for employment or educational purposes. It enables you to record and report accumulated college credit on a single document. Having all your college credits on a single Regents College transcript—with scores on most proficiency examinations taken on or after September 1, 1995, converted to letter

LINGO

A bachelor's degree by any other name

If you have studied in a school outside the United States and want to know what the equivalent of a U.S. school bachelor's degree is in another country, take a look at this list:

✔ United Kingdom or any country patterned after the U.K.'s educational system: Bachelor's degree with honors

✔ Canada: Within Quebec, a three-year bachelor's degree; from any other province, a four-year bachelor's degree

✔ France: Four-year diploma

✔ India, Pakistan, or Nepal: A bachelor's degree in engineering or master's degree in any other discipline

✔ Europe and Middle East (except for France): Four-year university degree

Regents also has just started a BA in Information Technology program (see Figure 7-4) that accepts professional certifications such as Microsoft Certified Systems Engineer (see Chapter 3) and allows you to build your degree program on the certifications you've already received. Check with your school administrators to see whether they accept such prior non-college education towards their degrees. If they do, you'll have to provide proof of the certification (a copy of your certificate will usually do).

Figure 7-4: Watch for other colleges to follow Regent's lead and begin recognizing professional certifications in future.

Do you have any references?

The school to which you are applying may ask you to supply letters of reference. These usually come from previous teachers, employers, or community sources such as a clergyperson or community volunteer organization. What schools are looking for in these letters is someone's assurance that you are hardworking, will stick with a program to its conclusion, and are a well-rounded person with varied interests.

Letters of reference have gone a bit out of fashion, but if you are asked to produce some, look for guidelines from the school for what information they want included in the letters, such as the title and relationship of the person writing the letter.

Completing the application form

Most applications consist of an application form, plus the scores, transcripts, letters of reference, and other supporting material. The application form itself asks for a few different kinds of information, depending on the school and the program you're applying for. For example, you may be asked about the following:

- Your contact information including phone, e-mail, and fax
- Previous education
- Employment history
- A list of personal and professional references
- Credit card information, if you're paying online
- Details about the program you're applying for (program title, start date, division of the school that runs it, and so on)
- Foreign student status
- Racial, ethnic, and gender information
- Whether you're applying for financial aid

If you are applying for a creative or design program, such as architecture or writing, you may also be asked to submit a portfolio of previous work with your application.

Most colleges today allow you to fill out an online application (see Figure 7-5) and submit supporting documents separately. Note that your school probably uses different application forms for undergraduate and graduate programs, special forms for foreign students, and possibly a different application form for continuing education and distance-learning students. Make sure that you have the correct form before you start the sometimes-lengthy task of filling it out.

Figure 7-5:
Oklahoma
State
University
allows you
to apply
online and,
if you
choose, to
pay online,
as well.

The form itself is often made up mainly of choices that you can check, as in the form from Oklahoma State University shown in Figure 7-6. However, you may occasionally encounter text boxes where you enter a written explanation or essay.

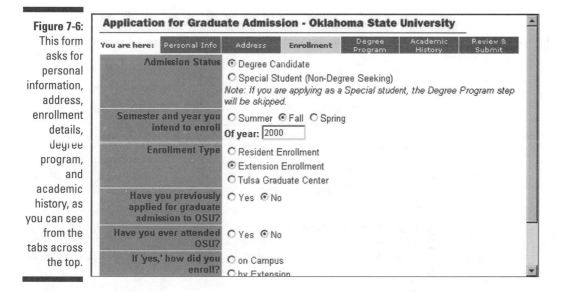

Figure 7-6:
This form
asks for
personal
information,
address,
enrollment
details,
degree
program,
and
academic
history, as
you can see
from the
tabs across
the top.

Some programs also require you to submit another application form for the division from which you want to take a degree. Read all application instructions carefully.

Before filling out an application, look around your school's Web site for a checklist of what you must submit, including test scores, letters of reference, transcripts, and so on, as well as advice about how to fill out the application.

Writing the application essay (Or "How I Spent My Summer . . .")

Quite often, perhaps just to see if you can put three words together and form a sentence, schools ask you to write an essay as part of your application. These essays tend to be about your educational objectives, your career goals, or why you think that the school should select you as a student. Essays typically run about 500 to 1,200 words and may include one or more questions or statements for you to respond to.

Schools are looking for a demonstration of your writing skills and a clear statement of why this specific program and this school would be a good match for you. But they are also looking for a clue as to what makes you special, what your thinking processes are like, and what your values are.

Don't underestimate the importance of the essay; when many students with similar credentials and similar interests apply, it is quite often the essay that helps the admissions department to make the final choice. In your essay, try to

- ✔ **Write well:** Your sentences should be crisp and clear and have no sloppy spelling, punctuation, or grammar errors.

- ✔ **Be engaging:** Try to let your own personality and enthusiasm for your education and the school shine through.

- ✔ **Be thoughtful:** Before you begin writing, think about why you want to attend this school and take this program. If you've done your homework, point out what you feel makes this program unique among others you've researched. You'll impress them with your thoroughness and flatter their school.

- ✔ **Highlight your strong points:** Show them that you bring as much to the school as the school can give to you. Don't make the mistake of talking about why the school is good for you and forgetting to tell them why you would be good for the school.

Registration, or What Fresh Hell Is This?

A college education isn't like a supermarket: You can't walk in the door and always expect to find milk in the refrigerator case and tomatoes in the vegetable aisle. The course you want to take, although listed in the catalog, may be cancelled or full. Or you may need special permission to get into a course. Because you can't always get what you want, knowing beforehand some of the variables associated with registering can be helpful.

Choose your courses and be ready with alternates

The first step in choosing your courses is to review the requirements for your degree program with your advisor. You can connect with your advisor through e-mail or by phone, or — if you are required to visit campus once for orientation — make an appointment to meet in person. Work with your advisor to make a list of core requirements (classes you must take to obtain your degree) and elective classes (classes that you can choose from among a broader group of courses, but that are relevant to the focus of your degree). You can then register online or by mail for the course or courses you want to take. The registrar then notifies you of whether you've been accepted into that course. (For more about working with advisors, see Chapter 10.)

Keep in mind that, in any one semester, the courses you want to take might not be available. Some courses are only taught every other semester. Others might be cancelled because of lack of enrollment. Others might be full. You might not yet have taken a prerequisite course that you need to enroll in a course.

You do have to create a slate of courses you want to take, but have alternates in mind in case you don't get your first choice. Because most distance-learning students take no more than one (or maybe two) courses a semester, finding some course that meets your needs and is available is usually pretty easy.

Your school's Web site may be able to help you choose your courses. For example, Figures 7-7 and 7-8 show an interesting feature of the Rochester Institute of Technology Web site (adm3.rit.edu/Careers). You can choose to search by jobs that interest you, classes that interest you, or what you like to do, and then fill out the resulting checklist (see Figure 7-7). When you submit this information, a search result (see Figure 7-8) returns the program that would be best for you, outlining the types of courses it includes, and the career choices it leads to. This system is useful in choosing electives: When you check topics that interest you beyond your degree focus, the system refers you to other divisions in the school that might have courses that match those interests.

Figure 7-7:
Rather than look through lists of courses, check the areas that interest you and you get a recommended program.

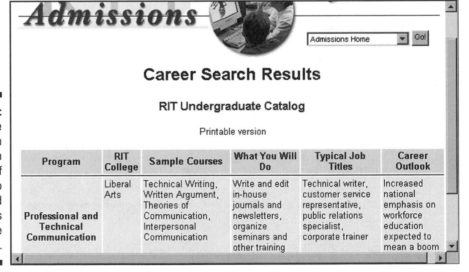

Figure 7-8:
Seeing the connection of certain programs of courses to real-world career goals can be helpful.

Some schools make student assessments of courses available, like the Course Evaluation Catalog from the University of Washington (www.Washington. edu/cec) shown in Figure 7-9. Scanning through student comments may help you find some courses that interest you.

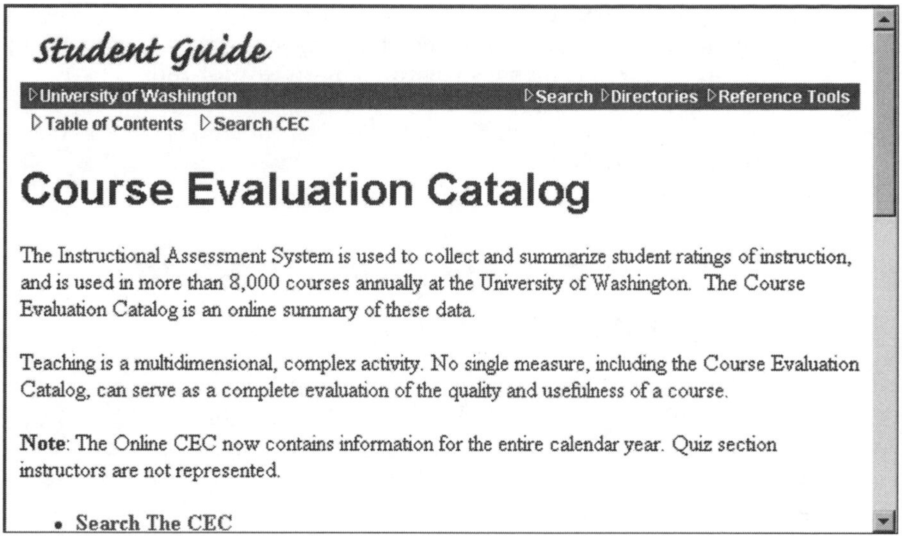

Student Guide

▷ University of Washington   ▷ Search ▷ Directories ▷ Reference Tools
▷ Table of Contents   ▷ Search CEC

Course Evaluation Catalog

The Instructional Assessment System is used to collect and summarize student ratings of instruction, and is used in more than 8,000 courses annually at the University of Washington. The Course Evaluation Catalog is an online summary of these data.

Teaching is a multidimensional, complex activity. No single measure, including the Course Evaluation Catalog, can serve as a complete evaluation of the quality and usefulness of a course.

Note: The Online CEC now contains information for the entire calendar year. Quiz section instructors are not represented.

• **Search The CEC**

Figure 7-9:
Stuck for an alternative course? See what other students recommend.

When you have a list the courses you want to take (and your alternates), take a look at your school registrar's Web page to see what is required to register. Many schools offer an online registration system, such as the SIRS (student interactive registration) system at the University of Wisconsin, described on the registrar's site shown in Figure 7-10. If your school offers such a system, you can see which courses are closed to you before trying to sign up for them. If you can't register online, you may submit a registration form and be told that a course you want to take is closed, and have to start over with an alternate.

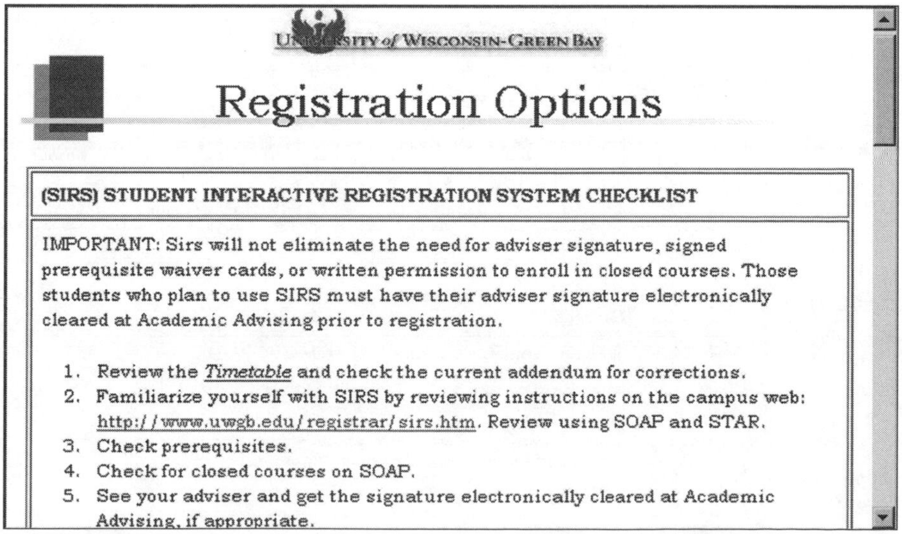

UNIVERSITY of WISCONSIN-GREEN BAY

Registration Options

(SIRS) STUDENT INTERACTIVE REGISTRATION SYSTEM CHECKLIST

IMPORTANT: Sirs will not eliminate the need for adviser signature, signed prerequisite waiver cards, or written permission to enroll in closed courses. Those students who plan to use SIRS must have their adviser signature electronically cleared at Academic Advising prior to registration.

1. Review the *Timetable* and check the current addendum for corrections.
2. Familiarize yourself with SIRS by reviewing instructions on the campus web: http://www.uwgb.edu/registrar/sirs.htm. Review using SOAP and STAR.
3. Check prerequisites.
4. Check for closed courses on SOAP.
5. See your adviser and get the signature electronically cleared at Academic Advising, if appropriate.

Figure 7-10:
Many schools have a sophisticated online registration system that lets you see which courses are available and which are not.

Registration typically involves filling out a form and getting your advisor to sign off on the courses. Distance-learning students can usually get such a signature electronically. Check with your advisor for the procedure at your school. Note that all schools have deadlines for registration, and missing those deadlines can result in a late registration fee, or not being able to get into a course at all.

The registration game: Adding, dropping, changing

What happens if you change your mind about taking a course after you register for it? For one thing, this change of heart might cost you. How much it will cost you depends on the timing of your withdrawal. Look for a calendar from the registrar's office that lists key dates and penalties for changes, like the one shown in Figure 7-11.

Here's a list of typical repercussions for making course changes:

- ✔ First three days after registration closes: No fee (grace period)
- ✔ One week after grace period: $25 withdrawal fee
- ✔ Second week after grace period: $50 withdrawal fee
- ✔ Third week after grace period: $100 withdrawal fee
- ✔ One month after grace period: Your withdrawal is noted on your official record (which doesn't look good)

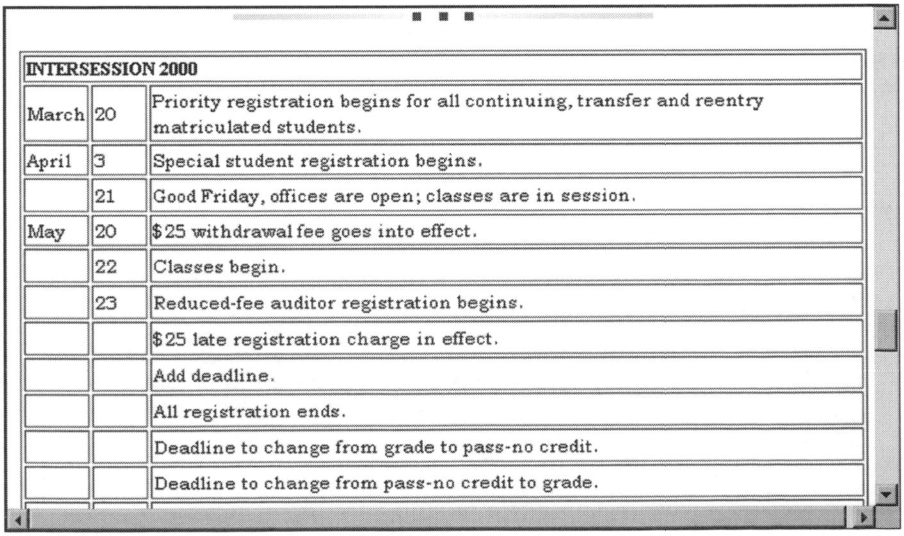

Figure 7-11: Find a calendar such as this one from the school registrar and note key dates and associated late fees.

INTERSESSION 2000		
March	20	Priority registration begins for all continuing, transfer and reentry matriculated students.
April	3	Special student registration begins.
	21	Good Friday, offices are open; classes are in session.
May	20	$25 withdrawal fee goes into effect.
	22	Classes begin.
	23	Reduced-fee auditor registration begins.
		$25 late registration charge in effect.
		Add deadline.
		All registration ends.
		Deadline to change from grade to pass-no credit.
		Deadline to change from pass-no credit to grade.

You can usually add a course up to a few weeks after it begins, but you sometimes have to get the instructor's permission to do so. You can also change from taking a course for credit to a pass-fail, non-credit status in many cases up to a few weeks after the course begins. If you're finding one course especially hard, consider shifting it to a pass-fail basis to save you from having a low grade on your record.

Paying the Piper

In this day of credit cards, making payments is painfully easy. But you should know a few things about the kinds of fees you may encounter, whether making your payments online is safe, and how you go about getting your money back if you have a problem or change in plans.

Deciphering school fees

Did you think tuition was the only thing you would have to pay to take a degree? I'm sorry to be the one to disillusion you, but a lot more is involved than that. If you think the IRS is the master of getting at your money from every direction, take a look at some typical school fees:

- Application fee
- Core course fee
- Reactivation fee (if you withdraw from a degree program and then reenter)
- Core course examination reregistration fee (if you miss taking a core course exam and have to schedule another exam)
- Core course examination second attempt fee (see the preceding item . . .)
- Late cancellation fee (if you register late for an exam)
- Degree completion plan fee
- Special assessment fee
- Independent learning contract fee
- Thesis fee
- Program completion and graduation fee (yes, you have to pay to get out of the program, too!)
- Returned check fee

I'm not going to try to explain all of these fees because, if you're lucky, your school doesn't inflict them on you. But do ask your registrar's office about any hidden fees and be prepared for them to mount up.

Paying online: Is it safe?

Most schools don't offer any kind of payment plan, so your tuition and fees are due in full before you start class. Schools usually offer you the option of paying online or paying by mail by a certain date. In my experience, however, I have often received a bill for a course only a few days before the course begins. The snag is that you're not allowed access to the course site until you've paid. This situation forces you to pay online or by phone, because you just don't have time for mail to reach the school before the course begins.

I'm not one to worry about secure transactions on the Internet; most of the time, there's little danger of anybody nefarious getting at your credit information. However, in my opinion, school sites may not be quite as secure as most Internet business sites, because so many students are wandering around in there. Not that students are ever hackers or crackers: God forbid. But due caution isn't a bad idea here. Registration sites are usually secured by standard means used by other businesses, so you're probably okay using a credit card. But if it makes you at all nervous (as it does me), just phone in your credit card to the registrar's office.

If your company is paying for courses (lucky you), some schools will bill tuition directly to the company. The company is usually required to open an account with the school to make this arrangement.

Some schools accept an *interbank wire,* which is a way to have your bank transfer funds directly to the school's bank. However, be warned that this transaction often requires a week or so, so it's not much of a timesaver.

The customer is always right: Getting refunds

If you get closed out of a course for any reason, or if you withdraw from a course, you can usually get a refund — up to a point. Be aware that you must withdraw from courses by the dates listed on the school's academic calendar to obtain a refund. After a certain date, you may only receive a portion of the tuition or none at all. Be sure to keep a record of any course changes and the dates you made them in the event that you need to request a refund. A refund typically comes in the form of a check sent to you by regular mail, although occasionally the school will credit your charge card.

If you are taking a course from an online training provider, rather than from a university, check the organization's refund policy. In some cases, you can get a full refund even after completing the course if you are not satisfied with its quality or if you experience technical difficulties. Universities, on the other hand, never refund money because of customer dissatisfaction.

Chapter 8

Orientation Express

- -

In This Chapter

▶ Fitting face-to-face interaction into your distance learning

▶ Getting textbooks and software before you begin class

▶ Taking advantage of school services

- -

*T*hink of this chapter as your trip to the store with Mom to get all the supplies you need for your first day of school. Of course, what this chapter helps you assemble isn't new sneakers and a lunchbox. Instead, it shows you how face-to-face contact can play a role in preparing for distance learning; where you can go to get textbooks, supplies, and information you need to study; and how you can use the various support services of a school, even from a distance.

So grab your class syllabus and the address of your school's Web site and begin to prepare for school days.

Getting in Your Face: When It's Not All Online

Although the many proponents of distance learning often discount arguments about the value of constant face-to-face interaction in learning, almost to a person they do see the value in at least one face-to-face meeting among those in a college-level distance-learning class.

Given this preference for a student/instructor get-together in the distance-learning academic community, if you're taking a distance-learning course from a college or university, consider the possibility that the course will require at least one face-to-face meeting. If a large group meeting isn't possible, the instructor may ask you to meet with a smaller group of students living near you at a regional center.

If you're taking a course from an online training company rather than a university with a campus, you can put away your travel agent's phone number: These courses are not likely to expect you to visit in person.

Getting oriented

Before the first class starts, many colleges ask distance-learning students to attend an on-campus orientation. Schools have a few reasons for requiring this in-person contact, the most obvious being that it helps the instructor and students to begin to bond as a group. A campus visit is useful in a few other ways, too:

✔ Instructors can demonstrate the software you'll be using or the Web site you'll be accessing for discussions and assignments. You can even try the software yourself with someone there to look over your shoulder and help you out if you encounter any problems.

✔ You can go to the bookstore and purchase textbooks or visit the library to see what it has to offer.

✔ You can meet with any support departments with whom you may need to interact, such as the group that supports foreign or disabled students. During this face-to-face meeting, you can discuss any issues you might have as classes begin.

If you've met your classmates in person, you are more likely to be sensitive to their feelings when communicating online during the course of your class. This bond helps all of you to avoid e-mail rage towards a faceless recipient.

Any brochure or informational listing about a distance-learning class or degree program should include the requirements for visits to a campus or regional study center. Look for this information and accommodate it in your study budget when you're applying to a school. (For more information on setting a budget for your distance learning, see Chapter 3.)

Small group get-togethers

Whether as a substitute for an on-campus orientation or as a support group you can work with during the course of your class, small group interaction is another way that schools provide personal contact within the context of distance learning.

Where will you meet? Some schools, like The Open University in England, maintain brick-and-mortar regional centers where students are required to meet on a regular basis. Statewide systems of colleges in the United States, such as the State University of New York (SUNY), whose many centers are shown on the map in Figure 8-1, have distributed campuses. Distance-learning students are sometimes able to take advantage of a nearby campus, even though they have registered through another school in the system.

Whatever form of in-person contact your distance-learning program offers, you should try to participate in it, even though it might be a bit expensive or inconvenient. Occasional face-to-face interaction will make you feel much less alone as you progress through your distance learning-experience.

Getting Your Supplies Together

I have a friend who wouldn't even take a tennis lesson until she had assembled a cute tennis outfit, a professional tennis racquet, and a fancy designer tote bag for her pro-signature tennis balls. Knowing that you have your material stuff together before tackling a new venture can sometimes give you that little edge of confidence that makes everything go more smoothly.

In distance learning, the items you need to assemble before class begins include information, textbooks, any special software you may need to go online, a contact list, and supplies.

Figure 8-1: SUNY has a whole network of universities, specialized colleges, technical colleges, and community colleges serving its student population.

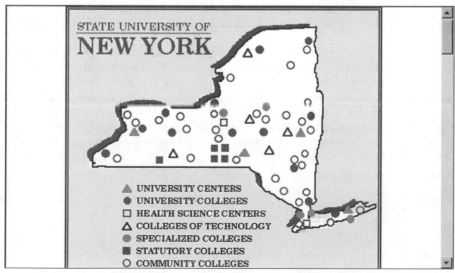

STATE UNIVERSITY OF
NEW YORK

▲ UNIVERSITY CENTERS
● UNIVERSITY COLLEGES
□ HEALTH SCIENCE CENTERS
△ COLLEGES OF TECHNOLOGY
● SPECIALIZED COLLEGES
■ STATUTORY COLLEGES
○ COMMUNITY COLLEGES

Information, please

Because, in many distance-learning programs, so much information is disseminated online, you probably won't get much printed material by mail. The start of a new course is the exception. When you sign up for a distance-learning course or program, you can expect to get a packet from your school that will be jam-packed with all kinds of information to get you started.

Schools typically include the following items in a packet for a distance-learning program:

- An enrollment confirmation and letter of welcome that outlines key dates
- A registration form to submit with payment
- Information on using the school telephone-conferencing bridge
- Directions for logging onto the class Web site
- Instructions for participating in online discussion areas
- Student user name and password
- Study tips
- A brochure on the university bookstore
- Special offers for discounted computer hardware and software
- A campus and city map
- A textbook list for the first course
- A copy of the university grading and ethics policy for students

Whatever information your welcome packet contains, take the time to read through it before the first class starts, and ask questions if something is unclear.

At this stage, you may not have instructor contact information. In most cases, you can direct any inquiries to the registrar's office or the office of the extension division running your program if you need an answer before the class begins. They can usually provide you with the appropriate contact.

Buying your textbooks

Just because your online education is high-tech doesn't mean you can get away from old-fashioned printed textbooks. You're likely to need a few of them for each class.

Your instructor may either post online or mail you a list of texts you need for the course a few weeks before the start of class so that you have time to place an order and receive the books in time.

If you can't make it to the campus bookstore, you can buy your textbooks from a variety of other sources:

✔ You can use an online bookstore, such as amazon.com (www.amazon.com) or barnesandnoble.com (www.barnesandnoble.com), to buy new books at a discount off of the retail price. Keep in mind that these stores do not specialize in textbooks, but they can often order most books in print, so they're worth a try.

✔ You can search for an online textbook bookstore such as bigwords.com (bigwords.com), whose Web site is shown in Figure 8-2. In addition to new books, these virtual-campus bookstores offer used textbooks that might be a bit battered, but will save you money.

✔ Some online bookstores, such as efollett.com (efollett.com), share information with university bookstores. These sites partner with schools to list courses with information about the assigned texts. If your school is on their list, you can use these sites as an easy way to order your texts. In Figure 8-3, you can see the result of searching for textbooks assigned by the State University of New York at New Paltz; from here you can order from efollett.com without having to return to your school site to find out what books your instructor has assigned.

Figure 8-2:
The textbook portion of bigwords. com offers a wide selection of used books to cost-conscious students.

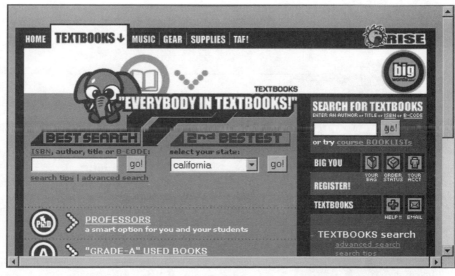

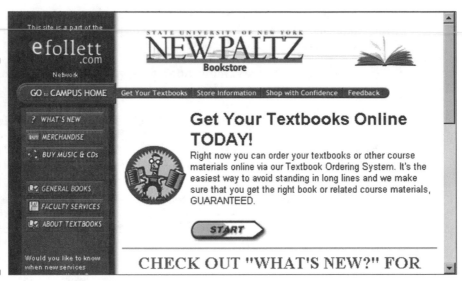

Figure 8-3:
efollett.com offers course information from various colleges so you can find your own course and buy the assigned texts.

✔ Usually, you can go directly to your own school bookstore (see Figure 8-4) through your school Web site. These bookstores typically offer both new and used versions of texts for many classes, and many allow you to order online.

Keep in mind, however, that if your text is available through large retailers like Amazon.com, you can usually get a 30-percent or more discount by ordering from them rather than through your school's bookstore. Also, textbook sites like efollett.com frequently have a better supply of used textbooks than campus bookstores do.

Figure 8-4:
The University of Wisconsin bookstore offers not only books but also school clothes and other paraphernalia online.

You can find listings of several more online bookstores in the Online Directory section of this book.

If you're taking a course from an online training company, and you have an assigned textbook, the company usually either includes the text in the price of the course or has copies of the book for sale to students.

Using special software

Many schools support online learning with a client-server model on a Web server: You go to the site and interact using the software interface they provide online. In this case, you don't have to load any software onto your own computer to participate in your virtual class.

Some schools provide a proprietary software product that you are required to use to access or run course material. Be sure that you get that software and install it before the first class. Allow time to contact the school's technical support in case you have problems getting the software to work.

You may also need to get some mainstream software products, such as the multimedia player RealPlayer or Adobe Acrobat Reader which enables you to read certain types of files you may encounter during your class. You can download many of these products from their manufacturer's site for free (see Chapter 4 for details).

Also check to see whether your own school has licenses for some software products that you can download from its Web site, similar to the Software Guide site from the University of Washington, shown in Figure 8-5.

Figure 8-5: Some software companies license their products to universities so all students can use them.

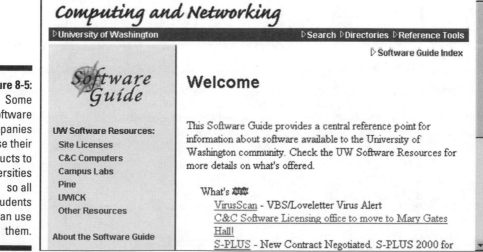

You may also find a collection of Web tools located in a reference area of your school's Web site, such as the Reference Tools page shown in Figure 8-6.

Your program may also expect you to have some standard software products loaded on your computer before class begins, including

- A word processor, such as Word for Windows
- A Web browser, such as Internet Explorer or Netscape Navigator
- An e-mail program, such as Outlook or Messenger, or any of the free e-mail providers such as Yahoo!
- Specialized software, depending on your course topic, such as a spreadsheet program for an accounting class or photo-imaging software for a design class.

Most computers come with many programs already built in when you purchase them that might take care of all the preceding needs, including a basic but useable word processor such as WordPad, which is built into Windows Accessories, or Notepad, the Macintosh equivalent; a Web browser; and often a suite of software such as Microsoft Works. See Chapter 4 for more about hardware and software for distance learning.

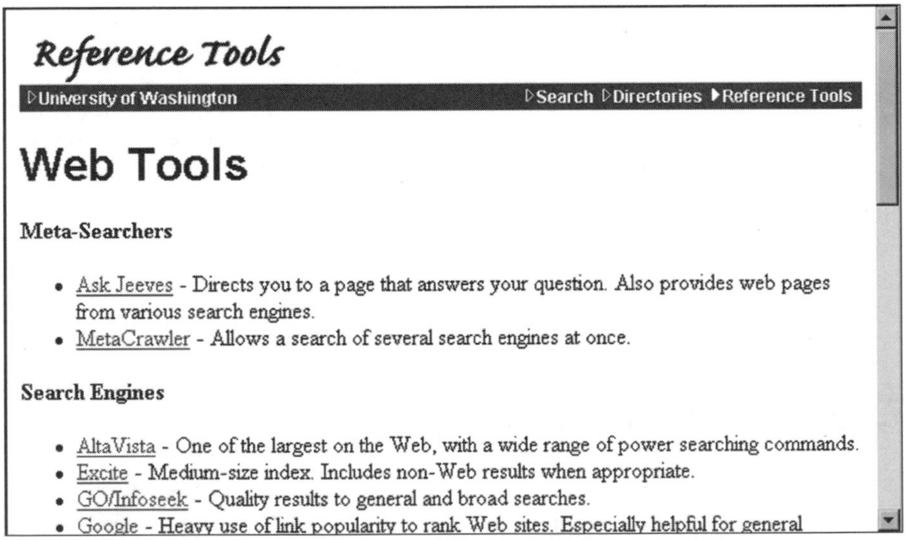

Figure 8-6:
The University of Washington offers a centralized place for Web tools and database references for students.

Reference Tools

▷University of Washington   ▷Search ▷Directories ▶Reference Tools

Web Tools

Meta-Searchers

- Ask Jeeves - Directs you to a page that answers your question. Also provides web pages from various search engines.
- MetaCrawler - Allows a search of several search engines at once.

Search Engines

- AltaVista - One of the largest on the Web, with a wide range of power searching commands.
- Excite - Medium-size index. Includes non-Web results when appropriate.
- GO/Infoseek - Quality results to general and broad searches.
- Google - Heavy use of link popularity to rank Web sites. Especially helpful for general

Assembling your school contacts

You know the old saying: It isn't *what* you know, it's *who* you know. If that's true, gathering information about the people you might need to support you as you begin your distance-learning journey is a good idea. Here are just a few of the contacts to make a note of:

✔ Registrar's office address, phone number, and e-mail

✔ Instructor's phone number and e-mail

✔ Academic advisor's phone number and e-mail

✔ Library phone number and Web site

✔ Technical support phone number and e-mail for Web site problems

✔ Bookstore phone number and Web site

✔ Support staff for the distance-learning division: names, phone numbers, and e-mail

✔ The phone number and code for the school teleconferencing bridge

Online training companies have several counterparts to these college-based contacts; for example, a customer service department may help you with payments instead of a registrar. With online training companies, you can still expect to have a support staff for technical problems and some way to contact your instructor, if only by e-mail.

Your school may provide you with a listing of these contacts in your welcome packet. If it doesn't, browse through the school Web site in search of a listing like the one shown in Figure 8-7.

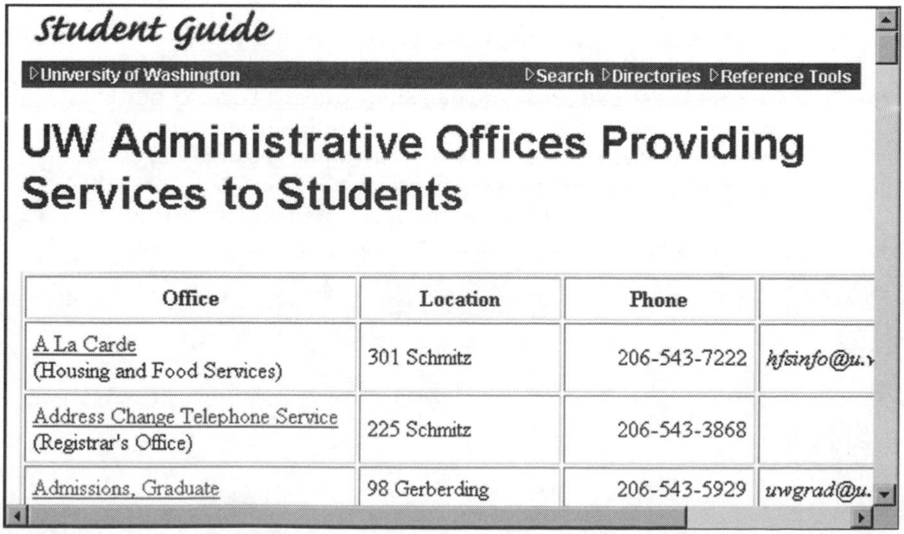

Figure 8-7:
The
University of
Washington
centralizes
phone
numbers of
interest to
students on
this Web
page.

Student Guide

▷University of Washington   ▷Search ▷Directories ▷Reference Tools

UW Administrative Offices Providing Services to Students

Office	Location	Phone	
A La Carde (Housing and Food Services)	301 Schmitz	206-543-7222	*hfsinfo@u.v*
Address Change Telephone Service (Registrar's Office)	225 Schmitz	206-543-3868	
Admissions, Graduate	98 Gerberding	206-543-5929	*uwgrad@u.*

Wherever you get your contact information, keep it in a handy place, either taped to the side of your monitor or at the front of a loose-leaf binder that holds your course materials. Having this list handy will save you from having to fumble to find a number when an urgent need arises.

A trip to the online office-supply store

Some people figure that the Internet will lead to the dawning of a paperless world. It may someday, but probably not before you complete several four-year distance-learning degree programs. The items you need to keep your studies organized are still very nonvirtual.

If you haven't been to school for a while, you may not have on hand the supplies you need to keep your school materials in place. Use this handy checklist to stock up before class begins:

- ✔ Loose-leaf binder for course materials you print out
- ✔ Dividers for the binder to keep lessons organized
- ✔ Three-hole punch
- ✔ Paperclips
- ✔ Stapler with staples
- ✔ Formatted computer disks with labels to keep copies of your coursework or important files
- ✔ A disk holder to keep your disks organized
- ✔ Index cards where you can print key learning points for quick review
- ✔ Post-it notes to mark pages in books or add notes to printed material
- ✔ Pens, pencils, and highlighters in as many colors as you can find

To get these supplies, you can simply take a trip to your local office-supply store, or you can order by phone or online from any national chain, such as Staples (www.staples.com) or OfficeMax (www.officemax.com). Don't forget your school bookstore; online campus bookstores, like the one shown in Figure 8-8, offer a wide assortment of products to choose from, often at as great a discount as major office-supply chains.

Figure 8-8:
The University of Wisconsin bookstore claims to feature over 25,000 products in their supply department.

At Your Service

Many distance-learning experts believe that the most important thing to look for in a school is the infrastructure they offer for supporting students. They may be right: From a good library to foreign-student support programs, the effort a school puts into making you a happy and productive student can be key to your success in distance learning.

If you're studying with a college or university, just because you're not on campus doesn't mean that you can't take advantage of many student services and facilities that are campus-bound. What different schools have to offer may vary, but some of the services to look for are library access, special student discounts on products and services, and counseling support for students in crisis.

Using the library

One advantage a college has over an online training provider is the established reference resource it has built up over the years in the form of a library. Good colleges offering distance-learning programs create several ways for remote learners to benefit from that resource.

As you can see on the main Library Web page for the University of Washington, shown in Figure 8-9, libraries have gone beyond just books. You can access databases, reference tools, news, and library events, as well as links to specialized collections.

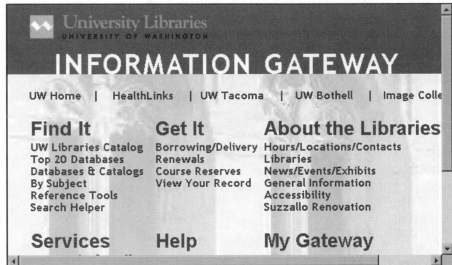

Figure 8-9:
The
Information
Gateway is
a central
location for
information
resources at
this
university.

Some school libraries have programs to mail printed books on loan to remote students, although this isn't always the policy. Because so much information is going online these days, you can access a wide selection of journals, articles, and other information through your school's online library.

If you can't get what you need from your school's library remotely, or if you're studying with a training provider who doesn't have such a resource, don't forget your handy local public library.

Taking advantage of student deals

Universities can have a student population of 10 or 50 thousand. When you add the ability to expand that student body through distance learning, you're looking at an organization with a lot of buying clout. As a result, schools can offer students discounts on many products, often through the school bookstore (see Figure 8-10). Other deals are available through banner ads on school Web sites or through student activity offices.

Check out what your school has to offer in the way of discounts on

- Computer hardware and software
- Music CDs
- Travel
- Insurance
- Electronic equipment such as CD players

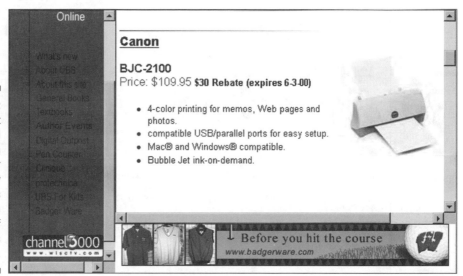

Figure 8-10: You can get a good deal through discounts or rebates by using sites like the University of Wisconsin's bookstore.

Credit card companies sometimes offer special accounts to students; check your school Web site to see if someone's touting a card with a good interest rate.

Getting guidance

Just because you may live halfway across the country from your school doesn't mean that you aren't a person. You're likely to have the same needs as a campus-bound student has. Before you begin your distance-learning program, check out any support services your school offers that might be useful to you.

Some of the services you can expect to access, either over the phone or online, include

- ✔ Foreign student assistance to help those studying from a different country
- ✔ Disabled student support programs to provide information on access, technical assistance, and special programs
- ✔ Tutor programs for students who need academic help
- ✔ Counseling help for personal problems like addiction or stress
- ✔ Work placement programs (see Figure 8-11) that provide assistance in finding potential employers, or brushing up on resume writing or interviewing skills (see Chapter 16 for more information)

Figure 8-11:
The Career
Services
division
of this
university
can help you
leverage
your
education
in the
workplace.

UNIVERSITY *of* WISCONSIN-EAU CLAIRE

Your link to the future . . .

Career Services

To assist with career
education and
development from
the time of
orientation to the
university throughout
the alumni years.

UPCOMING
EVENTS   ABOUT US   STUDENTS/ALUMNI   EMPLOYER
GUIDE

Upcoming Events

About Us

Students/Alumni

Employers Guide

Blugold
CareerLink

Vacancy Bulletin

Drop-in hours are available Monday-Friday, 1:00-3:00. This is a chance to
meet with one of our career counselors. If you have questions about career
planning, internships, the job search, resumes, or any other concern, please
drop in.

Part IV
Communicating in Cyberclass

The 5th Wave   By Rich Tennant

IT WAS ACTUALLY ON THE WEB ONE NIGHT THAT CAPT. AHAB CAUGHT UP WITH HIS OBSESSION.

WHALE CHAT

White? Really? Where can we meet?

In this part . . .

Before communication, there were just a few grunts and sighs in a dark cave somewhere, and you can guess how much fun *that* was. Communication is one of the areas in which humans excel. It allows us to share knowledge, exchange ideas, and make friends.

In an online education setting, communication takes a different form than it does around the water cooler at work. You have to master certain techniques, and even improve your writing skills to succeed. The chapters in this part explore the distance-learning classroom environment, and just how people interact and communicate there. You may already know about sending mail, chatting, holding discussions, and even forming study groups in the real world — but this part shows you how to do all those activities online.

Chapter 9

Ready? It's the First Day of Virtual School

In This Chapter

▶ Entering your virtual classroom

▶ Interacting with others

▶ Viewing course material and submitting assignments

▶ Locating your online teacher

*W*e've all been through those first-day-at-a-new-school jitters. Our nervousness probably stemmed from the fact that we didn't know what to expect, and above all, we didn't want to look like a jerk in front of the other students. So that you'll experience a minimum of anxiety about your first online learning experience, I've included this chapter to give you a preview of some typical online classroom experiences. Refer to this chapter for information about how to enter the classroom, where to find the other students and your teacher, and what a live lecture becomes when it's delivered over your computer. After reading this chapter, you can look like the class president instead of the class clown on your first day of virtual learning. This chapter gives you a look at a couple of online classroom environments and points out certain features that you're likely to encounter in your own classes.

Setting Your Expectations

The format of online distance learning varies from program to program. It can range from an entirely self-paced experience where you're the only player, to a learning community where student and teacher interaction occurs on a daily basis. However, most classes have certain elements in common:

✔ Use of the Web to disseminate information in text format

✔ Discussion areas for students to interact

> ✔ The capability to e-mail the school or an instructor to ask questions
>
> ✔ Links to help you navigate around the course or to related information

Beyond that, the way the course uses multimedia like audio and video, the extent to which self-paced tutorial and live interaction are included, and the learning approach (student discussion, project-based, and so on) may differ significantly.

This chapter gives you a look around a college-level classroom at the University of Washington, and walks you through an online class from Cardean, a virtual university whose courses combine self-paced learning with instructor interaction. (If you're taking a purely a self-paced tutorial, you can get a feel for that environment in Chapter 14.)

College Bound

The University of Washington is one of the leading institutions in distance learning in the United States. It retains a group of about a dozen online-course designers on staff to work with instructors on converting classroom courses to online courses. The focus here is on building learning communities among the students in a course. Instructors post information, and students discuss and interact online to share ideas and real-world experience. The instructor serves as a facilitator to that interaction. The course that this chapter uses as an example had no tests, only assignments to which the instructor replied with comments and suggestions. The course ran over a nine-week period and was part of a certificate program where the medium was part of the learning experience, because these distance-learning courses were all about distance-learning design. A team of instructors from the university taught the courses.

Logging on

In a face-to-face classroom, a student can wander into a classroom pretty much at will. But if his name isn't on the roster for that class, he'll be asked to leave. A similar qualifying process exists in an online class. So that only paying students can enter, your classroom is hidden behind a high-tech fence. To enter an online class, you have to obtain a password and follow a log-on procedure.

When you register for an online class, you receive information about the Internet address (URL) of the class, instructions for finding your specific class, and some kind of user name and password. You will have to provide your user name and password each time you enter your class; this process is known as *logging on* to a site. You may have encountered the log-on process at your office when accessing your company network, or if you have ever used an online service like AOL that requires that you register and use a password to enter the service.

Look for a log-on link on your school's welcome page for distance-learning courses, which may look something like the one shown in Figure 9-1 for the University of Washington.

In case you forget your password, the school in Figure 9-1 has provided a link on the welcome page to help you out. Click on that link and you get a form (see Figure 9-2) where you can enter your e-mail information. To protect you, and ensure that you are actually the one requesting the password, the system is set up to send the information directly to your e-mail account. Not all schools offer this reminder service, and those that do may take a few minutes, a few hours, or even a day or more to get your password to you. My advice is to write your password and user name down and don't lose them.

Figure 9-1:
The distance-learning division of your school probably maintains its own welcome screen for all classes it offers online.

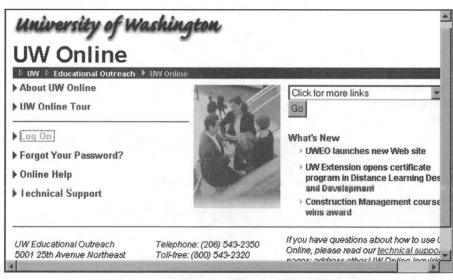

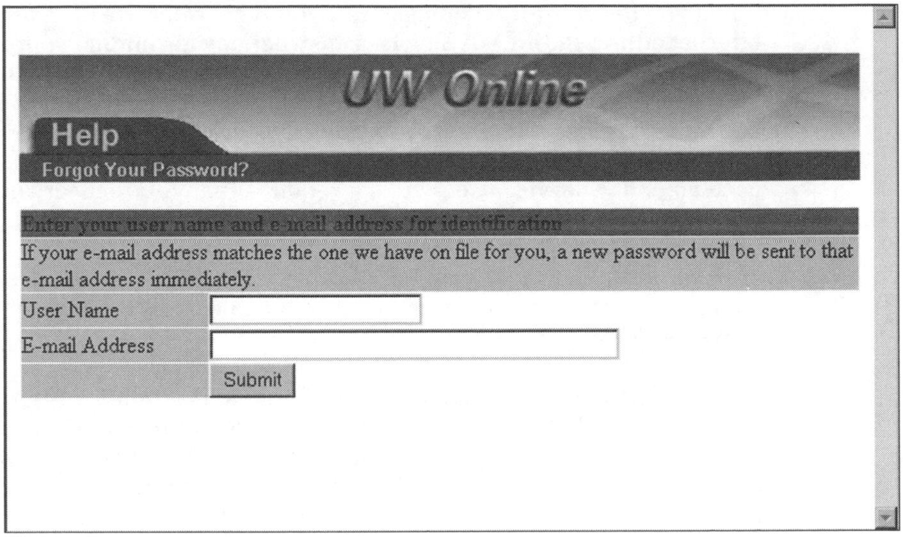

Figure 9-2:
If you lose
your
password,
some
schools
provide a
form such
as this so
they can
re-send it to
you.

If you know your password, you can click on the Log On link on the welcome page. Next, you can expect to see a form like the one shown in Figure 9-3, where you can enter your log-on information. Here, you fill in your user name and password, and then click OK to log on to the school's system. In this example, the next screen you see lists the courses you're registered for; you simply click on a course to enter that classroom.

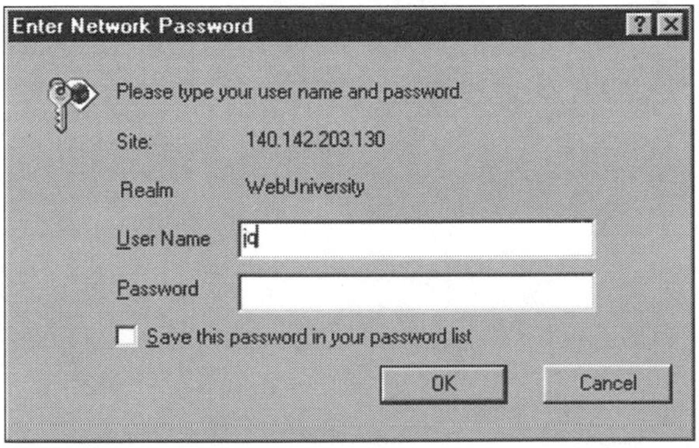

Figure 9-3:
When you
log on to
your
school's
Web site,
you get a
form like
this asking
for your
user name
(sometimes
called a
student
name) along
with your
password.

TIP

If you don't want to have to enter your user name and password information every time you log on, look for and check an option to Save the Password before closing the log-on dialog box. Just be aware that after you choose this setting, anyone can log onto the site from your computer and pretend to be you — not such a bad deal as long as they go ahead and take your tests for you, too!

Viewing the class syllabus

When you enter a class, what you see will vary, depending on your school's Web site design. However, a *class syllabus,* or outline of the topics the course will cover, is usually displayed or available through a link at this point. In some cases, this syllabus contains links to your actual course material and class discussion areas, as is the case with the syllabus for this course, shown in Figure 9-4.

This course is broken into modules for each of the nine weeks of the course. Dates for completing reading and class assignments appear to the right of each module. By clicking on a module, you can access the course material for it. Each module also has a discussion area where students post assignments and exchange comments.

The left side of the page includes a list of links to help you move to other areas of the course. You can use these links to jump back to the syllabus if you are viewing course material for a module, or to go to a help system or back to the welcome screen to enter a different class.

Figure 9-4:
This syllabus lists each module of the course along with dates for completing reading and assignments.

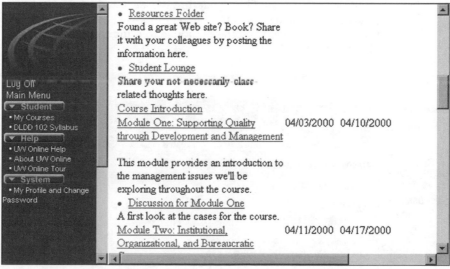

However you navigate it, a course syllabus or outline is a typical feature for both university and training classes. Like the table of contents of a book, it helps you find where you want to go and see where you've been. In many cases, you can find due dates for both tests and assignments right on the syllabus as well.

Raising Your Hand

When you first log onto your school's Web site and enter your class syllabus, you're likely to feel as though you showed up for class but nobody else did. That's because you haven't yet ventured into the areas of the course where people interact. Interaction can take place in discussion areas, chat rooms, or even through e-mails directly to your instructor's or other students' online accounts.

One thing you should understand about online classes is that the lecture model used in face-to-face classrooms has gone out the window. Rather than an instructor standing at the front of the room spouting information, information is available through textbooks and posted notes. The give and take of a classroom debate or questions to the teacher takes place through the exchange of messages online. See Chapter 10 for more information about using discussion areas, chat rooms, and e-mail.

Participating in discussions

Online discussions, also known as threaded discussions, are areas where you can post a message and read and respond to other people's messages. The term *threaded* refers to the fact that the discussion contains threads of conversations that you follow from first message to last to get the logical flow of people's comments to each other. Figure 9-5 shows a discussion area; note the second message and the response to it indented beneath, constituting a short thread.

Figure 9-5:
In this discussion area, you can view discussions by author, date of posting, or thread.

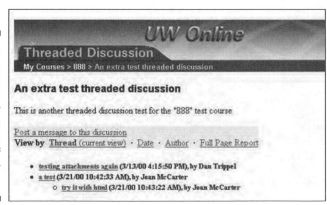

Although the particular features of a discussion area may vary, they all work in the same general way. In the case of the discussion area shown in Figure 9-5, you can read a message by clicking on it. You can post a message by clicking on the link that is titled *Post a message to this discussion.* When you click this link, you see the form shown in Figure 9-6, where you can enter a title, type a message, and even attach a file.

Conversations on a discussion area don't take place in real time, as a face-to-face conversation does. You might post a message on Thursday morning and find that no one responds to it until Saturday night; in other words, expect some lag time between comments. This type of communication is called *asynchronous.* Asynchronous communication does have advantages, because it allows students flexibility in the timing of their participation in a discussion. This flexible timing also enables you to create longer, more thoughtful comments than you might in a real-time discussion. However, it also means that you have to schedule regular visits back to the discussion area to see whether someone has responded to your comment, or asked a question you should respond to.

Chatting in real time

In the online world, chatting is as close as you get to an in-person conversation. That's because, with chatting, all the participants are "there" at the same time, typing in and sending comments and responses on the spot. This kind of communication is called *synchronous.* With synchronous communication, an online exchange happens almost at the pace of a spoken conversation (depending on how fast each person can type).

Figure 9-6:
By reading through messages in a discussion area, you can see how people build a dialog that resembles a classroom discussion.

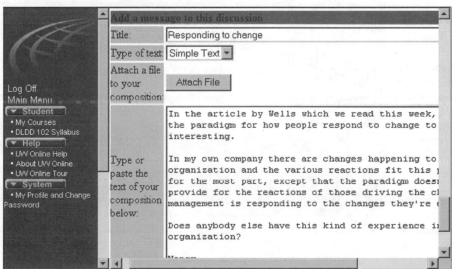

Chat rooms (areas online where chats take place) are very popular in distance learning because they bring a sense of personal interaction to what can sometimes feel like a one-person learning experience. In a chat, people are more likely to crack jokes, ask about each other's lives, and come up with seat-of-their-pants innovations. Chats are also one place where you can encounter online conflict in communication. (For more about communication styles and conflicts in distance learning, see Chapter 11).

If chat rooms are available as a feature in your classroom, a link to the chat room will appear somewhere either on the main page or within a discussion area. When you click on this link to enter the chat room, you will see a list of people who are in the chat room at that time, and a note announcing that you have just entered the room to let others know of your arrival. You will also see a text box where you can enter your comments or a question, and buttons to post a comment or exit the chat room (see Figure 9-7).

To contribute to the discussion, just type a comment in the text window and then click on the button to post the comment. Your message appears in the chat window. When someone responds, his or her comment is then posted on the next line of the chat window; the conversation scrolls down when a new comment appears so you can follow the comments as they come in.

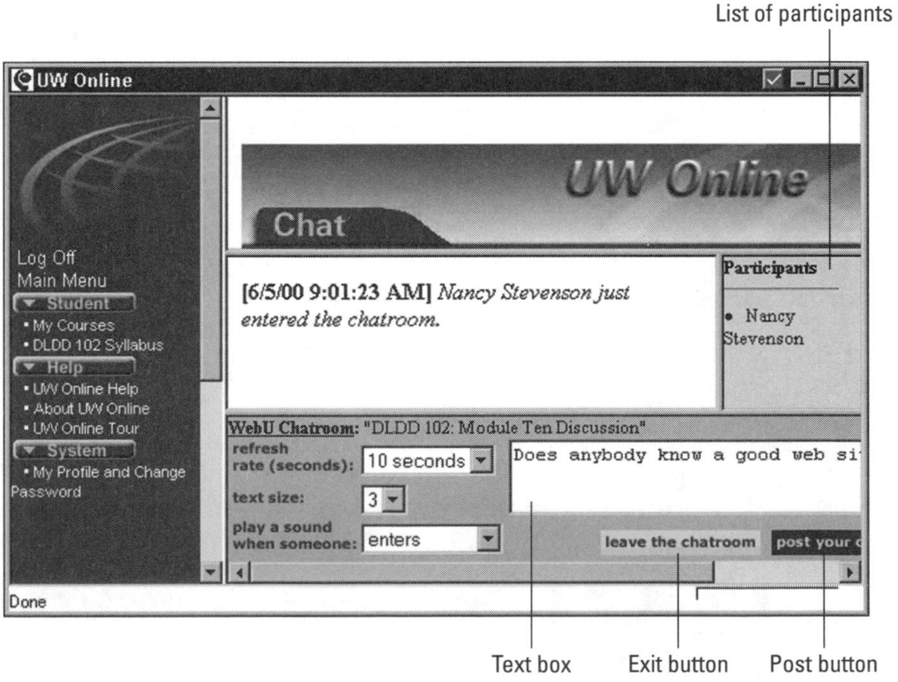

List of participants

Figure 9-7: Comments you post to the chat and notices of people entering and leaving the chat room appear in the chat window of this page.

Text box   Exit button   Post button

Some chat rooms allow you to scroll up and down to review earlier comments in the chat, or to view transcripts of the entire conversation after it's over, like the transcript shown in Figure 9-8. Transcripts are very handy because you can simply print them out and keep them with your class notes.

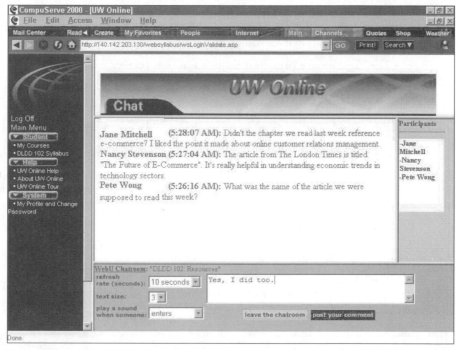

Figure 9-8:
You can use chat rooms just to touch base with another person or to hold formal, live discussions.

E-mailing to get your message across

Your school should give you your instructor's e-mail address so that you can contact him or her with questions or problems at any time. In some courses, the school also provides the e-mail addresses of your fellow students, so that you can contact them directly to discuss an issue or get help from each other. However, some schools will not provide student contact information for various privacy reasons.

Specific instructions for how to use e-mail are beyond the scope of this book (for that information, check out *E-Mail For Dummies,* 2nd Edition, by John R. Levine, Carol Baroudi, Margy Levine Young, and Arnold Reinhold, published by IDG Books Worldwide), but I do want to advise you about *when* to use it. The trick to using e-mail in a distance-learning class is knowing when e-mailing is preferable to posting a message in a discussion area. Typically, you use e-mail when

- You have a complaint about the instructor or course material that is more tactful for you to communicate to the instructor in private.

- You have an issue with another student that you want the instructor to mediate, whether it involves an irresolvable conflict in a discussion or some form of improper behavior or harassment.

- You are confused about a point that everybody else seems to be getting; you can then ask another student or the instructor to help you out, without wasting everyone else's time.

- You have a procedural question that relates only to you. (For example, you're going on vacation and want to know how to make up an assignment that week.)

Instead of sending e-mail, post a message to a discussion when

- You have a helpful suggestion of something that might make the course go better for all students.

- You think an idea or concept you have would be a good topic for a group discussion.

- You are confused about something that you think others might be confused about, too, and you think that posting the issue in a discussion area might help everybody in the course.

- You have a procedural question that affects everybody (for example, an instruction about an assignment gives dates contradictory to the syllabus.

Finding the lecture hall

In place of a teacher standing at the front of the classroom with chalk in hand, distance learners often get lecture information online. Usually, a regular lecture is posted, along with reading assignments from textbooks, links to online articles or related Web sites, and class assignment information, as with the information for Module Six of the course in distance-learning design, shown in Figure 9-9.

Some critics of distance learning say that this format merely shifts the burden of printing out course materials from the textbook publisher to the student, and they have a point. Most students prefer to print out lecture information and save it in a binder, rather than read it online; you can probably count on doing a fair amount of printing in your distance-learning life.

In addition to course information posted online, some schools send out regular packets of materials for courses by mail. These packets might include audio- or videotapes, lab material for science courses, or hardcopy printouts of articles or visual aids. Your school may also use videoconferenced lectures or teleconferencing to provide course content.

Getting and posting assignments

Your instructor is likely to post assignment information along with lecture material on a weekly basis, or around whatever timeframe your course is structured. Assignments for distance-learning courses often include:

- Reading assignments from textbooks or online material
- Assignments to post reactions to a reading or your perspective on a topic to a discussion area (This type of assignment often involves reading and responding to fellow students' comments on the same topic.)
- Written assignments that you submit directly to an instructor
- Lab work that you must complete and submit a written summary of
- Group assignments where you have to work with others students on a project or role play

In some classes, you complete assignments at your own pace. However, in a college course, you are more likely to receive a due date for assignments; keeping up with the pace is up to you.

Looking for your instructor

The teacher's role in distance learning is still evolving, but the current popular description of this role is that of a facilitator. An instructor for a distance-learning class is usually involved in creating materials that mirror in-person class lecture content, including assignments and textbook reading. But contrary to the traditional lecture model of teaching, one of the most important functions of the online instructor is to monitor student discussions and chats, and to post responses to questions or comments on dialogs that facilitate student learning. In academic jargon, they're building learning communities and fostering *constructivist learning* (that is, learning that relies less on rote memorization than on practical application of ideas).

Many distance-learning courses are designed so that much of the learning takes place between students through their discussions, rather than through a lecture-delivery method from teacher to student. For an adult learner in particular, this interaction with others who are working in the real world and interested in the same topic often gives a very practical and applied dimension to textbook knowledge.

Beyond their involvement in designing the course and creating and posting lectures and other materials, teachers also address general issues and concerns by posting messages to the entire class in discussion areas. Instructors also make themselves available to students with online office hours — that is, hours when they are in a chat room available for a discussion — or by their e-mail address or phone number for one-on-one communication. Finally, teachers provide feedback on assignments and facilitate group efforts such as teleconferences or videoconferencing.

Test Driving a Class

This section walks you through a partially self-paced course, which offers a different style of course design than many traditional college courses that have been moved online. The course I use as an example is Corporate Finance from Cardean University, which is an entirely virtual school run by unext.com (www.unext.com). This online school offers MBA courses to corporate clients, and plans to make these courses available to the general public in the future. Although this class is at the college level, it combines the self-paced and interactive aspects of many online training providers with the content richness of university study.

Cardean University partners with schools like Columbia Business School and London School of Economics to create course content, so the quality of the material is impressive. It also has a large full-time staff of designers and writers who work with the academics at these schools to design courses that take full advantage of the online format. Cardean uses a project-based approach to learning, challenging the learner to take a typical real-world problem and work to resolve it.

Getting started

After you enroll in an online course, you enter the virtual classroom by going through a log-on process that identifies you as a registered student. Each program's log-on process is a little different, but most programs work something like Cardean's, where you simply click the Login link on the main Cardean Web page, shown in Figure 9-10, to log on.

In most cases, after you click a button to log on, you see a dialog box where you can enter your user ID and password, which the school sends to you when you register for a course. On the Cardean site, after you enter this information and click OK, the next screen you see is the Welcome screen, shown in Figure 9-11. If you need help with technical information or more information about Cardean, you can get it here. You click on the go to your course link to access any courses for which you are registered.

Figure 9-10: You have only one option here: Log in to your courses.

Click here to log on

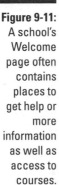

Figure 9-11:
A school's
Welcome
page often
contains
places to
get help or
more
information
as well as
access to
courses.

When you click the go to your course link, the Cardean University Courses page, shown in Figure 9-12, appears. This page lists courses available with links to view a description of the course at the top of the page, and a list of links to enter courses themselves near the bottom. To enter the course in this example, you click on the Corporate Finance: Asset Valuation link.

Cardean University Courses

We're pleased that you have chosen Cardean University as part of your employee development program. Cardean offers working professionals an MBA-level curriculum in a rich, engaging, online learning environment. We are truly delivering world-class business education with the convenience of anywhere, anytime access.

Cardean currently has several business management courses available. To learn more about these courses, select the descriptions below.

Corporate Finance: Asset Valuation	Description
Principles of Marketing: Price	Description
Financial Accounting: Assessing Profitability	Description
Leading and Managing Organizations: Managerial Problem Solving	Description

You can also view the courses and the Discussion (the Cardean online community message boards) to witness online collaboration in Cardean courses. Feel free to browse the courses at any time. To enter Cardean courses, select the course name below.

Corporate Finance: Asset Valuation
Financial Accounting: Assessing Profitability

Figure 9-12:
Several
courses
may be
available to
you on this
page.

Viewing your course material

The course material in a largely self-paced environment is set up with a logical flow of information that students can step through at their own pace. That information may be in the form a series of Web pages containing text, charts, graphic images, videos, or animations. A course may also use an audio narration at any point in the material to give you the feel of an instructor presence.

Because Cardean's courses are project-based, the first screen you come to presents the Project Guide (see Figure 9-13). In this case, the project is a case study of an energy company that needs to select the proper investment strategy. The student plays the role of a financial consultant who will study the company and the possible strategies, and make a recommendation to the hypothetical company. The Project Guide serves as a visual roadmap to the course, enabling the student to click on any element of the project at any time. This is student-driven learning, which allows learners to move around and access information that is useful to them as they need it, rather than getting weekly assignments from an instructor in chronological order.

When you click on the Getting Started link, you move to an overview of the course, as shown in Figure 9-14. Scrolling down this page reveals information about the designers of the course and a video introduction to the designer. Courses like this one that provide a video instructor presence do so to give students the sense of a real person behind the course.

Figure 9-13: This visual guide provides links to various elements of the learning project.

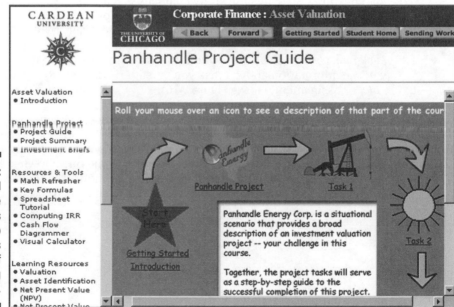

Figure 9-14:
This course
introduction
includes a
video
overview
from the
instructor;
you can also
access a
transcript of
this
information
if you don't
want to
view the
video.

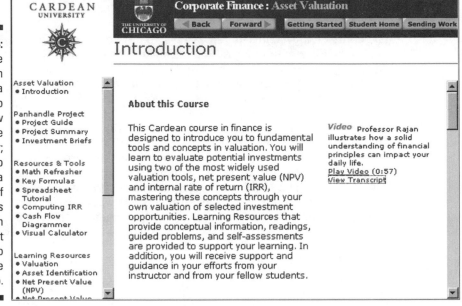

The Project Guide (refer back to Figure 9-13) provides a graphic overview of the project. Clicking on any of the topics in the project brings up a narrated animation sequence, one panel of which appears in Figure 9-15. This animated overview of the case study company gives you an idea of the challenges you, as a student, must overcome in this project. Self-paced training often uses animation to set out a scenario or graphically explain a concept.

Task Links are available throughout the project material. If you click on one, you see information about a task you must perform and what your *deliverable,* or assignment, is (see Figure 9-16).

If you need additional information about concepts or terminology involved in a task, you can click on links within the task descriptions to get more detail, or click on a link along the left side of the screen under the Learning Resources area. You then see a screen similar to the one shown in Figure 9-17 describing Net Present Value. Notice links to additional readings, a self-assessment test, and even video descriptions from the professors on this page.

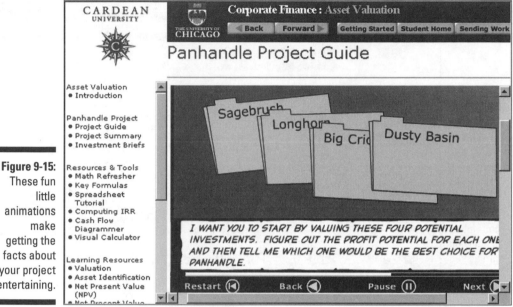

Figure 9-15:
These fun little animations make getting the facts about your project entertaining.

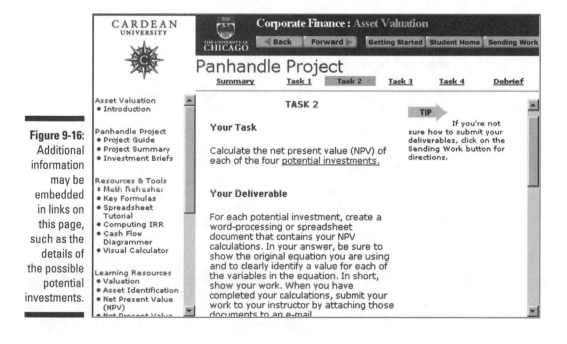

Figure 9-16:
Additional information may be embedded in links on this page, such as the details of the possible potential investments.

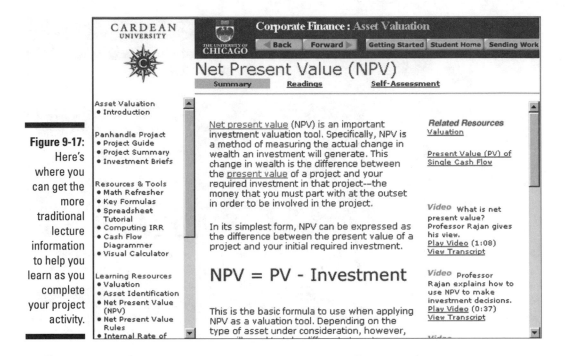

Figure 9-17:
Here's
where you
can get the
more
traditional
lecture
information
to help you
learn as you
complete
your project
activity.

When you finish reviewing a project and work through its tasks, you access a Project Debrief. The Debrief reviews the skills and concepts you've been exposed to in working through the tasks, and makes a final assignment for the course that calls on all of the knowledge you've picked up during the project. Summaries of key concepts are typical features of self-paced learning that help students to identify and retain important ideas.

Getting help and resources

A good self-paced course provides several types of help for students. This help may include an online glossary, software tools such as calculators, or a database of frequently asked questions (FAQs) about how to navigate around and use the course itself.

The left side of the Cardean course screen includes a section called Resources & Tools. What you find in this list differs from course to course; in this example, the designers have included calculators, diagramming tools, and even a tutorial on how to use a spreadsheet. The Visual Calculator available in this course lets you enter information about an investment and generate a chart.

In a Cardean course, as in most online courses, in addition to accessing these resources and tools you can also send questions to your instructor by e-mail at any time. You also have the option of posting questions to a discussion area for the instructor or other students to answer. Although a discussion area isn't always part of a self-paced course, it's a very useful feature for interacting with other students when it is available.

Checking your progress

When you learn something new, having a way to gauge your progress — to spot areas where you need a little more study and others where your new knowledge seems to be on a solid footing — can be helpful. In any self-paced course, being able to assess your own progress and knowledge is especially important because no one else may be there to give you feedback. This assessment can take the form of a multiple-choice test that you fill out online; such tests are graded automatically and return your score instantly. In other courses, you may submit a test to an actual instructor who grades questions — which, unlike in automatic tests, may include essays — and returns a score and comments to you.

The Cardean course includes a self-assessment section that you can access from a Self-Assessment link (refer back to Figure 9-17). Figure 9-18 shows a typical multiple-choice test. If you get the correct answer, a screen appears (see Figure 9-19) with further information about the question topic.

Figure 9-18: Make your choice and check your answer to see how you're doing.

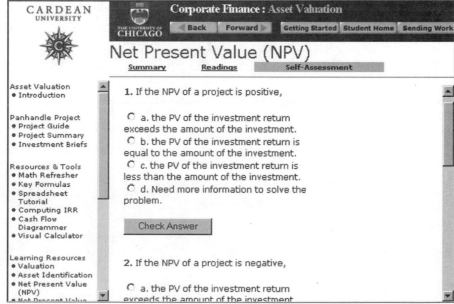

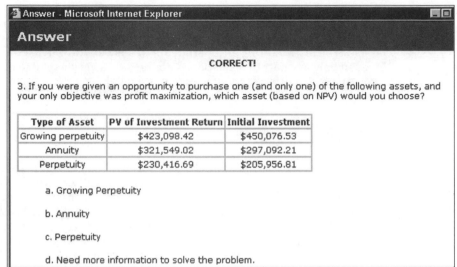

Figure 9-19:
Your course
gives you
information
to support
why your
answer was
correct.

As in all good online courses, this one also gives you feedback on assignments that you submit to your instructor. You must complete all assignments to complete the course. Assignments in distance-learning courses are often noted in specific module lectures, or are listed on the course syllabus. Students typically e-mail assignments directly to an instructor or post them online in a discussion area. Instructors may give feedback individually to each student via e-mail, or may post a more general comment online.

Chapter 10

Interacting in a Virtual Classroom

∙∙

In This Chapter

▶ Using e-mail, discussion groups, and chat rooms to communicate

▶ Participating in videoconferences

▶ Interacting with instructors

▶ Planning your degree with an advisor

∙∙

*T*he word *education* comes from a Latin word that means to draw out. In the purest sense, education doesn't consist of sitting alone reading a book; it's a process of interacting with others to exchange information, share ideas, and make discoveries. This kind of interaction requires communication.

Communication is every bit as important in a distance-learning setting as it is in a face-to-face educational experience. Because you can't take advantage of body language and voice inflection when you're not in the same room with the people you're talking to, the way you manipulate the written word to communicate becomes all-important.

This chapter explores some of the tools and formats for interacting in a virtual classroom, and reveals how to communicate with your instructors and advisors to get the most out of your education at a distance.

Putting It into Words

The three main venues for communicating in distance learning are e-mail, discussion groups, and chat rooms. In each of these methods, you use the written word to communicate; however, each has a slightly different purpose and rhythm for how you can convey information.

Of course, you can always communicate with your classmates, instructors, and advisors over the telephone, but remember those long-distance charges! Because you call a local phone number to access your e-mail account, communicating online is far less expensive if your school is long distance.

E-mailing 101

Nowadays, you hear about e-commerce, e-learning, and e-shopping, but what started the whole e-thing is e-mail. Electronic mail (e-mail for short) is, quite simply, the transmission of a message from one person to another over a network, such as the Internet. E-mail can go out to a single recipient or to the whole world (if you have everybody's address). When you send e-mail, it goes to a holding place on your Internet Service Provider's server until your recipient logs on and accesses it using a mail program such as Outlook Express. You can also attach files to your e-mail messages; this approach allows you to send graphics, lengthy documents, video clips, or sound files to anyone with an online e-mail address.

Distance learners typically use e-mail for one-on-one communication, either with an instructor or one or more fellow students. E-mail works best for shorter messages, say messages of no more than two or three paragraphs, because these messages are usually read on a computer screen. Anything lengthier than a few paragraphs becomes cumbersome to read online. For longer messages, you can always attach a document to an e-mail that a recipient can download and print to read offline. (For ideas about when it's appropriate to use e-mail in the online classroom, see Chapter 9.)

Here are a few tips for composing effective e-mail messages, such as the one created in Outlook and shown in Figure 10-1:

- ✔ Write a subject line that makes clear what the message is about.

- ✔ Include optional contact information, such as a phone number, if you think the recipient might want to respond in person.

- ✔ If you are sending a message to your instructor, include the course name, number, and section, if any, in your message. Instructors may have dozens of students each semester, and can't always remember which class you're in just from your name.

- ✔ If somebody else should be aware of the contents of your message, send him or her a carbon copy (Cc:).

- ✔ If you want someone else to receive a copy of the message but you don't want the other recipients to know that you're copying that person, use the blind carbon copy feature (Bcc:).

- ✔ If the e-mail includes a key piece of information, such as a deadline, consider formatting that portion differently so that it jumps out at the reader.

Most e-mail programs have settings for handling an e-mail message that might help you work more efficiently. For example, Outlook's Message Options, shown in Figure 10-2, allow you to

Copy-recipient's address Specific Subject Concise message

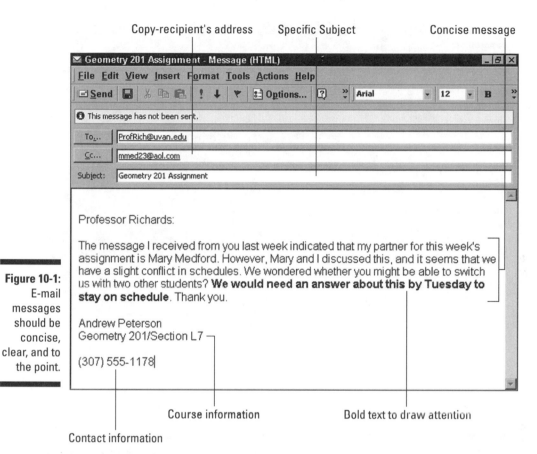

Figure 10-1:
E-mail
messages
should be
concise,
clear, and to
the point.

Contact information

Course information

Bold text to draw attention

✔ Set the importance and sensitivity of a message — for example, marking it as *urgent* so the recipient sees an urgent flag and might act on it more quickly.

✔ Set the security level for your message to allow or exclude messages that contain what are called *active scripts;* active scripts can run programs such as viruses on your computer.

✔ Arrange to copy someone on any replies to your message.

✔ Set the timeframe for the message delivery by specifying that the message shouldn't be delivered before a certain date, or that a message should not be sent after a certain point in time. You choose these settings by checking either the Do not deliver before or Expires after option and selecting a date from a drop-down calendar in that field.

✔ Get a receipt when the message has been received and read.

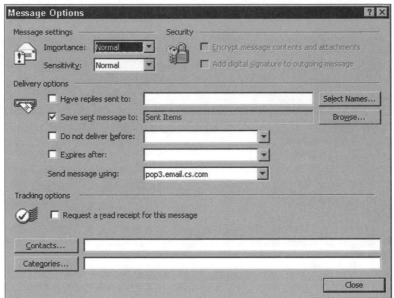

Figure 10-2:
Your own
e-mail
program
may have
settings,
such as
these from
Microsoft
Outlook, that
control the
handling of
your
messages to
make
communica-
tion easier.

Check your own e-mail program to see whether you can take advantage of settings such as these.

Airing your ideas in discussion groups

Whereas e-mail goes to specific individuals' e-mail accounts, discussion areas (sometimes called *bulletin boards,* as in Figure 10-3) are places located on your school's Web site where you can post a message. Whoever wants to come by and read it can (assuming the person has access to that area). Discussion areas, like e-mail, are asynchronous, giving you time to think about what you're going to say before sending your words out for others to view. Discussions are arranged in *threads*: strings of messages on the same topic that form a conversation.

Don't assume that, just because you put information in a discussion area, it has reached everybody in your class. Some students, and even your instructor, might skip some messages in a discussion, whereas most people read all their e-mail (eventually!). If you have an urgent message, stick with e-mail . . . or even a plain, old-fashioned phone call.

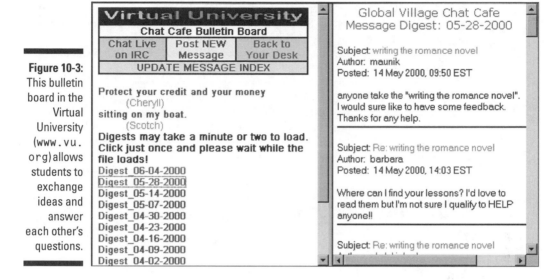

Figure 10-3:
This bulletin board in the Virtual University (www.vu.org) allows students to exchange ideas and answer each other's questions.

As with e-mail, messages posted to a discussion area are typically read online as part of a discussion thread. For that reason, these messages — like e-mail — should not be too lengthy. If you want to include a greater amount of text, you might consider attaching a document to a discussion group message. Then, those who wish to read in more detail can download and read that document, and those who don't can read your main message and move on.

You can usually sort messages in discussion areas by the date of the message, the author, or the thread that the messages fall into. If you want to be sure that you read all of your teacher's messages, for example, sort by author.

You have two options for creating a message in a discussion area: You can respond to an existing posting and add your message to that thread, or you can begin a new thread by posting a new message. If you're replying to another person's message, it's sometimes useful to copy and paste a portion of the original message into your reply message to help readers understand the context for your comment.

How and where you perform the functions of replying, posting, attaching files, and so on depends on the structure of your discussion group page, so check to see if your school offers a help document about using its discussion areas.

Keep in mind that your instructor probably monitors your class discussion areas. Although a message that isn't quite on target for that particular discussion is likely to be overlooked, a blatantly inappropriate comment of an aggressive, racist, or sexual nature will probably earn you a private e-mail from your instructor suggesting you modify your messages in future.

If you plan to compose a lengthier message, consider writing it in a word processing program before you log onto the discussion group, and then cutting and pasting the text into a discussion message form. This approach will save you from having to retype a lot of text if the school server crashes or disconnects you before you've posted the message.

Chatting away in chat rooms

A *chat room* is a location on your school's Web site where you and anyone else who is in the chat room at the same time can exchange text messages. If your school doesn't provide a chat room and you want to chat with other students, check your Internet Service Provider to see whether it has chat rooms you can use.

In a chat room, you can hold a live (albeit written) conversation, as in the chat room called Virtual U Chat Café from Virtual University in Figure 10-4. Sometimes, distance-learning classes use chat rooms to hold formal student discussions lead by an instructor. Schools also make chat rooms available so that students have a way of getting together to chat and share ideas in real time.

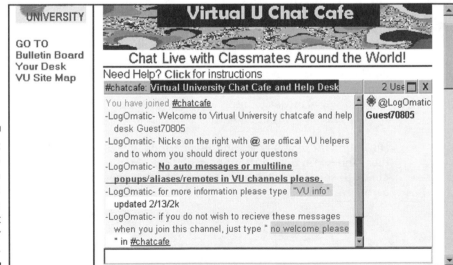

Figure 10-4: Those in the chat room are listed here, along with the text of their messages.

In a chat, one person types and submits a comment that everyone else in the chat room can read immediately. The next person types and submits a reply. These comments appear one after the other in the chat area of the room, and you can read the conversation as it moves along. Of course, because the participants can't see each other to get visual clues, people often interrupt each other, with one person starting a new topic before another person submits a comment about the current topic. This setup can make chat communication disjointed until you get the rhythm of it.

If you are using a chat room to have a conversation that has a specific topic and agenda, setting some guidelines as to how people will contribute is essential. To add some organization to your chat, consider these tips:

- ✔ The group should designate one person as the facilitator; the facilitator states the focus of the chat and any goal or outcome of the discussion.

- ✔ People who want to "speak" raise their hands by typing a message such as "Next?" or "Speak?" to indicate that they want to make the next comment. Everybody then sees who will speak next, so they don't jump in with a comment too quickly, causing confusion.

- ✔ Set a pattern whereby each person in the group makes a comment in turn; you can do this alphabetically or just assign everybody a number and have each person start off his message by typing his number. If the next person in the pattern doesn't want to make a comment, she simply sends the message "Pass."

- ✔ If a conflict arises, or if the discussion wanders away from the topic at hand, the leader is authorized to step in to mediate the dispute or have all the members refocus their comments.

You can set whatever rules work for you and your group; just be sure that everybody understands the rules and agrees to follow them before you start.

You're the Star: Videoconferencing

With all the wonderful things that distance learning can bring to you, there is still no real replacement for meeting people face-to-face now and then. Using videoconferencing technology, you can meet face-to-face in cyberspace.

Videoconferencing is an interactive technology that allows the transmission of a live video signal among different locations. Videoconferencing takes two basic forms:

✔ **Facility-based videoconferencing:** Groups of participants gather at various locations (often called *electronic classrooms*) and use special transmission lines and televisions to interact during the conference (see Figure 10-5). Signals sent from video cameras and microphones at each site enable everybody to see and hear each other at the same time, making the process similar to an in-person classroom in many ways. Transmission usually takes place over high-bandwidth telephone lines, but may sometimes occur via satellite links in remote areas.

✔ **Desktop videoconferencing:** With this technology, individuals can participate in a videoconference from their respective computers using videoconferencing software, such as White Pine's CU-SeeMe (`www.cuseeme.com`) and a small camera called a Web cam.

A great site to visit to find out about how videoconferencing is being used in education is `www.kn.pacbell.com/wired/vidconf/classroom.html`.

Attending videoconferences

Many schools have videoconferencing systems set up for instructor and student use. In distance learning, students in remote locations may be invited to attend a videoconference that is hosted at the school's campus by visiting a site near them, perhaps a local community college or a hotel conference center. One other option for videoconferencing is to look in your phone book: A store such as your local Kinko's copy store, whose Web page on videoconferencing (`www.kinkos.com/atkinkos/videoconferences.html`) appears in Figure 10-6, may offer videoconferencing facilities in your area.

Figure 10-5:
Iowa State
University
uses video-
conferencing
technology
to transmit
information
to groups of
students.

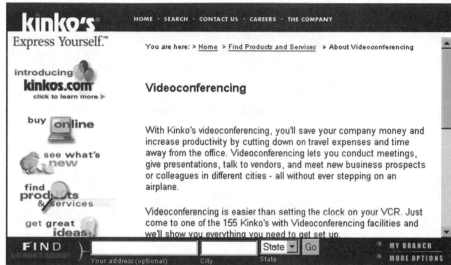

Figure 10-6:
Kinko's offers video-conferencing services in stores in many parts of the United States.

Of course, renting these facilities or equipping a campus-based electronic classroom costs your school money, so don't expect one to be available in every town where your school has a distance-learning student. The more typical scenario is that a college, say in New York, might host videoconference sites in Chicago, Atlanta, Los Angeles, Dallas, and Seattle. The school then expects students in each region to travel to the closest facility. No matter where you attend a videoconference, you can expect to find experienced people there to handle the technical side of things.

Many schools offer free training in the use of videoconferencing equipment. If you have an interest in this technology, check with the department that runs videoconferencing at your school to ask whether they have information or advice that might be useful to you.

Accessing conferences online using desktop videoconferencing

By far the hottest trend in videoconferencing is desktop videoconferencing. This technology enables everybody in the class to participate in a live video-conference from his or her own computer. To participate with both audio and video, each person must have videoconferencing software and a Web cam, which is a small camera that you place on top of your monitor. This camera transmits either still photos or streaming video using your connection to the Internet.

You have several options for interacting using desktop videoconferencing:

- ✔ Point-to-point connections involve two people connecting with each other via their IP addresses — similar to "calling" someone by using your computer and modem to dial the person's Internet address instead of his telephone number. (For more information on working with IP addresses, see *The Internet For Dummies* by John R. Levine, Carole Baroudi, and Margaret Levine Young, published by IDG Books Worldwide.)

- ✔ Group videoconferences use a server to host the conference. Instead of each person connecting with the others directly, all participants connect with the server site. See Figure 10-7 for an example.

- ✔ Multicast conferences involve a group connecting with each other directly rather than through a server.

- ✔ Cybercasts involve one person transmitting video and audio, and everybody else receiving it. This option is a logical choice for an online lecture, for example.

- ✔ Programs such as NetMeeting from Microsoft use a service to locate people online and connect them, similar to the way your phone company sets up a teleconference among several people. With NetMeeting, you don't need any video hardware to receive video images. If you want to transmit video images, though, you have to get a Web cam.

Figure 10-7:
The National Guard trains people from several locations through a central server, as outlined in this diagram.

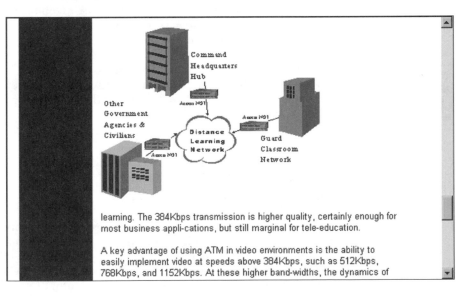

learning. The 384Kbps transmission is higher quality, certainly enough for most business appli-cations, but still marginal for tele-education.

A key advantage of using ATM in video environments is the ability to easily implement video at speeds above 384Kbps, such as 512Kbps, 768Kbps, and 1152Kbps. At these higher band-widths, the dynamics of

The typical low-end desktop videoconferencing setup allows people to speak one at a time. When one person is talking, everybody else's video stops transmitting, leaving only a still photo on-screen. Video quality is not especially crisp, and size is typically limited to a small window, but the desktop setup can provide at least some sense of community among geographically separated distance learners. What's more, the technology for lower-end systems is improving all the time, and increases in bandwidth for Internet access are making individual desktop videoconferencing more closely approximate the higher-end facility-based experience. In the next few years, you will probably see the use of desktop videoconferencing creeping into many distance-learning courses.

Speaking to the group

The use of two-way audio and video in videoconferencing means that you can receive audio and images from people at another location even as they are receiving audio and images from your site. Although videoconferencing technology is improving, be aware that the quality of the video will not be quite what you're used to on prime-time TV. That's because videoconferencing uses a technology called compressed video, which leaves a slight distortion, especially when someone moves or gestures quickly.

In group videoconferences, one site typically serves as the host, with a speaker or moderator kicking off the session and controlling which site or individual can speak at any point during the session. If a videoconference is set up with groups of people at different sites (as opposed to participating from their individual desktops), each group usually designates a leader to help control the participation of people at that site and coordinate with the host site. The leader at your site will let you know when you can ask questions or make comments, and you may be asked to step in front of a camera or before a microphone to do so.

Videoconferencing etiquette

Participating in a videoconference comes with some do's and don'ts. These tips help make the communication efficient, and avoid some technical glitches that videoconferencing is still prone to.

Follow these guidelines when participating in a videoconference:

✔ Make sure that you obtain any printed information or agenda before the conference starts so that you can understand the focus of the meeting.

✔ If you want to send any graphics to other sites during the meeting, let the recipients know that the information is on its way via fax or e-mail. Better yet, make sure that it gets to them before the meeting starts.

✔ Don't speak before another site has finished with its current comment; you can cause a technical problem called *rapid site switching,* which causes both your and the other site's audio to become garbled. Videoconferencing technology typically includes a mute feature that ensures your site's silence while it is activated.

✔ Try to be concise in your questions and comments, and don't monopolize the discussion. Most videoconferences have time limits because of cost; give others a chance to participate.

✔ Speak into the microphone at a natural pace.

✔ Try not to cough, snap fingers, click a pen, or make other distracting noises or side-comments during the conference because these sounds may be picked up and broadcast to every location.

Don't wear bright reds or plaids when you participate in a videoconference; they can cause your video image to shimmer on the screen, resulting in slight distortions for those watching you. Also, bright white clothing can cause glare. Pastels and blues are perfect for video.

Interacting with Instructors and Advisors

How many times during your school days did you wander up to the teacher at the beginning or end of class and ask a question about an idea you didn't quite get, or an assignment detail you wanted clarification of? Or perhaps you passed your professor in the hall or cafeteria now and then and struck up a conversation about an upcoming group project. Well, I have news for you: You don't have hallways, cafeterias, or even a front of the classroom in distance learning. As a result, you have to find other ways to get your instructor's attention.

Asking questions

These days, both on-campus and distance learning students have access to their teachers by e-mail, and the teachers are probably missing the days when they were only reachable in their offices from 3:00 to 4:15 on Thursdays. E-mail is probably your best ally for reaching your instructor for one-on-one interaction.

At the beginning of a course, be sure to ask your instructor whether he or she keeps regular virtual office hours. That could be a time during the week when the teacher is checking e-mail or is available in a chat room for live discussion. More and more instructors are trying to fit such a time into their schedules as they take on more distance-learning students.

However, not every question should be kept between you and your instructor. In a campus course, some questions are best asked in front of the class; in distance learning, you should ask those same questions in an online discussion area. Any question whose answer might benefit all students in the class should be asked in a discussion; any question that pertains to your situation or a personal issue should go directly to the instructor.

Getting and giving feedback

Because tests are more rare in distance learning than they are in a face-to-face class, you don't always have that handy ranking of your performance to depend on. So where does your feedback come from? Feedback on assignments and your progress in a distance-learning course may come in a couple of ways.

✔ You submit several assignments over the course of most-distance learning classes. In some cases, your instructor may formally grade these assignments and return them to you with detailed comments. In other instances, especially in non-credit courses, you might just get a comment from the instructor with no formal grade. The instructor may post this comment in a discussion area for the benefit of other students, calling everyone's attention to a good point you may have made or an area for further study. Or, the instructor may e-mail a comment to you directly. In some cases, one comment might be sent to all students in the group, summarizing their performance on an assignment.

✔ You must feel free to ask your instructor at any point in time what he or she thinks of your progress in class. This method of getting feedback is very important, considering that you don't have the non-verbal clues of a classroom to tell you whether the instructor thinks your questions are brilliant or mundane. Remember, most teachers are new to this distance-learning stuff, too; they might forget to give those clues, just as new managers sometimes forget to give praise to their employees. Always remember that this is *your* education; if you aren't making the grade, you need to know about it sooner rather than later.

Planning your long-range education with an advisor

If you're taking a college-level degree program, in addition to instructors in your various classes, your school also assigns an advisor to you. *Advisors* (also called *tutors* in England and some other countries) are members of the faculty of the division that is granting your degree, for example the School of Engineering or Education. You are likely to get a notice with your advisor's name and contact information in any welcome packet you receive from a school.

The advisor's role is to guide you as you make choices of which classes, in addition to your core requirements, to take in order to complete your major.

As in the description from Penn State shown in Figure 10-8, your school course catalog provides information about how many hours of work you must complete to obtain your degree, as well as the core requirements for the degree. *Core requirements* are the specific courses that you must take to complete the degree. You also have to take a certain number of non-core classes — called *electives* — to tally up your total credit hours for degree.

In addition to academic goals planning, you can also look to your advisor for help with or advice about

✔ Analyzing how your academic goals can help you in your career (For more about leveraging your educational credentials in the job market, see Chapter 16.)

✔ Any problems you're experiencing keeping up with work or getting acceptable grades

✔ Registration

✔ School policies and procedures

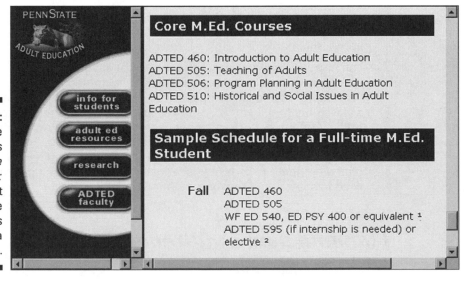

Figure 10-8: All degree programs have *core requirements:* classes that all degree candidates in that area must take.

Core M.Ed. Courses

ADTED 460: Introduction to Adult Education
ADTED 505: Teaching of Adults
ADTED 506: Program Planning in Adult Education
ADTED 510: Historical and Social Issues in Adult Education

Sample Schedule for a Full-time M.Ed. Student

Fall   ADTED 460
        ADTED 505
        WF ED 540, ED PSY 400 or equivalent [1]
        ADTED 595 (if internship is needed) or elective [2]

You can usually reach advisors by e-mail or phone, and you can expect to have scheduled appointments with yours at regular intervals during your program. If you are working towards a degree, I recommend at least one in-person meeting with your advisor as you start your classes. After all, this process may last three years or more, and a little planning and communication at the start will help you feel comfortable with your advisor and save you some costly mistakes in designing your education.

Your advisor may also be able to help you get credit for life experience, such as employment or projects that you might have worked on in your area of study. Because your advisor specializes in your degree area, he or she may be able to help the registrar assess the value of your work in that field.

Chapter 11

Building Relationships Online

In This Chapter

▶ Finding your distance-learning communication style

▶ Building learning communities

▶ Dealing with online conflict

▶ Working with groups online

A lice in Wonderland author Lewis Caroll wrote, "'What is the use of a book,' thought Alice, 'without pictures or conversations?'" In distance learning, communication with others about the ideas contained in your textbook or course material is what makes your learning a true educational experience.

Because communication is one of the most important elements of any community and any learning experience, you have to master at least the basics of it to succeed in distance learning. Chapter 10 explores some tools and media used for communicating in a distance-learning setting, but how you communicate is every bit as important as the mechanics of communicating.

Although not every distance-learning course is interactive, most require at least some person-to-person interaction, and many use student interaction as their key ingredient. In this chapter, you get some advice about communication skills that may help you succeed in the interactive portion of your online learning courses.

Writing Your Way to Success

The fact is that much of your communication in distance learning occurs in writing. In addition to submitting written assignments just as you would in any in-person course, almost every conversation, question, and even argument is likely to take place in writing. That means that those who are good writers have an easier time of it than those who aren't.

Improving your writing skills

Can you learn to be a better writer? Absolutely. Can you learn it between now and the class that you're starting next week? Probably not. But you can begin to pay attention to how you write and, taking advantage of all the practice you're about to get in your online class, work to improve your style with every message you send and every assignment you write.

Good writing involves two things: mechanics and style. *Mechanics* are things like correct punctuation and grammar, choosing accurate vocabulary, and spelling things correctly. Style relates to how well you organize and focus material, and the author voice that you bring to your work. An author voice might be humorous, long-winded, concise, technical, serious, or sarcastic. It might give the reader the impression that you're friendly, standoffish, down-to-earth, or adventurous. Writing style is the personality that comes across in your sentences, and the extent to which you engage readers in what you're saying.

Becoming a word mechanic

If you're uncomfortable with writing, the simplest place to start is with the mechanics. Buy a good guide to punctuation and grammar, and start using the grammar and spell check features of your word processor and e-mail program. Although these software features can be less than perfect, they do help you spot some common problems with things such as tense or number agreement.

Get a good dictionary and use it. Most dictionaries have a section at the front that provides a review of the basics of grammar and punctuation, in addition to serving as a tool to improve your spelling.

You can learn the mechanics of writing by a combination of memorization, practice, and example:

- ✔ Memorize rules of grammar and punctuation from a good reference book.

- ✔ Practice those rules in your writing or get a workbook that provides practice sentences and exercises.

- ✔ Read examples of good writing and pay attention. The textbooks for your classes have been edited by professionals who know grammar and punctuation rules as well as you know the Thursday night TV line-up. As you read, notice how the text fits the rules you've been memorizing and follow their example.

Getting some style

Style is a little less cut and dried than mechanics. However, think of it as learning musical scales before you can play a concerto: After you are comfortable with the mechanics, you can begin to play around with your style by refining things like the rhythm of your sentences and the pacing of your material. You can start to work on the style of your writing by following some of these guidelines:

✔ Make sure that every paragraph begins with a topic sentence that clearly states the focus of the paragraph.

✔ Use order patterns to bring organization to information. For example, using chronological order to organize things as they occur in time works well when conveying a sequence of events to your instructor in an e-mail (first I completed my assignment; then my dog ate it). Spatial order (putting things in the order that they are placed in space, such as top to bottom or left to right) might work well in an engineering document. Other patterns are priority, cause and effect, and numerical or alphabetical.

✔ If you can't find a place for a certain idea or comment that makes sense in relation to your outline, store the idea away for another day. Keeping your writing focused and on topic is important.

✔ Avoid passive voice (for example, "The book was given to him by them.") and instead use active voice ("They gave the book to him."); active voice is shorter and much easier for your reader to understand.

✔ Keep your writing concise, avoiding run-on sentences and overly wordy phrases.

✔ Vary your sentence structure to break up the rhythm of your writing. For example, use a simple sentence followed by a compound sentence, like this:

"Hamilton was dead. Aaron Burr dropped to his knees slowly, and the early morning silence grew deeper."

✔ Read your writing out loud to a friend; if your friend doesn't understand what you're trying to say, or if the writing doesn't sound natural, simplify or rephrase it.

Some classic guides for writing style are *The Elements of Style* published by Allyn & Bacon and *The Chicago Manual of Style* published by the University of Chicago Press. You can also visit the FAQ site for *The Chicago Manual of Style,* shown in Figure 11-1, at `www.press.uchicago.edu/Misc/Chicago/cmosfaq.html`.

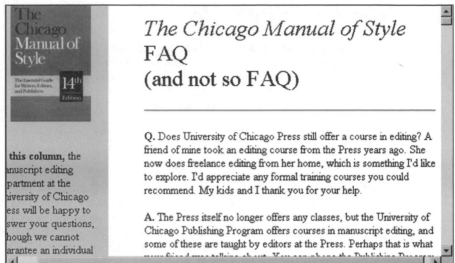

Figure 11-1:
You can find
out about
some
common
writing style
issues at
this Web
site.

The Chicago Manual of Style
FAQ
(and not so FAQ)

Q. Does University of Chicago Press still offer a course in editing? A friend of mine took an editing course from the Press years ago. She now does freelance editing from her home, which is something I'd like to explore. I'd appreciate any formal training courses you could recommend. My kids and I thank you for your help.

A. The Press itself no longer offers any classes, but the University of Chicago Publishing Program offers courses in manuscript editing, and some of these are taught by editors at the Press. Perhaps that is what

this column, the anuscript editing partment at the iversity of Chicago ess will be happy to swer your questions, hough we cannot arantee an individual

Developing a process for writing

Many people describe writing as an *iterative process;* that is, you write a draft, you go back and revise it, you add to it, and then you go back and cut things out, slowly crafting a finished document. This approach enables you to focus on one thing at a time, such as organization, content, mechanics, and refining your style, and it helps you catch errors or problems with your writing. The next time you write something, try this process:

1. Draft an outline consisting of key ideas with sub-topics listed beneath.

2. Throw out any ideas that seem irrelevant.

3. Write the first draft.

4. Read and revise the draft for clarity and content. Again, throw out what doesn't seem relevant.

5. Read and revise the draft for mechanics such as punctuation and spelling.

6. Proofread the document one more time for errors before sending it off.

Some people proofread with a team method; one person reads the material out loud while another checks the text. This helps keep the person who wrote the piece from missing errors because he or she has become too close to the material during the revision process.

Many online courses on writing are available, such as the ones listed on the writers.com Web site shown in Figure 11-2. Consider taking one of these courses before you start your other courses. Good writing is invaluable not only in class, but also in your career and your life.

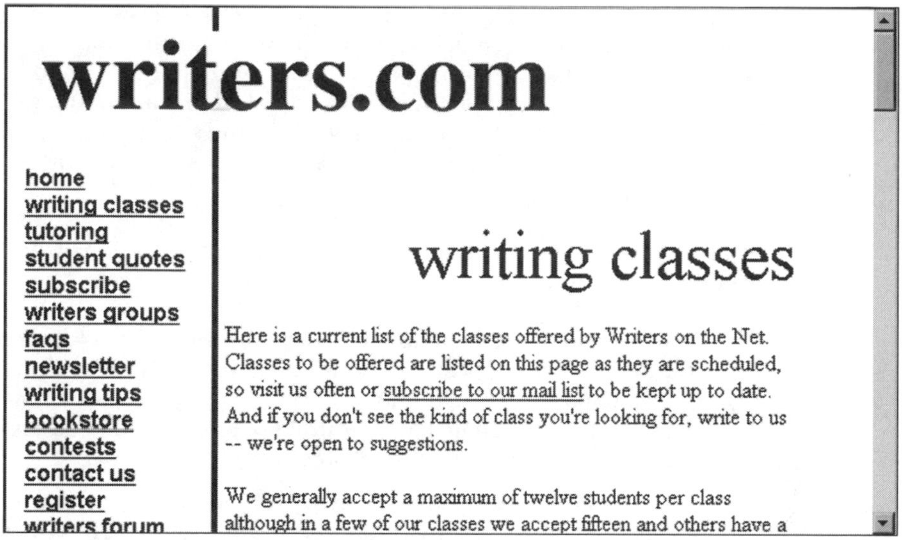

Figure 11-2:
Professional
and aspiring
writers can
find a class
to help at
www.
writers.
com.

Finding the Right Approach
to Communication

Even if you are the best writer in the world, you may need some improve-
ment in the way you approach communication online. For example, consider
your answers to these questions:

✔ Are you open to other people's ideas?

✔ Are you willing to ask a question and risk appearing less knowledgeable
than others in the class?

✔ Do you feel comfortable asking for help?

✔ Are you willing to share your experience with others?

✔ Can you step out of the spotlight and praise someone else for being right
when you are wrong?

✔ Can you avoid getting emotional or defensive when someone attacks
your ideas?

If you answered yes to all the preceding questions, you are probably a mar-
velous communicator and a truly wonderful human being. If you didn't (like
99 percent of us), then you'll find distance learning the perfect place to hone
these attitudes, because they'll come into play on a regular basis.

In many distance-learning courses, your instructor measures your performance to some degree by how much you participate in discussions and how well you support the larger learning community with your ideas and cooperative attitude. Many schools offer advice to help students approach their distance-learning communications successfully, as on the site from the University of Illinois (Illinois.online.uillinois.edu/model/ studentprofile.htm) shown in Figure 11-3.

Follow these guidelines to approach online communications with the most productive attitude:

- ✔ Don't be afraid to speak up if you have a problem or complaint about the course, but make any suggestions constructive. You also want to be careful to make the right choice of delivery method for a complaint (for example, sending an e-mail to your instructor versus posting a message in a discussion area open to all students).

- ✔ Listen to what others have to say by reading their postings carefully and asking questions to clarify points they are making before responding or attacking their statements.

- ✔ Be open to other people's suggestions about your work; your peers are a significant source of knowledge.

- ✔ Participate actively by contributing to discussions where you have expertise or experience to offer, and asking questions of those who are more expert in other areas.

- ✔ Be as professional in your conduct in class as you would be at your job. This is not the place for e-mail rage, personal attacks, or inappropriate emotional reactions.

Figure 11-3:
You can learn what succeeds online and what doesn't on Web sites like this one.

Everybody's different

In this new global community that makes up distance education, you are likely to run into cultural and language differences that can be enlightening, but also challenging.

If your class includes students who are from different countries and whose primary language is not English, mechanical difficulties (for example, their grammar or vocabulary is imperfect) or by psychological differences (for example, in their country women don't aspire to management positions in business) can hamper communication. Either one of these issues can be the cause of misunderstanding and even conflict.

And don't think that just because you speak the same language you won't have problems. My British husband and I have been married for 17 years, and we still have a misunderstanding about our two languages (British and American) almost weekly. Even people from different regions of the same country can use different vocabulary, have different standards for behavior, and harbor different prejudices that can all interfere with good communications. When you are communicating online, try to be open minded about others' ideas and the way they express themselves, whether they are from around the world or around the corner.

You can deal with these communications challenges in two ways:

✔ Open your mind and listen carefully: Don't assume that everybody thinks alike, and appreciate the differences.

✔ Practice patience when someone doesn't understand your words or can't comprehend your meaning. Working at understanding is one of the most rewarding things you can do; when you both finally connect, it's a great moment.

So, here's my sermon for the week: Your mission in a distance-learning course is to take advantage of the diversity among the students and instructors. Your goal should be to learn about other cultures and attitudes as much as to learn about the topic of your course. The globalization of education is merely mirroring the globalization of business and society at large. No matter whether you are studying astronomy or business communications, this exposure to diversity will serve you well.

Building a Learning Community

Any proponent of distance learning will tell you that the future is all about building learning communities. What does that mean? It means that the lecture model of education is dying a fast death, and what's replacing it is a model in which student interaction becomes the vehicle for learning. That interaction may involve sharing real-world experiences, role playing, or working through case-study scenarios to solve a problem, or simply kicking around ideas in a discussion area. This new mode of learning is a natural for some, and a struggle for others. So, what do you need to do to succeed?

Becoming a better online citizen

Part of your responsibility in an online class is to help to build this new virtual learning community that is at the heart of distance learning. Good communication is key to that effort, but the way you involve yourself in your course is also important:

✔ Strive to be neither the center of attention nor a fly on the wall, merely observing but never taking part. Every student's participation is required to build a successful community.

✔ Be comfortable with working on your own for much of the time, but also be happy to join a group effort if one is assigned. Don't think of distance learning as solitary confinement. Although you do spend a great deal of time alone, you also have to work well with others.

✔ Be self-disciplined and self-motivated because, with distance learning, you — not a lecturer — drive your learning.

✔ Be generous with your knowledge and take it upon yourself to ask questions to explore the knowledge of others.

Many distance-learning schools offer advice, checklists, and even tests to see whether you have what it takes to work in this new educational model. For example, refer to the site from University of Illinois shown earlier in Figure 11-3 (Illinois.online.uillinois.edu/model/studentprofile.htm) and the Is Online Learning for Me? quiz from Colorado Community College shown in Figure 11-4 (ecollegelogin.cconline.org/Index).

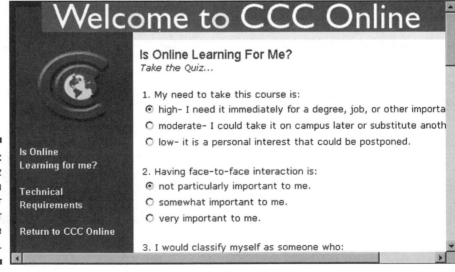

Figure 11-4:
This quiz helps you assess your aptitude for distance learning.

Take this advice seriously: Signing on to a distance-learning class isn't a matter of reading some material and collecting your degree or certificate. It can be a highly interactive and involving experience that takes time, commitment, and the ability to work with other people.

Resolving conflict

Any community is likely to encounter conflict eventually. The very act of bringing together differing points of view to broaden everybody's perspective can also cause clashes among ideologies.

When you do encounter conflict in an online class, consider these options for resolving it:

- ✔ Try to restate your idea or belief as simply your point of view and not a fact that applies to everybody. Ask the other person to do the same.

- ✔ If what you're claiming is a fact, back it up with specific information about your sources and ask the other person to do the same.

- ✔ Take some time to cool off before responding to a heated e-mail or discussion posting.

- ✔ Never bring the dispute to a personal level and never knowingly exhibit prejudice. Calling people names or blaming their lack of understanding on their race or gender is unacceptable and unproductive.

- ✔ If the conflict arises in a chat room, let a few other people post comments before you join in again. One of them might make a point that bridges two ideas and resolves the conflict for you.

- ✔ Ask your instructor to comment so that he or she can act as a moderator or facilitator for the discussion and turn it in a more positive and productive direction.

- ✔ If your conflict is with someone in a project group that your instructor has assigned you to and you can't resolve the problem, as a last resort you can ask your instructor to assign you to another group.

Working with groups online

At some point in your online studies, your instructor may ask you to work with others to complete a project or participate in a small group discussion. You may also want to form a study group during the courses of your classes. The principles of teamwork and good communication that apply to your larger class apply here, as well. However, participation in workgroups also has some of its own rules of etiquette:

- ✔ If the group arranges a time to meet by phone or online, be prompt.

- ✔ Establish a group leader early on to facilitate discussions and hold the group accountable for action items.

- ✔ If the group assigns you a task, complete it.

- ✔ If, after taking on a task, you realize that you can't complete it, let the group know as soon as possible and take full responsibility for the failure.

- ✔ Use e-mail effectively; if you're writing to one member of the group and others in the group should be aware of what you're saying, copy all the members of the team to keep everybody informed.

Part V
Virtual Study Hall

The 5th Wave   By Rich Tennant

"It happened around the time George signed up for a class online. Taking tests makes him nauseous."

In this part . . .

*I*t's midnight. The smell of burning coffee wafts out of your kitchen, blending with the intense scent of pure panic as you realize that your assignment is late, your test is due tomorrow, and your brain has turned to mush.

Quite simply, the chapters in this part are here to help you to avoid the above scenario. This part exists to get you back into the swing of good studying and test-taking habits, and to give you insights into the form that assignments and tests take when you're studying online. Along the way, you pick up some tips about good time management, a vital skill for any successful distance learner.

Chapter 12

Online Study Habits 101

. . . .

In This Chapter

▶ Managing your study time

▶ Motivating yourself

▶ Performing research online

▶ Getting feedback

. . . .

*P*erhaps your high school or college yearbook has turned to dust in an upstairs closet. Or maybe you're a full-time student for whom studying, caffeine, and cramming are as much a part of your life as breathing. Whether or not you've taken a classroom-based course recently, you'll find that online study habits are a bit different from — and a bit the same as — those you cultivate for a face-to-face class.

Developing good study habits involves understanding things about yourself: things like how, when, and where you study best and whether you need total quiet or rap music to concentrate. The fact is that study habits are very personal. Only you can find your own quirky balance of cajoling yourself with candy bars and disciplining yourself with mental slaps on the wrist.

One of the main differences in online study habits is that, to a great extent, you're the one driving the bus. Nobody's sitting at the head of the class a few times a week telling you what to do and watching to make sure that you do it. The self-directed nature of distance learning, and the isolation that can accompany it, make good time-management and planning vital. You also have to find ways to study that take best advantage of what the online world has to offer. And, if you know how, you can build online relationships with your instructor and fellow students that help you stay focused and accountable.

It's a Matter of Time

Einstein might have disagreed, but online time is different than offline time. There's a black hole of online time just waiting for you out there, and if you're not careful, you may get sucked into it and disappear forever. Because online courses often offer little in the way of structure, it's easy to get lost. In many cases, classes don't start and end at specific times, and, although assignments may have due dates, sometimes the assignment is merely to check into a Web site several times a week and post responses to other students' messages. Who decides when to go online and how much time to spend there? Nobody but you.

Winning the battle of you versus time

The first element of structuring your online studying habits is time management. You can start taking steps today to become a better manager of your time:

- ✔ **Make a list and check it twice:** This is an old-fashioned method, but a good one. Make to-do lists and check off items as you complete them. You can use the To Do List feature of software like Microsoft Outlook to help you.

- ✔ **Set reminders:** You can go low-tech and make a note on your desk calendar, or you can set automatic reminders for important obligations in your personal digital assistant, such as a Palm. You can also set reminders in software that includes a scheduling feature, such as Outlook or Lotus Organizer. Try using an old fashioned alarm clock to flag you when you're halfway through your planned study time so you can be sure that your online focus isn't wandering.

- ✔ **Prioritize:** With distance learning, you have to prioritize not only the various tasks involved in your online study, but also the major areas of your life. This can be tricky when your kid has a big game, you have a test, and your boss has an immovable project deadline, all on the same day. When you're making the decision to sign up for a class, consider where the class fits in the hierarchy of your life and plan accordingly.

- ✔ **Put off till tomorrow:** Sometimes the temptation is strong to finish that one little thing that isn't terribly important just so you can cross it off your list. ("I'm just gonna handle this itty-bitty task before I tackle that great, big, monster of a task.") Don't do it. If something can wait until tomorrow, let it — and get what's more important done now.

- ✔ **Let somebody else do it:** So who do you think you are, the center of the universe? You're not the only one who can fix a broken faucet, drive little Maisie to her band rehearsal, and come up with the perfect tag line for that new advertising account, so stop pretending that you are. Whether you call it delegating, asking for help, or just plain keeping your mouth shut when someone asks for volunteers, you have to control what you commit yourself to.

Taking it one week at a time

If you look at a six-week course and all the reading and assignments involved in that course as one giant obligation, it may seem insurmountable. On top of that, when you take on a distance-learning experience, you're often doing so in addition to many other life commitments. But if you plan your tasks out week by week, everything becomes more manageable.

Follow these steps to create your weekly study plan:

- ✔ **Choose your study time in advance:** Sit down at the beginning of your course and pick your study times. Choose times when you are very unlikely to have a conflict — perhaps early morning, every lunch hour with your office door shut, or late at night after the kids or your significant other have gone to bed. Mark these times on your calendar every week as if they were an appointment with your CEO.

- ✔ **Plan for online rush hour:** When you pick times to study, take into account whether the congestion in the online world or at the institution you're working with might cause you to have problems connecting to the school Web site. Sometimes system administrators do weird and wonderful network things in the wee hours that make it difficult or impossible to access a site. This becomes problematic if a student is in a different time zone: The network guy at the West Coast college may have thought 3 a.m. was a great time to schedule a network overhaul; little did he know that some poor student living in Boston, picked 6 a.m. as prime study time. For students studying with a school in another country, the problem gets even worse. If you are in a different country than your school, try keeping a clock set to the host country's time by your computer to help you out.

You can save time and money by downloading messages or documents and then reading them offline. You should also compose assignments and even responses to e-mails offline. The time I lost having the computer crash halfway through typing a lengthy e-mail response to an instructor still haunts me late at night.

- ✔ **Don't be a stranger:** Checking in and reading other students' comments is part of many distance-learning course designs. You have to check back in on a regular basis to participate in the to and fro of online conversations. In addition to time you spend reading and writing assignments, plan to go online at least four or five times a week to post assignments and read messages from the instructor or comments from other students. If online discussion or chat rooms are part of your course, plan time for them, as well. (See Chapter 11 for information about communicating effectively with others in an online class.)

✔ **Pace yourself:** Don't schedule your study time all at once each week. Breaking up your study time into a few sessions makes the work more manageable, enables you to absorb what you've read before writing a response or assignment, and allows you to have a life.

Unlike a face-to-face class where you ask a question and get an answer, getting an answer from your online instructor may take a day or two of phone tag or e-mail lag. If getting an answer will hold you up in completing an assignment, plan for that delay in advance, if possible.

"My computer ate my homework"

When you don't have classes to attend at a specific time, the one thing you can use to keep yourself on track is assignment deadlines. Because instructors can't watch your face to see whether you're "getting it" the way they can in face-to-face situations, they're likely to give you regular assignments to be sure that you're following along.

Don't put off your assignment until the due date. Getting an assignment done may involve a few steps, so plan what you need to do to complete the assignment when it's first assigned. Even if you have a week to get your class work done, locate and read through the *deliverables* (assignments, postings to discussion boards, and so on) the first day. That way, you can tackle the items that will produce material that's visible to your instructor first, and leave the nondeliverables (like writing notes in your own student journal) till last.

Online learning: It's not all online

The fact is, most of what you do in a distance-learning environment doesn't occur at a set time, which is what makes the structure of distance learning so student driven. However, no matter what anybody tells you, not everything can be handled online. You'll have to plan for a few offline interactions in addition to your solo studying times. These might include phone conferences, video conferences, phone calls to and from instructors, or trips to meet with your class face-to-face.

Many distance-learning programs, especially at the university level, strongly recommend — or even require — an in-person orientation session to help students get to know each other and lay the foundation for communication throughout the course. Other courses consist of both an in-person and distance-learning element (quite common for full- or part-time students within commuting distance of campus).

A well-designed program includes a detailed syllabus that helps you anticipate the few scheduled offline interactions during the course of your class. Write these dates down and plan to be available.

Now I wouldn't want you ever to be late handing in an online assignment, but in case you are, use this handy conversion chart to help smooth the waters with your teacher.

Low-tech excuse	*High-tech excuse*
My dog ate it.	My computer crashed.
I was sick.	My computer got a virus.
I was robbed.	A hacker broke into my network and deleted everything.
The library closed early.	My ISP went bankrupt.
I dropped it in a puddle.	My printer ate it.

Of course, your online teacher is likely to receive these excuses with as much compassion as your fourth-grade math teacher showed, which is to say, not much! Bottom line: Plan ahead, and excuses won't be necessary.

Motivating Yourself

If you're taking a lengthier class, say a few weeks or more, you're going to reach a moment when you feel overwhelmed, frustrated with technology, and, well, just plain tired. It's the equivalent of the mid-afternoon slump at your desk when you've had a heavy Mexican lunch an hour or so earlier. You get through that moment every day; you'll get through this, too.

If you did your research in making the distance-learning choice (see Chapters 2 and 3), you are doing all this work for very solid reasons. The first thing you should do when you hit a slump is review those reasons, which are likely to include

- ✔ Improved career opportunities
- ✔ More money
- ✔ Personal growth
- ✔ Change of career (perhaps even starting your own business)
- ✔ Because it's there (that is, the bottom-line personal challenge of it all)

Just remember that the class will be over in a few weeks; the degree program will end in a year or two. Yes, you have to put off some personal pleasures and work hard until that time, but when it's all over, you'll have a reward that is likely to make a significant difference to your life. Try these techniques to keep motivated:

✔ Project yourself to graduation day and feel just a bit of the pride you'll feel on that day now. This exercise helps you remember why you're doing what you're doing.

✔ Put up a picture near your study station that represents your goal. If you're studying to get a better job, put up a picture of a well-dressed professional in a corner window office; if you're studying to get more money, put up a picture of a boat, fancy car, or house in the country.

✔ Take a day off. That's right. Even if you're feeling overwhelmed by the amount of work, sometimes just getting away from your studies for a bit gives you the perspective to attack them all the more efficiently.

Talk to your instructor about the problems you're having. He or she may be able to direct your study time so you can be sure that you're focusing on the most important material. Your instructor may even give you extra time to finish some of the work. Online learning time tends to be a bit more flexible than courses built around face-to-face classes.

The only reason to ever give up on a course of study is if you decide it's not the right school or the right topic for you to be spending your time on. If you come to this realization part way through your class or degree program, meet with your advisor and, if you have to, make a change. But if the class is worthwhile, the degree useful in furthering your career or personal goals, and the outcome worth having, stick with it.

Online Research: Your Best Friend

To many, learning online suggests exciting multimedia presentations, interactive computer learning games, and lively, real-time intellectual exchanges. Despite the logical assumption that an online class moves learning away from traditional classroom tools, the reality of distance learning today is that a great deal of what you study will be textbooks, articles, or instructor-created materials that you read offline.

Be that as it may, distance-learning assignments often require you to do research, and your instructors are likely to weave Web links into course materials so that you can visit relevant sites for more detail on topics. You have to be prepared to use the Internet not just as a communication tool, but a study tool, as well.

Searching for answers

Just as a V-6 engine powers a Corvette, search engines, in a very real sense, have powered the revolution in communication that is the Internet. Why are search engines so important? Well, a lot of great information is out there on the Web, but if you can't find the piece of information you need, it's not much use.

Many search engines have emerged over the past decade. Most, such as Yahoo! and Excite, work on the principle of a *keyword search,* a feature you may recognize from database programs such as Access. Others, such as Ask Jeeves (see Figure 12-1), work through a *natural language interface,* which simply means that you type a question in regular English rather than entering a keyword or keyword phrase.

Most Internet Service Providers and browsers give you access to a few different search engines from their home pages. Search engines also have their own home pages that host not only their search capability, but also links to categories of information that are helpful when performing research. Table 12-1 lists some of the major search engines and their Web addresses.

Figure 12-1:
Ask Jeeves
(www.ask.
com) is like
a personal
information
butler
waiting to
provide
answers to
your every
question.

Table 12-1	Popular Search Engines
Name	*Web address*
About	about.com
AltaVista	www.altavista.com
Ask Jeeves	www.ask.com
Excite	www.excite.com
Google	www.google.com
GoTo	goto.com
HotBot	hotbot.com
InfoSeek	infoseek.com
LookSmart	www.looksmart.com
Lycos	www.lycos.com
Northern Light	northernlight.com
Snap	snap.com
WebCrawler	www.webcrawler.com
Yahoo!	www.yahoo.com

You can find entire books devoted to online research techniques. Your distance-learning school may provide research guidelines of its own. But to get on the fast track of online research, brush up on these basic search techniques right away.

Keywords are terms that a search engine such as Yahoo! uses to locate relevant documents in an online search. Learning to use keywords efficiently is one of the key skills of accurate searching. Too general a keyword can result in millions of options to weed through. Too specific a keyword or list of keywords can screen out the very site you want. Here are some guidelines for using keywords:

✔ **Spelling counts:** A search engine can only find matches for the word you enter, not the word you meant to enter.

✔ **Use a plus sign (+) to indicate mandatory keywords:** If you're using more than one keyword, type a plus sign immediately before each word that you want the search engine to consider mandatory. For example, typing **audio +video** gets you results that include both video and audio, and results that include only video, but not results that include only audio.

✔ **Use a minus sign (-) to exclude words:** If you don't want a particular word to be included in the Web sites that your search returns, use the minus sign (hyphen) immediately before each word that you don't want in your results. For example, searching for **Star Trek -Klingons** results in Web sites that mention Star Trek but don't contain the word *Klingons*.

✔ **Wildcards help find variations:** Wildcard characters are placeholders that some search engines use; these characters allow you to find words with a similar root word or spelling. For example, typing **veterinar*** would locate *veterinarian* as well as *veterinary*. **Judg*ment** would locate matches including both *judgment* and *judgement* (American and British spellings of the same word). Common wildcards are *, #, and ?.

✔ **Use quotes for phrases:** If you want to find a match for a whole phrase (for example, you want to find sites that include the phrase "Christmas Carol," but not sites that only include Christmas or Carol) enclose the phrase in quotation marks.

Find centralized depositories of links on topics related to your class work at the start of the class. These sites, which are often run by professional or academic organizations, make a much better place to start in many cases than a general search of the whole Web. To find these sites, perform an initial search on a keyword or combination of keywords, and from the results, select a Web site that claims to be a clearinghouse of information on that topic, or the site of a professional association dealing with that area. For example, if you are taking a class on education, a search result on the keyword *training* might turn up the American Society for Training and Development (ASTD). That site, in turn, offers a collection of relevant links and information, helping you avoid the wealth of irrelevant sites a general search brings. Table 12-2 lists some examples of sites that service specific topic areas, such as the Science Online site shown in Figure 12-2.

Table 12-2	Centralized Depositories of Web Links	
Category	*Site*	*Web address*
Science	Science Online	www.scienceonline.org
Business	Online Women's Business Center	www.onlinewbc.org
Computers	AOL Webopaedia	aol.pcwebopaedia.com
Art	CultureFinder	www.culturefinder.com
Religion	Catholic News Service	www.catholicnews.com
Psychology	Human Nature	www.human-nature.com

Figure 12-2:
Find links to
science
sites,
databases of
information,
publications
on science,
and more all
on Science
Online.

Use subject directories. *Subject directories* are groupings of information, such as travel or finance, that a search program has collected in one place. Most search-engines include a list of subject directories on their home pages. Just click on one to see what it includes, and follow useful links.

Above all, set parameters for your research:

✔ Have a goal for your research clearly in mind when you start. (Are you looking for information to write a specific assignment, or to get a general understanding of a topic?)

✔ Try not to wander off to tangential sites just because they look interesting.

✔ Set a specific amount of time for researching, and stick to it.

Try a natural-language search engine, such as Ask Jeeves (`www.ask.com`). These programs allow you to type a question in regular English, rather than entering a keyword. They then suggest some ways to narrow the search; in this way, they often produce more targeted results than a keyword search.

Navigating Web waters

When researching online, you are sure to spend a great deal of time moving around the Internet: from Web site to Web site, among pages within a Web site, and jumping back and forth among sites you've already visited once. Mastering some basic Web-navigation techniques is a good idea:

✔ Save Web sites you visit frequently as favorite places or bookmarks in your browser. You can then select them from a list rather than having to locate and enter lengthy URLs. Look for a Favorites or Bookmark item in one of the menus of your browser and start using it.

✔ To follow a Web link, you click on it. After you click on a link, it changes color to help you remember where you've already been.

✔ Use the navigation arrows on your browser to move backwards and forwards through series of sites you have visited during the current search.

✔ You can use the history feature of your browser to view the sites you've visited recently and to go there again. Many browsers include a list of sites you've visited as a drop-down list from the address box where you enter Web addresses. Others have a history feature you select from a menu. Check out your browser's Help feature to find out how to use its history feature.

See Chapter 4 for more about browsers and other hardware and software setup for distance learning online.

Downloading files

While studying online, you may find that you need to download files, for example, from a location where they've been posted on a school's server, from a Web site you've located while researching, or as attachments to e-mails. In most cases, the bulletin board, Web site, or e-mail program you're using has an obvious button to click to download files; in other cases, you can display a file and save it to your hard drive by using the Save command in your browser menu.

Some Internet services, such as AOL or CompuServe, offer a download management feature. This feature enables you to place all files for download in a central location, where they wait for you to download them all in one operation. This approach usually takes less time than downloading files one by one.

Before your class starts, create a new folder on your hard drive to which you can download all files associated with your class. Use this folder to save class assignments, as well. Doing so makes everything associated with your class centralized and easy to find.

Unzipping: It's a must!

If unzipping makes you think of a seedy Las Vegas nightclub act, you need an attitude adjustment. *Zipping* refers to a process of compressing files, making them smaller in size and therefore faster to send online. Using a zip program, you can also bundle multiple zipped files into a single, easy-to-send file. Odds are, you're going to download compressed files from someone along the way in your online classes. It's up to you to decompress *(unzip)* these files before you can work with them.

Many Internet Service Providers (including AOL and Prodigy) provide software that automatically decompresses zipped files when you download them. But some don't. Get a copy of a software product, such as WinZip (`www.winzip.com`) for your Windows-based PC or Stuffit (`www.aladinsys.com`) for your Macintosh, to help you unzip files you download and zip files you want to send. These types of products are often either free or available for a very low price ($15 or so), and they're worth every penny!

To give you an idea of how simple using this software is, I'm including the steps you follow to open a compressed file and extract files with Winzip:

1. **From the Windows desktop, click Start➪Programs➪WinZip➪ WinZip 8.0.**

   The WinZip main screen appears. (Note that if you haven't yet registered the product, a registration screen appears first. Either register at this time or click I Agree to bypass this screen.)

2. **Click the Open button in the toolbar along the top of the window.**

   The Open Archive dialog box appears (see Figure 12-3).

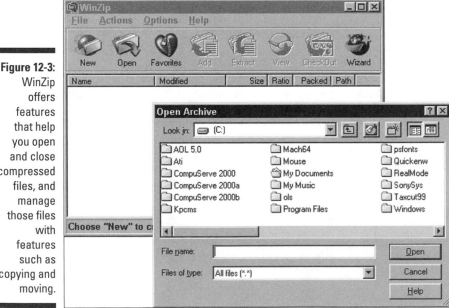

Figure 12-3: WinZip offers features that help you open and close compressed files, and manage those files with features such as copying and moving.

3. **Use the Look In drop-down list to locate the file you want to unzip and then click the file.**

4. **Click Open to open that file.**

   All the files contained within that zip file are now displayed in the WinZip window, as shown in Figure 12-4.

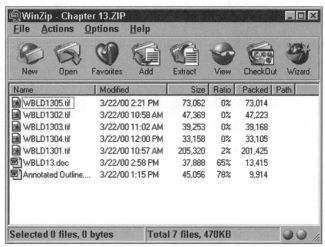

Figure 12-4: Notice the original size of files and the packed (or zipped) size: The ratio column tells the story of just how compressed this material is.

5. **To extract a file (that is, to decompress it and place it on your hard drive, a network drive, or a floppy disk), click Extract.**

   The Extract dialog box appears.

6. **Click a radio button to extract either all files or a file you selected before opening the dialog box.**

7. **Using the Folder/Drives settings, locate the folder and drive where you want the file(s) to be extracted and saved.**

8. **Click Extract.**

   The file is decompressed and saved in the selected location.

9. **When you finish, you can close WinZip by choosing File⇨Exit.**

Note that, rather than opening WinZip and then opening the file from within it, you can alternately locate the file on your hard drive and double-click the file name to open WinZip with the file displayed.

To create a new zip file using WinZip, follow these steps:

1. **From the Windows desktop, click Start⇨Programs⇨WinZip⇨ WinZip 8.0.**

   The WinZip main screen appears.

2. **Click the New button.**

   The New Archive dialog box appears.

3. **Type a filename in the File name text box, and choose a location for the zip file using the Create in drop-down list to browse folders and drives.**

4. **Click OK to save the new file.**

   You return to WinZip's main screen.

5. **To add files to the zip file, click Add.**

   The Add dialog box, shown in Figure 12-5, appears.

6. **Using the Add in drop-down list, locate and click on the file you want to add.**

7. **Click Add to add the file.**

   The filename now appears in the WinZip file list.

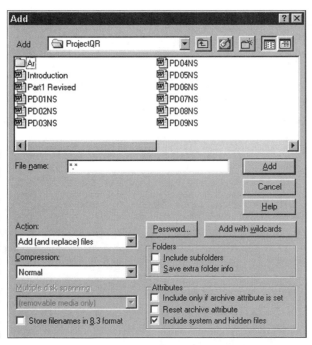

Figure 12-5:
You can add as many files as you want to a zip file from any location on your computer, network, or floppy disk.

8. **Repeat Steps 5 through 7 to add all files you want to include.**

9. **When you finish, you can close WinZip by choosing File⇨Exit.**

   Now you can attach the file to any e-mail or post it on a class bulletin board just as you would with any other file.

Dealing with file formats

Would you know a file format if you saw one? Because online courses require you to exchange files with other students and instructors, and to work with files you've found during online research for your class, you can expect to see many different file formats, each associated with the software program a document was created in. A file format is indicated by that little three-letter extension at the end of a filename. (For example, you know that termpaper. doc is a Word for Windows file by the .doc extension; you know that sunset.jpg is an image file by the .jpg extension — a common graphics format.) You may have to save files in other formats so that others can read them, or open files people send you and save them in another format so that you can read them properly.

When you save a file in the program it was created in, you typically can choose from several formats in the Save dialog box. For example, if you want to save a Word for Windows file as a Word for Macintosh file to share it with your Mac-loving instructor, you can follow these steps:

1. **With your document open in Word for Windows, choose File⇨ Save As.**

   The Save As dialog box appears.

2. **Type a name in the File name text box.**

3. **Click the arrow next to the Save As Type box (see Figure 12-6), scroll through the available options, and select a format option.**

4. **Click Save to save the file in the selected format.**

For text files, if the format you want isn't offered, you can use what I call *lowest-common-denominator formats* such as Text Only or MS-DOS Text Only formats. These formats display bare-bones text with much of the formatting of the original document (things like special fonts, bold, or even line breaks) taken out. The result may not be pretty, but it will usually be readable by a variety of computers and software, and get the information across. One alternative to Text Only is RTF (rich text format), which maintains most of the formatting in your document but is accessible by just about as many programs as Text Only.

Figure 12-6:
Most
programs
offer several
common
format
alternatives
for saving
files.

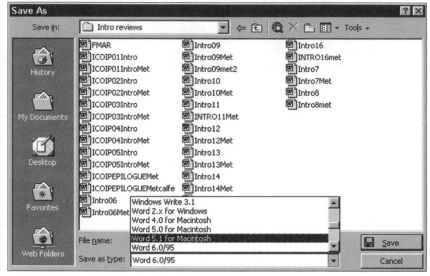

Chapter 13

No All-Nighters: Taking Tests

In This Chapter

▶ Considering the consequences of cheating in online classrooms

▶ Exploring the different types of online tests

▶ Planning for test-taking success

*Y*ou may have spent high school hiding under the bleachers in the gym to avoid taking tests, but the fact is that tests help you gauge how you're doing in a course. In the world of distance learning, where you're on your own so much of the time, the feedback tests give you can be surprisingly welcome.

This chapter examines the types of tests that you're likely to run into in a distance-learning course, how schools keep remote test-takers honest, and how instructors grade online tests. But perhaps the most important information in this chapter (and the stuff that should keep you out from under the bleachers) is solid advice for preparing for and taking a test successfully.

How Tests Fit into Distance Learning

You may run into different attitudes about testing for the distance-learning student. Some schools and instructors see no issue with self-administered testing; students who want to cheat will find a way to do so whether within the classroom or in their own living rooms, they claim, so online testing is no less valid than any other form. Others see too great a potential for cheating when it's impossible to see who is answering the questions on the test, and so some distance-learning courses put emphasis on assignments over testing as a way to judge performance.

If your distance-learning experience does including remote testing, be sure that you understand the ground rules. In some cases, the teacher intends for you to treat the exam as an open-book test, with the intention of measuring your ability to reason or draw conclusions, rather than to memorize facts. In other cases, the test is a way to see whether you've memorized the facts and figures that made up your class; in that situation, you are probably not allowed have research materials at hand when answering questions.

Motivation is key

Learner motivation is often the reason that some instructors completely trust the distance learners administering their own tests. Think about it: When you went to school the first time around, you probably figured that you'd never use some of the things you were learning. After all, how many times does the average rainfall in Bora-Bora come up in conversation? That was the perfect setting for doing only what you had to do to get a good grade, but not worrying about whether you really knew the material.

However, most people taking distance-learning courses have a different motivation: They want to learn the information being taught so that they can put it to use in the real world. They realize that if they cheat on tests, they won't get a true picture of how well they're assimilating the material, and so they'd simply be cheating themselves. So instead, these motivated learners stay honest.

Testing, Testing, 1-2-3

If you are taking a combination of online coursework and in-person classes, the odds are your teacher will test you when you attend class. But if you are truly remote from your school and in-person visits happen seldom if at all, your instructor will typically give your tests and quizzes online, either posting them to a discussion area or attaching them to an e-mail. If you are taking courses from an online training provider, self-assessment tests are likely to be embedded throughout the self-paced training materials. In some cases, these tests are for your information only; in others, test scores are automatically reported back to the instructor when you complete the test.

For tips on taking tests in a self-paced learning environment (classes you take without an instructor), see Chapter 14.

What types of tests can I expect?

A definite trend is emerging in online tests: More and more are in a format that an automated program can grade. Multiple choice (see Figure 13-1), one-word fill in the blanks (see Figure 13-2), and matching items in a list (see Figure 13-3) are all popular formats of questions whose answers can be fed into an electronic template and graded in seconds. These formats lend themselves to testing the memorization of facts. To a lesser degree, they can test your ability to draw conclusions or analyze situations by presenting you with a case study or problem and allowing you to pick the solution you think works best from a list.

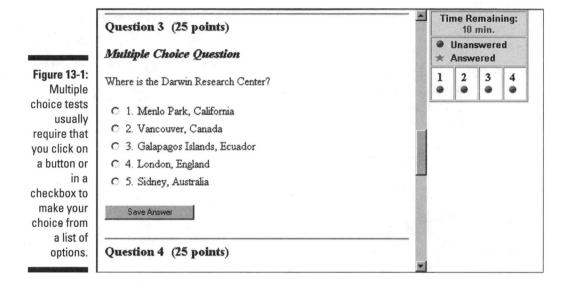

Figure 13-1:
Multiple choice tests usually require that you click on a button or in a checkbox to make your choice from a list of options.

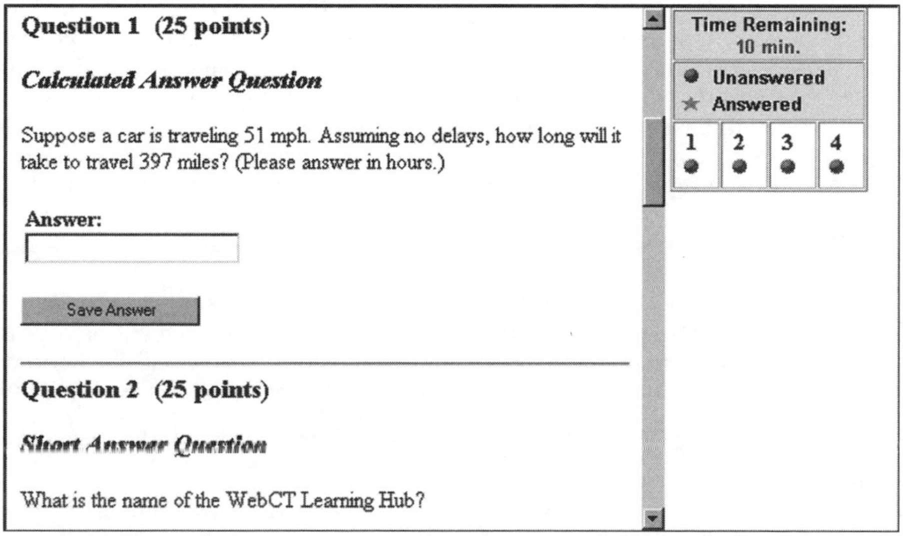

Figure 13-2:
Questions that require you to enter an answer may ask for a word or phrase, or for an amount resulting from a calculation.

You may also encounter essay-style questions in tests administered at a distance, but probably less often; instead, the material that you turn in for assignments is your opportunity to expound on a topic in a more robust way.

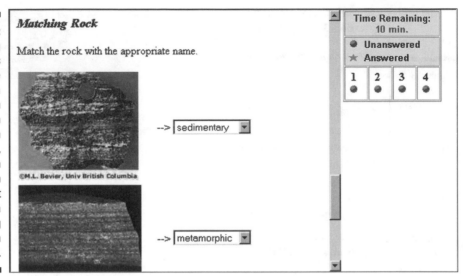

Figure 13-3:
Matching questions may have you select a match from a drop down list, as in this example, or drag an item from one list over to a corresponding item in a second list.

One area where online testing does shine is in enabling you to actually work through a simulated procedure and get graded on how well you perform. This function is useful for technical topics such as engineering, computer science, and medicine. For example, an online test may ask you to design a simple database in Access within a simulated software environment. As you move through the steps to create the database form, the simulation records incorrect steps, generating a message that the choice was wrong and directing you to the correct choice. Each time you make an incorrect move, you lose points in your overall test score.

Whatever form your test takes, if its results are submitted to your instructor (as opposed to being there for your own self-assessment of your progress), your instructor will provide a timeline for completion. The good news is that, with remote testing, you can take the test when it's convenient for you; the bad news is that you have to complete it by a certain point in time, sometimes indicated on your course syllabus.

Online tests are sometimes timed. If your test has a time limit, you will be cut off from entering any more answers when the time is up. Look for a clock or counter on the computer screen to alert you to how time is slipping away.

How do online tests get graded?

Some tests are completely automated, in which case you get your results immediately. The testing software calculates these results and usually provides a summary of your scores, such as the one shown in Figure 13-4; often, you also receive the option of going through question-by-question to see what you got wrong and view the correct answers.

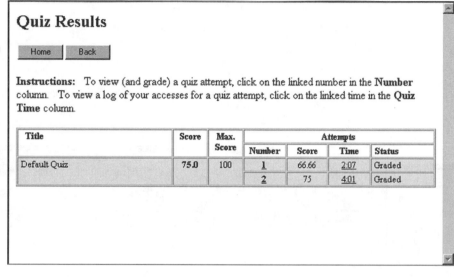

Figure 13-4:
Summaries
of quizzes
often list all
the tests
you've taken
in one place
so you can
see how
your grades
are
improving
(or not).

Quiz Results

[Home] [Back]

Instructions: To view (and grade) a quiz attempt, click on the linked number in the **Number** column. To view a log of your accesses for a quiz attempt, click on the linked time in the **Quiz Time** column.

Title	Score	Max. Score	Attempts			
			Number	**Score**	**Time**	**Status**
Default Quiz	75.0	100	1	66.66	2:07	Graded
			2	75	4:01	Graded

Tests that involve essay questions and those that are not set up for automated grading must be graded either by your instructor or by grading resources that your instructor relies on, such as teaching assistants. The degree of feedback you receive on distance-learning tests varies from school to school and from instructor to instructor, just as it does in an in-person course. If at any time you get a poor grade on an essay question or a confusing comment on your answer, e-mail your instructor and ask for clarification (since you can't confront him or her after class!).

Automated testing programs quite often provide you with useful information about your performance on tests, ranging from how much time it took you to complete a test to where your score fits in with the overall class average.

When an online test goes offline: proctored exams

Perhaps as a result of the school of thought that mistrusts tests taken out of sight of an instructor, many schools have begun to set up *proctored testing sites* (locations where students can go to take a test under the watchful eye of someone in authority). This practice occurs in both universities and training groups that offer certification on technology or professional topics, such as networking or accounting. If your school arranges for a proctored site, your instructor will provide details about when and where you must attend. These test sites are close to remote students (at least closer than the school itself!), and might be administered by any of the following:

✔ Your company Human Resources department

✔ Your commanding officer, if you're in the military

✔ A local community college

✔ A local training company

✔ A regional testing center, such as Sylvan Prometric (`www.prometric.com`), shown in Figure 13-5

Figure 13-5:
A search of the Sylvan Prometric Web site for tests for certification in Adobe software given in French in Vietnam came up with these results.

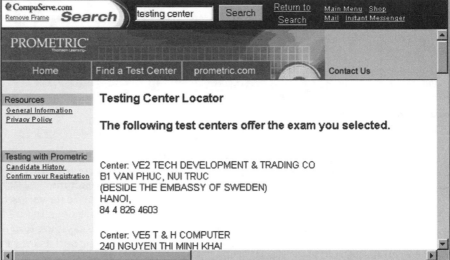

Some university systems also give degree-qualifying tests at the very end of your studies, such as comprehensive exams given in the United Kingdom. These tests are always given face-to-face, and, although you may be able to arrange a proctored test, be aware that you may be required to sit for your exam at the school campus.

Making the Grade

Perhaps you never mastered the art of test taking. Or maybe you've just forgotten all you ever knew about it. Because most distance-learning students are adults returning to the educational scene after a hiatus, I've provided the following sections to help you brush up. They offer some tried-and-true techniques for getting ready to take a test, and for getting through the test with your nerves and grade-point average intact.

Preparing for success

You can win half the battle of test taking before you even begin the test. The way you study and the attitude you have towards the test itself can go a long way towards making you successful when you put pen to paper (or mouse pointer to checkbox). Try some of these techniques to prepare for your next test:

✔ **Analyze your previous results:** If you've taken other tests of this type, look at them to see if you can discern the types of questions you seem to have problems with, clues in questions that you frequently miss, and concepts that you tend to struggle with. After your electronic test is graded, you often receive details of what questions you got wrong along with the correct answer, as the test in Figure 13-6 shows. Use these results to prepare for future tests.

✔ **Study the instructor's testing style:** When reviewing previous tests, notice patterns in questions. Does your teacher seem to appreciate essay answers that focus on details or broad concepts? Do multiple choice questions tend to test concepts or facts and figures?

Find out whether your school library has archived copies of your instructor's face-to-face tests that you can review. These exams might differ slightly from the online versions, but they can give you an insight into the types of questions the teacher focuses on.

✔ **Periodically review course content:** Don't leave the review of key concepts to the day before you have to take a test. Every few weeks, do a quick summary sheet of your notes to reinforce what you've learned.

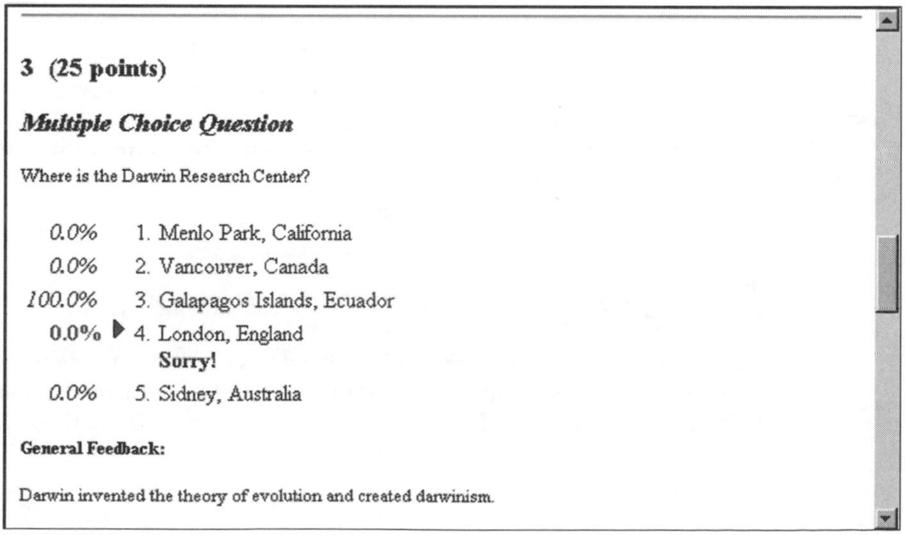

Figure 13-6:
If you're slack on your knowledge of Darwin, you might have chosen London in this test, too!

3 (25 points)

Multiple Choice Question

Where is the Darwin Research Center?

0.0%	1. Menlo Park, California
0.0%	2. Vancouver, Canada
100.0%	3. Galapagos Islands, Ecuador
0.0% ▶	4. London, England **Sorry!**
0.0%	5. Sidney, Australia

General Feedback:

Darwin invented the theory of evolution and created darwinism.

- ✔ **Review chapter summaries:** Many textbooks offer summaries on a chapter-by-chapter level that make a quick review of reading material easier.

- ✔ **Form a study group:** Distance learning makes creating a study group easy. You can share ideas or summaries of concepts in real time in a chat room or teleconference, or at your leisure by posting notes on a bulletin board or sending e-mail. See Chapter 11 for advice about working with other students remotely.

- ✔ **Create tip sheets with key points for review:** By creating concise summaries of key points, you can provide mental links to deeper levels of detail. Create these summaries on index cards, in a notebook, or in your PDA (personal digital assistant), but create them. Clarify with your instructor ahead of time whether you have permission to use such notes during the test.

- ✔ **Find out ahead of time how the test is scored:** If you don't lose any more points for a wrong answer than for no answer at all, take a guess. If you do lose more points for a wrong answer, avoid guessing. If essay questions are graded on structure as well as content, take a little extra time outlining your comments before you start writing.

- ✔ **Get some sleep:** Don't invite a poor mark by logging onto your computer with bags under your eyes.

- ✔ **Eat something before the test:** Low blood sugar will dull the edge of your mental sword. Have an apple, a cookie, or a bowl of rice, but eat something! However, just because you're on your own at your desk, don't eat *while* taking the test — that's just a distraction, and you could get chocolate on your keyboard!

- ✔ **Allow enough time:** In the world of distance learning, you may be completely in charge of your test-taking time. Don't grab a half an hour just before it's due to complete the test, only to find that you needed an hour. Plan an appropriate amount of time to take the test.

Be sure to find a time when you have no distractions, such as after the kids have gone to bed or while your spouse is at the dentist. That's because your first reaction to a question is often the right one. If you get interrupted after reading a question and you have to go back and read it again, you may lose that edge.

Fool-proof test-taking techniques

Okay, it's test time. Whether you're sitting in your den to take a test online or in a proctored classroom to complete a pen-and-paper exam, these tips for test taking might just help you improve your grade and get through the process with a little more aplomb.

Attitude and approach

The way you approach taking the test can be almost as important as how you answer any specific question. Instead of attacking your test without a battle plan, take the time to try these techniques:

- **Relax:** A little nervousness is natural, so don't berate yourself for it. But the more relaxed you are, the more you can keep your attention on the questions, where it belongs. Remote testing offers an advantage here: If you feel anxiety building, you can get up and walk around, put on some music, or drink a cup of hot cocoa to relax yourself.

- **Preview the test before starting and read directions carefully:** Try to pick up any clues you can about what's being asked of you and how you're expected to respond, and then complete the test accordingly.

- **Pace yourself:** If you've previewed the test, as suggested in the previous bullet point, you should have a good idea of about how long you will need you to complete each section. Don't spend too much time on any one section and then find that your time has run out — figuratively and literally!

- **Prioritize:** Answer questions you know the answer to first; then go back and take a little more time on the tougher questions. If you get caught without enough time, this approach ensures that you'll have taken your best shot.

- **Keep moving:** If you don't know an answer, don't panic; just go on to the next question and come back if you have time.

Master multiple choice questions

Some of us have trouble making choices. Being indecisive is tolerable when choosing a sandwich from a lunch menu, but it can be disastrous in a multiple-choice test. But take heart: You can find patterns to multiple choice questions that may help you choose the right answer:

- Eliminate answers that are definitely wrong first; then see what's left.

- Know whether you get a penalty for wrong answers; if not, guess away!

- If "all of the above" is one of your choices, it's often the right answer.

- If you don't know a numerical answer, choose the middle value. For example, if a question asks you to choose the percent of politicians who are less than truthful (20%, 70%, or 100%), and you're not sure of the answer, stick with 70% — although, in this example, you may be tempted to choose 100%!

- Consider the option that provides the most information. Generalized answers sometimes reveal themselves to be too general to be accurate.

Write dazzling essays

Some people fear essays as if the questions were being administered by the Spanish Inquisition. Of course, having solid writing skills helps a lot with formulating a successful essay response, but beyond good grammar, keep these techniques in mind:

- ✔ **Keep your responses concise and get right to the point.** The instructor has an answer in mind, and the more ink you use to get there, the more displeased he or she will be.

- ✔ **Outline your essay on a piece of scrap paper.** Organization of information is one of the foundations of good writing. Make a list of the key points you want to cover, and place them in a logical order. Try chronological order, alphabetical order, or order of importance — anything to give the reader (the person grading your test) a sense that you know where you're going.

- ✔ **Start with a clear topic sentence.** Every paragraph in your answer should establish the purpose of that paragraph. If you can't come up with a purpose for a paragraph, that paragraph doesn't belong in your answer.

- ✔ **Leave time to review your essay for spelling and grammar.** Some teachers will overlook these details completely (not English teachers), and others will weigh a portion of your grade by how well written your answers are. If you have time, take a few minutes to review your answer for mechanical mistakes.

For more tips on writing well, see Chapter 11.

Use language clues

No matter what type of question you encounter, you can usually get clues about the answer from the way the question is phrased:

- ✔ Negatives can fool you. For example, if the question is "When is an anti-social person not interested in social interaction?" read the question carefully to get the answer, "always."

- ✔ Qualifiers can be red flags. If the question asks for the name of a wife who was *somewhat* in favor with Henry the VIII, tread carefully! Qualifiers make the answer less black and white than you might assume on first glance.

- ✔ Watch for extreme qualifiers such as *never, always, completely,* and *only.* These qualifiers are so restrictive that they often signal an incorrect choice. For example, if a multiple-choice question asks whether men are always better at math than women, you'd be wise to choose No as the answer. Most rules have exceptions, and the use of the word *always* in this question suggests that agreeing with it would be chancy.

If at first you don't succeed . . .

We've all done it: left a test with that sinking feeling that we've really botched things up and, sure enough, found out later that we did. Can you do anything about a poor test grade after the fact? Perhaps. Here are few possibilities; after all, it doesn't hurt to ask:

- ✔ Many instructors are willing to let you retake a test if there were extenuating circumstances, such as a high fever or grief over the sudden death of your pet iguana, that made you perform badly on a particular day.

- ✔ Some teachers will disregard one of your test results if it's uncharacteristically poor.

- ✔ In some cases, instructors may be willing to let you do an extra assignment to help your grade recover from a disastrous test.

- ✔ Discuss your results with your instructor. If you misunderstood some of the questions, the instructor may just see your point and give you partial credit for some of the answers.

Keep in mind that almost none of the preceding requests are likely to be granted by even the most generous teacher if you consistently get poor grades on tests. That means it's up to you to make improvements after a bad test experience. If you do poorly on one test, review the answers you got wrong and then go back and study that information again. Take a look at your study techniques and make sure that you're organized and focused in your approach going forward. (For more about good study habits, see Chapter 12.)

Above all, if you get a low test score, don't lose heart. You need to attack your next test with confidence, not anxiety.

Chapter 14

You're in Charge with Self-Paced Courses

In This Chapter

▶ Touring what's available in self-paced courses

▶ Navigating around a self-paced tutorial

▶ Running multimedia files

▶ Using self-administered tests and practice exercises

▶ Getting help

A significant portion of what's going on in the world of distance learning falls into the self-service category called *self-paced learning*. The Automat of learning, self-paced courses let you pick and choose what you want to learn and in what order. The instructor is noticeably absent; rather, a software program offers structured material that you work through at your own pace.

This chapter explores some typical self-paced learning environments, with tips on navigating the learning material, tests, and multimedia presentations that make up your classroom-for-one.

Taking a Peek inside Self-Paced Education

Self-paced training material is typically available either online from a training company or school Web site, or on a CD-ROM. Whatever the media, what these courses have in common is that they offer information with some combination of text, graphics, video, animation, and audio that you can move through at your own pace. These courses have no instructor, although some form of technical or customer service may be available.

A few self-paced training courses do offer some form of certificate or certification on completion, but most do not result in any formal educational credit. Ask a representative about what you get on completing the course before you sign up. You can find out more about accreditation and educational credits in Chapter 3.

A variety of self-paced courses are available, and they all take slightly different forms:

  ✔ **Books online:** Some courses come very close to being a book you read online; you page through the text by clicking on an arrow or other icon, as in the course shown in Figure 14-1.

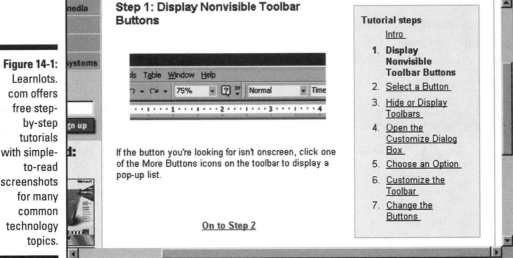

Figure 14-1: Learnlots.com offers free step-by-step tutorials with simple-to-read screenshots for many common technology topics.

  ✔ **Multimedia courses:** Some courses include video presentations or animated demonstrations of procedures.

  ✔ **Interactive courses:** These courses allow you to work with a simulation of a procedure or technical application, and get feedback in the form of automated assessment based on your actions.

  ✔ **Games:** These courses add a creative element, such as the clever history lesson shown in Figure 14-2, which turns the learning into a murder mystery.

Many organizations — including schools, associations, training providers, and companies — offer self-paced training to their customers or employees. Some of this material is free; other courses are available for a fee. When you pay the fee, you get the course either on CD-ROM or by downloading it, or, in many cases, you receive access to run the course on the provider's Web site. These courses last as long as it takes you to get through them, usually anywhere from 10 minutes to a few hours.

One of the nice things about a self-paced course is that you can go back and take the whole course, or pieces of it, as often as you want.

Getting around

Although the design, look, and organization of information in self-paced tutorials is as varied as the people who use them, you usually navigate around the material in a pretty consistent way.

✔ You typically start at a main page that offers access to whatever options the program contains, like the screen shown in Figure 14-3. In this example, which is the Welcome page to a course on creating a marketing campaign, you click on any of the buttons along the right side of the screen to get to specific areas, such as the course menu (a syllabus) or assessment (self-testing).

Figure 14-3: This course in marketing from SkillSoft (`www.skillsoft.com`) offers access to all course materials on its main screen.

✔ Most courses include a syllabus, offering a detailed outline of the course contents (see Figure 14-4). You can usually access this syllabus from anywhere in the tutorial and click on topic-area names to jump to another section of the course at any time you want.

Figure 14-4: In this syllabus, you can click on the arrows to the left of a topic to see the detailed lessons beneath it.

✔ Course-content screens, such as the one shown in Figure 14-5, contain a combination of text, graphic images, and hyperlinks that take you to additional content. You move through lessons using navigation buttons. In many courses, you also have access to other elements of the course, such as testing or help, from each content screen. In others, you have to jump back to the main screen to reach these options.

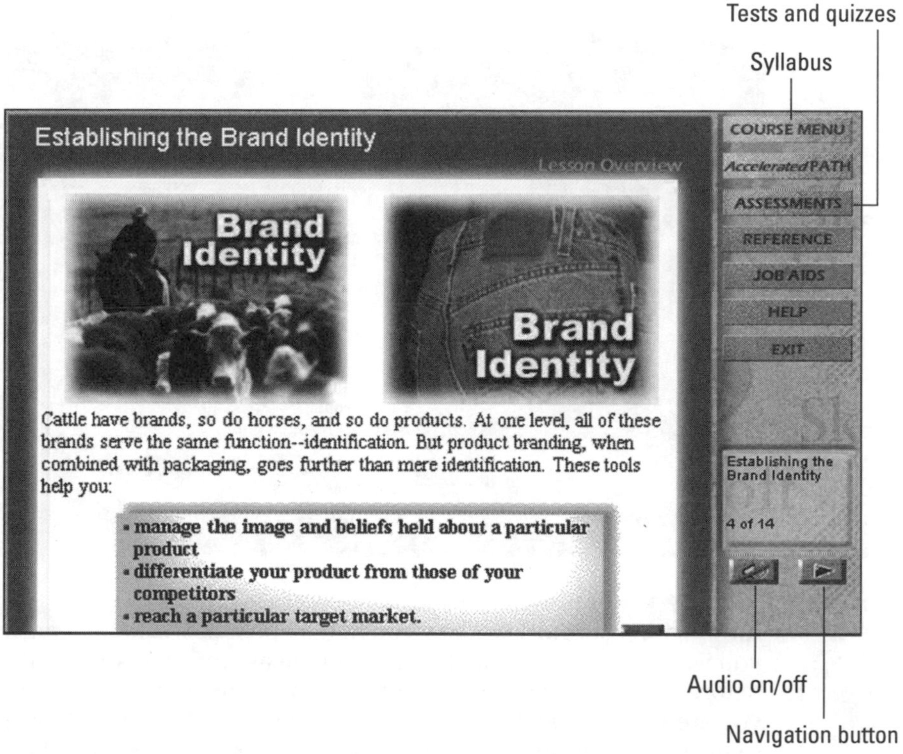

Tests and quizzes

Syllabus

Figure 14-5:
In this self-paced course, all the buttons to go to other parts of the tutorial are available to the right no matter where you are in the content.

Establishing the Brand Identity

Lesson Overview

COURSE MENU
Accelerated PATH
ASSESSMENTS
REFERENCE
JOB AIDS
HELP
EXIT

Establishing the Brand Identity

4 of 14

Cattle have brands, so do horses, and so do products. At one level, all of these brands serve the same function--identification. But product branding, when combined with packaging, goes further than mere identification. These tools help you:

- **manage the image and beliefs held about a particular product**
- **differentiate your product from those of your competitors**
- **reach a particular target market.**

Audio on/off

Navigation button

Many training sites provide demos of self-paced courses so you can get a feel for this environment. Check out demos at Headlight.com (headlight.com), SkillSoft (www.skillsoft.com), and Learn2.com (www.learn2.com) to get a feel for self-paced learning.

Testing your own mettle

Very few people are blasé about taking tests. Some people love them, and others quake in their boots when test time rolls around. But tests provide a way to find the weak spots in your learning. When you're managing your own education, this kind of feedback on your progress becomes even more important to your success.

Assessment of your progress in a self-paced environment typically comes through tests and quizzes. Often, courses include both pre- and post-assessment tests. The pre-assessment element (such as the one shown in Figure 14-6) serves a couple of purposes. First, it highlights what information you already know, so you can skip the material that's too basic for you. Second, it enables you to measure your progress by comparing a pre-assessment with a post-assessment test.

Figure 14-6: This program builds an accelerated learning path based on your pre-assessment test results.

Although most tutorials allow you to take post-assessment tests as often as you want, a pre-assessment test, which measures your knowledge level before taking any part of the course, is available for you to take only once. If you are serious about using a pre-assessment test as a yardstick against which to measure your progress, be sure you don't skim through half-heartedly. You may not get a second chance to take it for real.

Self-administered testing takes a few different forms. Some common formats are

- ✔ **Multiple choice questions (see Figure 14-7):** You remember these from high school, except that in a self-administered test, you make your response to a multiple-choice question by clicking in a box or button to mark the appropriate answer.

- ✔ **Procedures tests (see Figure 14-8):** Often, technical-skills assessments ask you to perform a procedure or enter some information, and the software then scores whether you did so successfully. For example, the course on a networking topic featured in Figure 14-8 asks you to enter the command that displays a certain file.

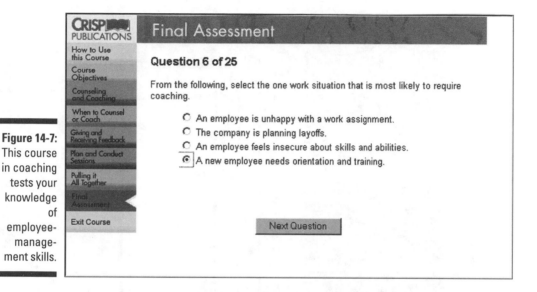

Figure 14-7:
This course
in coaching
tests your
knowledge
of
employee-
manage-
ment skills.

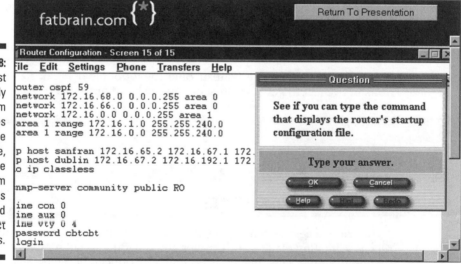

Figure 14-8:
In this test
you actually
perform
procedures
in the
software,
and the
program
grades
correct and
Incorrect
choices.

✔ **Questions that require a match or text entry:** In some cases, self-administered tests ask you to enter text to answer a question, or to match items from one list with the corresponding item in another list.

After you complete the answers in a test, the software scores your performance. At this point, you are likely to have a few other options; for example, in the course on Excel shown in Figure 14-9, you can review questions you got wrong, compare these results with other tests you've taken, or retake the test.

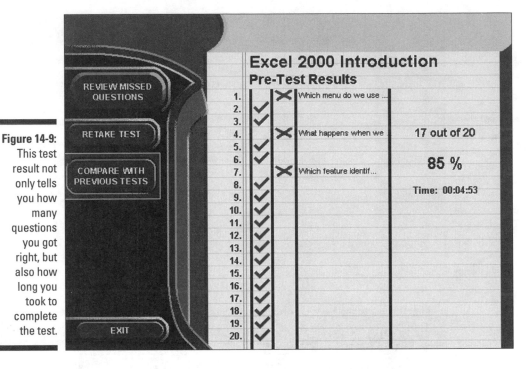

Figure 14-9:
This test
result not
only tells
you how
many
questions
you got
right, but
also how
long you
took to
complete
the test.

Don't think self-administered tests offer the loophole of memorizing the questions in the test to get a better score on the third or fourth try. Successive post-assessment tests often vary the questions to prevent that kind of virtual cheating!

Talking heads and other multimedia events

As Internet access speeds up, multimedia is coming into its own online. Until recently, multimedia files — whether audio, video, or animation — were less than impressive. They played back slowly, produced odd electronic hiccups periodically, and crashed more than one stalwart computer system. But newer computers pack impressive multimedia features, and faster Internet access speeds are making multimedia playback better all the time. Depending on your own computer hardware, phone line quality, and online access setup, you may able to run multimedia files at acceptable speeds. Figure 14-10 shows a short tutorial that uses RealPlayer to run; it includes both an audio narration and short video demonstrations.

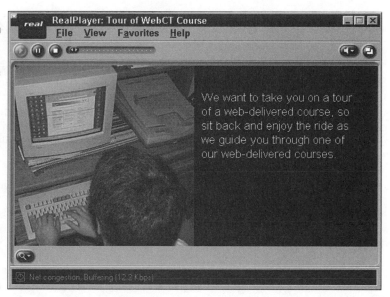

Figure 14-10: This playback of a course on how to take an online course by WebCT plays an audio narration while displaying both video and text information.

Some courses include a video file of a so-called *talking head,* that is, a video of a person talking to the viewer with no other action taking place. This videotaped individual who speaks directly to the student at his computer creates a sometimes-comforting illusion of a front-of-the-classroom teacher.

Another use of multimedia in self-paced training is for demonstrations. *Demonstrations* show you something: They can take the form of a graphic illustration of a concept (such as a flow chart that shows the hierarchy of an organization); video that shows the intricacies of a procedure (such as a film clip of how to paint a picture); or graphics that show a progression (such as an animated chart displaying the growth of a business).

Often, self-paced training courses use audio, video, and animation together. It isn't uncommon to see a video demonstration with an audio explanation, and with an animated character popping up to offer occasional tips.

You may need to install multimedia players to play back audio, video, or animation files. These players are almost always offered for free download on the site where you encounter the files. You can read more about this type of software and how it works in Chapter 4, and the Online Directory section of this book contains more information about where to obtain the software.

How do you get to Broadway? Practice, practice, practice!

Self-paced materials may include various forms of exercises or practice to help you with your learning. For example, I've seen role-playing exercises using *avatars* (3-D images of a character which represents the student in an on-screen interaction), written exercises you compile in a personal journal, and interactive exercises in which you practice a procedure (see Figure 14-11) and the software corrects you if you make a mistake. These exercises are often sprinkled throughout the lessons at regular intervals. Other programs combine all the exercises in a single section of the course; you can go to the exercise section for practice whenever you want.

Highlighted activity area   Instruction

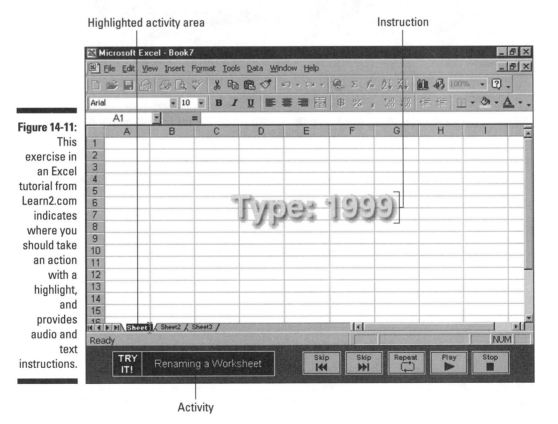

Figure 14-11: This exercise in an Excel tutorial from Learn2.com indicates where you should take an action with a highlight, and provides audio and text instructions.

Activity

Getting Help with Self-Service Learning

There's no doubt about it, you're flying solo with self-paced training. But does that mean that you don't even have a friendly air-traffic controller out there somewhere to help you when you get lost? Not at all. Self-paced learning software usually offers help in a few different formats:

- **A built-in help system:** This is essentially a searchable database of topics or frequently asked questions, similar to the help system you might find in your word processing program. Figure 14-12 shows an example of a help system directory for a self-paced course.

- **E-mail support:** Many training hubs offer the capability to e-mail the staff with questions. Remember, though, that an answer may take a day or two to reach you.

- **Phone support:** Phone support is not as common as e-mail support, but, if you buy training from a site rather than using it for free (and especially if your company buys a lot of training), you may find that phone support is part of the deal.

Some learning portals also have discussion areas where students of their courses can go to compare notes about their learning experiences. You may pick up a useful tip about a course in this online student lounge. Look for areas on the provider's Web site labeled *Student Discussion, Student Lounge,* or the like. To find out more about participating in online discussions, see Chapter 10.

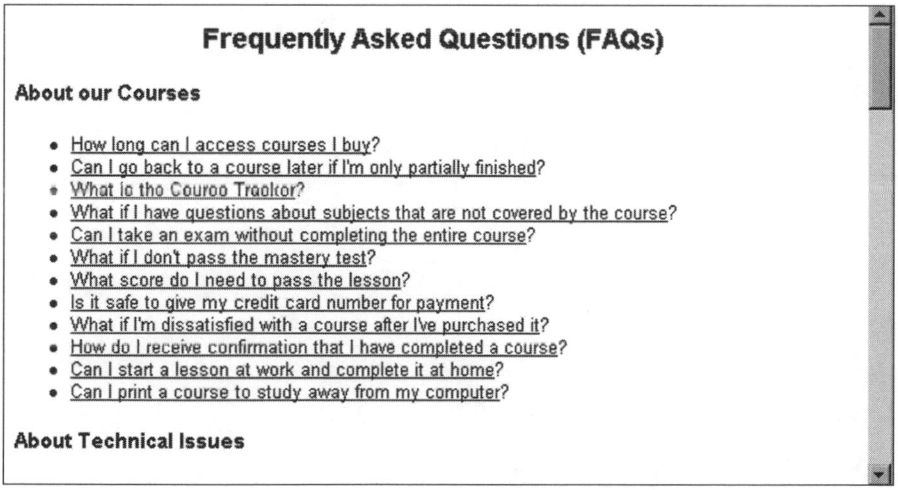

Figure 14-12:
The emind.com help system consists of frequently asked questions and technical help documents.

Frequently Asked Questions (FAQs)

About our Courses

- How long can I access courses I buy?
- Can I go back to a course later if I'm only partially finished?
- What is the Course Tracker?
- What if I have questions about subjects that are not covered by the course?
- Can I take an exam without completing the entire course?
- What if I don't pass the mastery test?
- What score do I need to pass the lesson?
- Is it safe to give my credit card number for payment?
- What if I'm dissatisfied with a course after I've purchased it?
- How do I receive confirmation that I have completed a course?
- Can I start a lesson at work and complete it at home?
- Can I print a course to study away from my computer?

About Technical Issues

Part VI
Distance Learning in the Real World

The 5th Wave — By Rich Tennant

"OH YEAH, AND TRY NOT TO ENTER THE WRONG PASSWORD."

In this part . . .

Sometimes it seems that education sits over there in an ivory tower spinning pretty philosophies, concepts, and theories, while the real world squats across the moat, counting potatoes and pricing potato peelers. In this Part, I intend to change all that by lowering a bridge between your education and everything it can do for you in your day-to-day existence.

For most people, the whole point of getting more education is to take that shiny new credential back to the real world and trade it for a promotion or raise. In this part, you discover how to find distance-learning opportunities in your workplace, and to leverage everything you learned online in your career.

Chapter 15

Distance Learning at Work

. . . .

In This Chapter

▶ Exploring training opportunities employers are providing today

▶ Finding ways to learn on the job

▶ Studying during business hours

▶ Learning with a workgroup

. . . .

*J*ust like Dorothy in *The Wizard of Oz*, you may not have to look any farther than your own backyard for your heart's desire, if your heart's desire
is to learn online. Today's employers, knowing the value of a loyal and
well-trained workforce, are doing more than reimbursing tuition for courses
taken outside of work. Many employers are bringing education to their
employees in the workplace. Because of their existing technology infrastructure, these companies are, in some cases, bringing even more cutting-edge
technology to the table for educating their employees than more traditional
schools do.

Companies today are creating their own distance-learning programs or are
partnering with educational providers to reach sometimes far-flung work-
forces. They're exploring technogies and delivery methods that utilize their
own internal intranet, as well as helping employees to take full advantage of
education on the Internet. This chapter explores some of the ways this in-
house education is happening so that you can know where to look for opportunities in your own place of employment. In addition, it offers some tips on
studying while on the job.

Exploring the Training Your Employer Provides

Today, companies are going beyond the obligatory sexual harassment class
and the half-day off-site seminar in word processing. Many companies are
building their own distance-learning courses, or partnering with training
providers or universities to provide customized education to their workers

on a wide variety of topics. Some of these topics are job-performance specific, but others are designed to help workers grow and take on skills that they can use somewhere down their career path.

What kinds of training are employers offering? Here are some topics you may see at your company:

- ✔ Management skills such as leadership, teambuilding, and communications
- ✔ Technical topics such as computer software and hardware, or programming
- ✔ Employee safety courses for supervisors in manufacturing settings
- ✔ Specific job skills such as operation of a piece of equipment or supply-chain management for purchasing professionals
- ✔ Internet skills such as researching, using a browser, or setting up an e-commerce site
- ✔ Customer-service and technical-support skills or procedures
- ✔ Sales and marketing
- ✔ Finance and budgeting

In short, whatever employees need to know to do their jobs better or improve their value as employees is probably being taught somewhere, and in many cases it's being taught using online distance learning.

Making use of your training department

Traditionally, a company's human resources department administers employee training, although some companies have a separate training department to tend to employees' learning needs. If you have a formal training department or program through your human resources group, your first move should be to visit them and ask what's available. Some companies, such as one Midwestern telephone company, Ameritech, offer both customers and employees educational opportunities online, as shown on the Ameritech Commitment to Education Web page (ameritech.com/education/commitment/index.html) shown in Figure 15-1.

Companies sometimes maintain a library of computer-based training (CBT) materials that you can borrow. CBT refers to course or training materials you can access from a CD-ROM. Many companies also post Web-based training materials (WBT) on their intranet; that is, courses that you run online, rather than from a CD-ROM. WBT that is available through your employer may consist of materials that in-house resources or contractors created for your company, or of courses that your company bought off the shelf from training vendors, such as American Management Association (www.amanet.org).

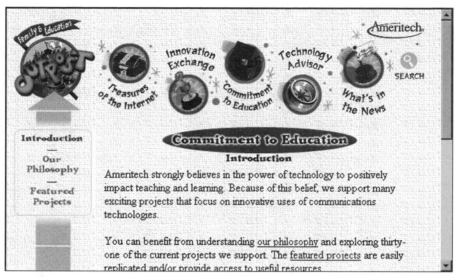

Figure 15-1:
As a communications company, Ameritech sponsors high-tech learning opportunities for customers and employees alike.

Many companies that do provide training post a training schedule, such as the one for Ameritech shown in Figure 15-2. Notice the use of e-mail, Internet, and other distance-learning methods for delivery. Look for such a training schedule on your own company's network to see whether they have upcoming courses that are of interest to you.

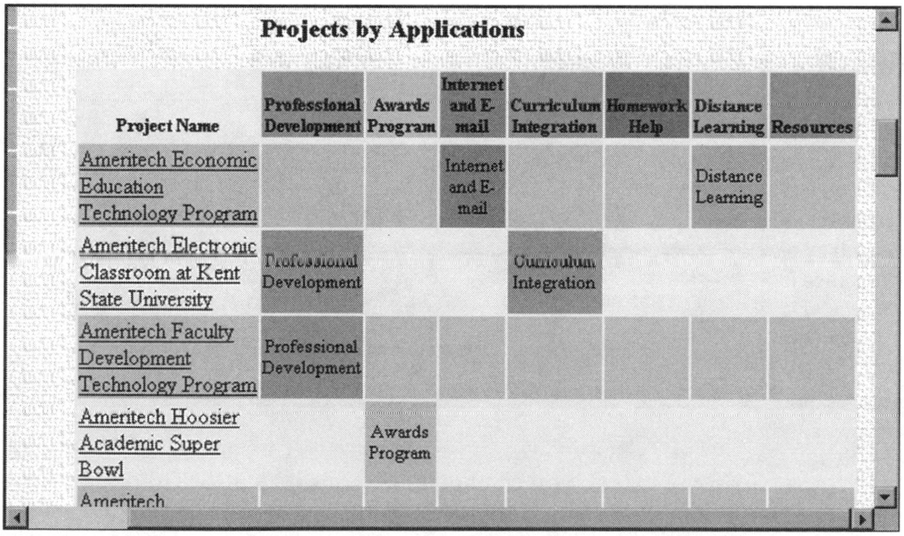

Projects by Applications

Project Name	Professional Development	Awards Program	Internet and E-mail	Curriculum Integration	Homework Help	Distance Learning	Resources
Ameritech Economic Education Technology Program			Internet and E-mail			Distance Learning	
Ameritech Electronic Classroom at Kent State University	Professional Development			Curriculum Integration			
Ameritech Faculty Development Technology Program	Professional Development						
Ameritech Hoosier Academic Super Bowl		Awards Program					
Ameritech							

Figure 15-2:
This company even sponsors an electronic classroom at a major university.

Some employers have a computer lab or classroom available for training; in addition to in-person training sessions, you may be able to use the computer lab to access distance-learning programs or to study CBT or WBT courses.

Learning at your service: Military distance education

If your employer is the military, or if you're in a reserve program like the Army Reserve Corps or National Guard, you may have some special distance-learning opportunities. As the United States Army Soldier Support Institute portion of the U.S. Army Web site (usassi-www.army.mil/orgs/orgs.htm) shown in Figure 15-3 suggests, military organizations include a strong educational component (in fact, education is one of their big recruiting carrots). Given the global distribution of its personal, the military has always been a proponent of distance learning; the U.S. military even runs its own distance-learning network via satellite. Many military organizations also use third-party vendors to supply distance learning or to design courses for their particular needs, just as corporations do.

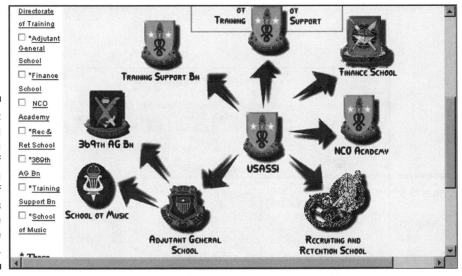

Figure 15-3: Everything from a school of music to a school of finance is available from the U.S. Army.

To some extent, you can negotiate your education from the military when you join up; some programs and courses are built into your military career plan at that time. If you have already enlisted, you have to make a request of your commanding officer to get into a program. The actual extent to which the military is using distance-learning technology varies from service to service and from country to country.

Partnering with educational providers

Many employers hire third-party vendors to provide training, either because they don't have an in-house training staff or because hiring out is more cost-effective. That training might be a generic class in a technology or management topic, or it might be customized training that addresses specific skills and information for your company's workforce.

More and more online training companies are partnering with companies to provide a distance-learning alternative. These companies offer quantity discounts for multiple students. If your company doesn't have a distance-learning alternative, you may want to suggest that they contact companies such as Headlight.com (www.headlight.com) shown in Figure 15-4, click2learn.com (www.click2learn.com), or MindEdge.com (www.mindedge.com).

Figure 15-4: Headlight. com offers volume discounts for corporate clients.

Some academics bemoan it, but the fact is that most universities today are working hand in hand with the business community to create curriculum that meets businesses' needs rather than some academic ideal of learning. Universities such as Jones International University (see Figure 15-5) are partnering with businesses, offering college-level courses for employees. Some of these courses are offered on campus or even at a corporate site, but many are offered through distance learning.

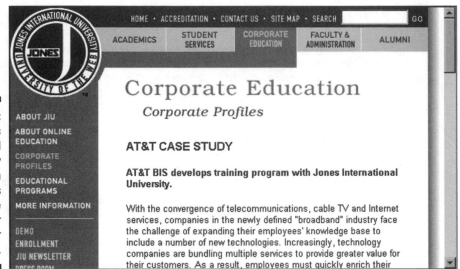

Figure 15-5:
Jones
International
University
works with
corporations
to provide
learning for
their
employees.

ABOUT JIU
ABOUT ONLINE
EDUCATION
CORPORATE
PROFILES
EDUCATIONAL
PROGRAMS
MORE INFORMATION

DEMO
ENROLLMENT
JIU NEWSLETTER
PRESS ROOM

Corporate Education
Corporate Profiles

AT&T CASE STUDY

AT&T BIS develops training program with Jones International University.

With the convergence of telecommunications, cable TV and Internet services, companies in the newly defined "broadband" industry face the challenge of expanding their employees' knowledge base to include a number of new technologies. Increasingly, technology companies are bundling multiple services to provide greater value for their customers. As a result, employees must quickly enrich their

Learning in a Cubicle

Many companies require that ongoing education happen outside of office hours, but some are willing to make time for learning right from your desk between 9 and 5. One company I know of offers a six-month educational sabbatical to each employee every five years. Other companies allow workers to study on company time, up to a point. If your company has agreed to provide a distance-learning experience and has designated a certain number of your regular work hours that you can spend on your education, you're in luck.

But what does studying while at work mean to you? Well, I'm not going to kid you: Studying in a work environment is not always easy (sometimes, *working* in a work environment isn't easy!). People encounter problems that generally center around distractions and lack or recognition for what they are doing.

Distractions differ depending on whether you have an office or cubicle, but even a closed door won't keep the phone from ringing, e-mails from popping up on your computer screen, or coworkers from sticking their heads in to chat with you. Ask your manager about the possibility of using a conference room or a computer lab to study. Or, if your company is conducting on-the-job studying on a large scale, suggest a scheme for letting others know when an employee is off limits, such as hanging a balloon on a cubicle or doorknob.

Sometimes, coworkers aren't aware of what you're doing, and so they don't understand your need for privacy. To a great extent, fixing this problem is up to your management. Although you can tell a few people around you that you need to study for an hour, having management make education a part of the corporate culture so that its value is understood by all is the foundation for coworker understanding of your needs. Also, having a supportive manager who understands that this time away from the job will pay off for all concerned down the road is a big help to any job training you pursue.

If your company agrees that you can spend part of your workweek studying, ask whether you might do your work-time studying at home, say a half day or full day every week. Not only does studying at home help you concentrate without workplace interruptions, it also saves you some commuting time.

Buddy Up! Studying with a Workgroup

Some companies send groups of students through a distance-learning class together. This approach provides a built-in learning community, because you all work for the same company, understand its procedures and issues, and can use that common knowledge to create realistic examples and fuel discussions in your course. This connection to the place where you'll all apply your knowledge can be a very useful thing.

Ask your training resource at work about the possibility of hooking up several employees with an interest in studying the same topic to take a course. Your company may arrange to purchase a class for several people at a discount, or you can informally agree with coworkers to sign up for the same class on your own. Then, if you get stuck or have a question, you can not only e-mail other members of the group but also get up and walk down the hall for a chat, taking a little bit of the distance out of distance learning.

Chapter 16

Marketing Your Distance Education

. . . .

In This Chapter

▶ Getting help from job placement programs

▶ Obtaining transcripts

▶ Understanding how employers view distance degrees

▶ Marketing your credentials

. . . .

1 once met a woman who had been taking distance-learning courses for 18 years. One day she realized that she'd qualified for a degree (probably a few degrees) but had never bothered to take the final steps to obtain it. Unlike this long-term college student, most of us don't learn just for the fun of it (although it certainly can be fun). We have specific uses for our education.

When you complete a course or degree via distance learning (or even before you finish), you should start thinking about the benefits you can reap from your efforts. If you plan to use your new educational credential to get a better job, are you aware of how potential employers will view your degree? If you expect your school to help you get a job, are your expectations realistic? After you have that sheepskin in hand, how can you promote your online education credentials in the job marketplace?

This chapter explores some of the ways that your studies fit into your future career goals, and how to document and promote your education in the real world.

Using Your School's Resources to Land a Job

When I went to college for my bachelor's degree, my school offered career counseling, but I was like a fish with a bagpipe when it came to knowing what to do with it. I hadn't been in the business world and didn't know what type of job I wanted. And, at that time, the Internet, the world's greatest job networking tool ever, wasn't even around.

Now that you (and I) are perhaps older and wiser about the job market, you can take greater advantage of a school's job placement and career counseling functions, if you know all that your school has to offer. Check out your school's Web site to see what career services are available (see Figure 16-1). These functions, which are often contained within an area called Student Support Services, may be called something like Job Placement, Work Placement, Job Counseling, or Career Counseling.

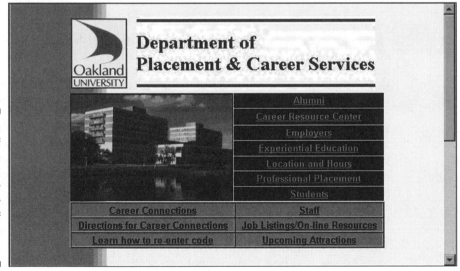

Figure 16-1: This part of the Web site for Oakland University offers many forms of help to the job seeker.

Services that may be available include

✔ **Job search tools:** Some schools offer their own job-listing service or job-search software online.

- ✔ **Career workshops:** These might cover topics such as interviewing techniques, resume writing, or searching for a job online. And they may even be available in a distance-learning format!

- ✔ **Web-site links:** Some schools include links on their Web sites to professional associations, online employment services, and classified job listings.

- ✔ **Alumni connections:** Some schools make an effort to match up alumni whose companies have job openings with students looking for work.

- ✔ **Career fairs:** Schools often set up interview sessions on campus and advice for getting the most out of them, such as the tips offered on the site shown in Figure 16-2. If you can't visit in person, you may be able to work with your school to have them submit your resume to employers at such an on-campus career fair.

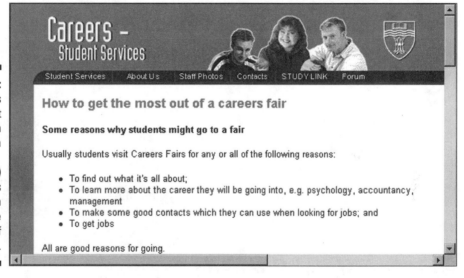

Figure 16-2: Charles Sturt University in Australia (www.csu.edu.au) offers advice on getting the most out of career fairs.

- ✔ **Employer services:** Your school may offer services to employers, helping them locate a student (perhaps you!) whose background meets a current job need. Some schools also provide a service to help employers verify applicants' degrees, such as the Degree Validation service at the University of Washington, shown in Figure 16-3. If your school offers this service, you can always mention it to potential employers as a way to help them qualify you quickly.

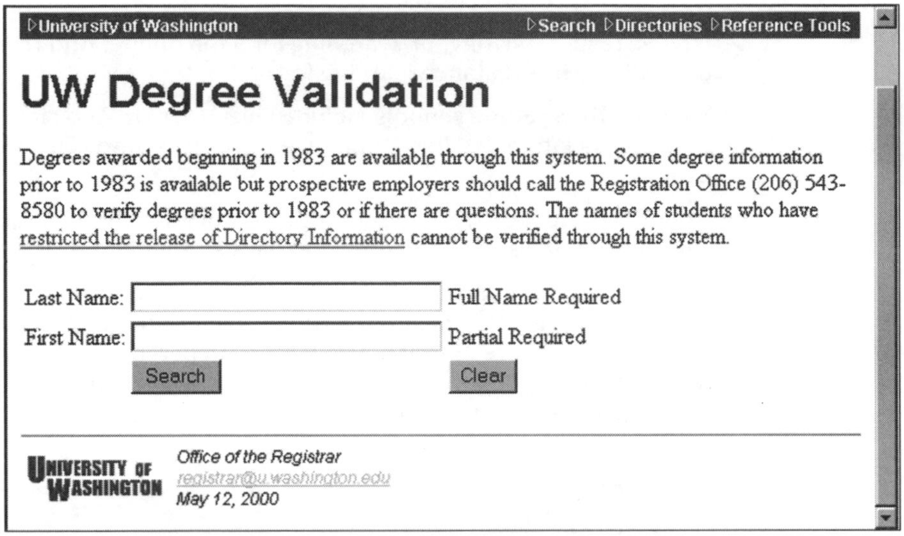

▷University of Washington   ▷Search ▷Directories ▷Reference Tools

UW Degree Validation

Degrees awarded beginning in 1983 are available through this system. Some degree information prior to 1983 is available but prospective employers should call the Registration Office (206) 543-8580 to verify degrees prior to 1983 or if there are questions. The names of students who have restricted the release of Directory Information cannot be verified through this system.

Last Name: [   ]   Full Name Required
First Name: [   ]   Partial Required

[Search]   [Clear]

UNIVERSITY OF WASHINGTON   *Office of the Registrar*
registrar@u.washington.edu
May 12, 2000

Figure 16-3:
Employers considering you for a job can search through this database to verify your degree.

For more about searching for a job online, read *Job Searching Online For Dummies,* by Pam Dixon, published by IDG Books Worldwide.

If you're unemployed at some point when working on your degree, you might consider work-study options offered by your school career office. In this kind of program, you can work part time for a potential employer and even get some credit for that work. A work-study job may lead to a full-time career, or, at the very least, it will keep you in practice in your field while you're looking for a new job and add one more experience to your resume. (See Chapter 3 for more information about financing your online education through work-study programs.)

Getting Your Records Straight

When I was about six, I got my first report card and, because I didn't like some of my grades, I erased them and wrote in my own. At six, this solution seemed logical enough to me. My parents pointed out the error of my ways, and ever since I've had a healthy respect for official records of achievement.

If you want to use your education to get a better job, you're going to have to prove your accomplishments to potential employers. The school or institution from which you took your courses can help you.

Obtaining transcripts, certificates, and degrees

Some employers require proof of your academic performance in the form of a transcript of your grades. You can order transcripts from your school, for a processing fee of about $5 per order. Contact your school's registrar's office to order your transcripts. Some schools allow you to order by mail, in person, or even online. The Web site shown in Figure 16-4 gives details on the methods available to the students of that school.

Typically, schools send a transcript directly to the recipient, which might be another school where you're applying for advanced study or a potential employer. This ensures the recipient that they've received an official record that no one has tampered with (not that you would!).

Figure 16-4:
This school doesn't offer an option of ordering online, but its Web site gives details of other methods of ordering.

UNIVERSITY *of* MARYLAND UNIVERSITY COLLEGE ▼ Search   ▼ Request Info.   ▼ Home

Questions and Comments

UMUC Transcript Request Form

If you have been issued a four digit PIN by UMUC Stateside
Please click here

To request a transcript directly from the European/Atlantic Divisions visit
http://fieldrep.ed.umuc.edu/pubs/umrg-035.html

Some employers also ask for a copy of your college diploma itself, or some proof of a certification credential you obtained from an online training company. In the case of a college degree, you usually have the option of attending an in-person graduation ceremony, where the school hands you your degree. If you can't attend, the school should mail your diploma or record of completion of a certificate program to you. Online training companies or certification granting companies also send you your hard copy credential through the mail.

What do you have to recommend you?

Before or just after you finish your studies, consider getting letters of recommendation from faculty members you've worked with closely. These references add some nice variety to your portfolio of employer references. In addition, because of fear of prosecution, employer references these days have become notoriously thin and neutral in their tone. Your instructors may not feel quite as bound by a company policy on references. Also remember that they saw you perform not for a paycheck or to impress a boss, but from a self-motivated desire to improve yourself. That's a perspective on your personality that those employer references don't provide.

It's probably best to ask your instructor for a letter of recommendation in person (that is, for the long-distance learner, by phone) rather than by e-mail or a letter. After all, you're asking for a favor, and that's always best to do on a personal level. When the instructor does send you such a letter, sending a thank-you note for his or her efforts is a nice professional touch.

If you have a certain career goal in mind (for example, to move into management), don't hesitate to mention that when you ask for the recommendation. That way, your teacher will know to stress the most relevant attributes (leadership, great team builder, and so on) in the letter.

Tooting Your Distance-Education Horn

You're not spending all this time getting an educational credential just to have it sit in your attic collecting dust. The first thing you should do upon obtaining your distance-education credential, whether you've completed a single course or obtained a full-blown degree, is to reflect that achievement on your resume.

Spiffing up your resume

Your resume, whether on paper or electronic, is your strongest tool in educating your potential employer about your qualifications. List your online coursework in the education section of your resume, which should be organized with the most recent schooling first. Although you don't have to differentiate the method of obtaining your credits on your resume, drawing attention to the fact that you took the initiative to complete the coursework online can work in your favor. One great place to do so is in the cover letter that you send with your resume. Use the cover letter as an opportunity to stress the self-motivation, hard work, and dedication to improving yourself that went into your studies.

How employers look at a distance

There was a time when a mail-order degree, one of the earliest forms of distance learning, was looked on as a poor substitute for a "real" college degree. The granting institutions were sometimes shady, the course material unchallenging, and the learning methodologies questionable.

Happily, things have definitely changed for the better, for several reasons:

✔ **Who is conferring the degrees:** One of the big problems with mail-order degrees was the caliber of the institutions granting them. As more prestigious schools, such as Berkeley and Stanford, grant distance-learning-based degrees, employers are changing their tune about this format of learning. In fact, most employers are more interested in the source of the degree (a good, accredited school) than the delivery method of the material.

✔ **Incorporation of technology in distance learning:** Today's workplace puts a strong emphasis on technology. Because distance learners function in the online world in pursuing their studies, they are more comfortable with technology than their classroom-bound counterparts in some employers' eyes. The distance learner is also likely to have developed strong online communication skills — another real asset in today's business world.

✔ **The emphasis on lifelong learning:** The workplace of today stresses lifelong learning, and the employee who continues to learn is looked at as one who will strive to acquire new or improved skills as needed.

✔ **Appreciation of self-improvement:** Being successful at distance learning means that you have to be self-motivated, organized, and able to take charge of your own learning experience. These abilities are highly prized in the business world, and highly transferable to any job.

Be sure, when you present your distance-learning achievements to a potential employer, that you are clear about the quality of the institution from which you obtained them, the accreditation held by the school, the equivalency of the content of the courses you took to in-person classes, and the skills you gained in use of technology along the way.

If you're not looking for a new job, but rather for a better job at your current place of employment, make sure that you revise your resume to reflect your new academic credentials. Then, present a copy of your updated resume to human resources and your own boss so they are aware of your achievement when new openings come up.

If you took your courses through an extension program of a university or the distance-learning arm of a school, do you need to specify that fact in your resume? The answer depends somewhat on whether the courses you took and credit you obtained were the same as those offered through the regular academic department. If they were, listing Acme University as opposed to Acme University Extension Program is probably preferable and perfectly legitimate. However, if you took courses for Continuing Education Units rather than regular college credits, or the course content was not of the same scope as those offered to on-campus students, that's different. In that case, you probably should specify that you studied through the Extension Division, Continuing Education Division, or whatever title your school applies to that program.

Publicizing your credentials

After you complete your online course or receive your degree through a distance-learning program, you're ready to take the next step in your career. If you want to advance within the company where you already work, you can contact your own human resources department and search current listings to see whether you now meet criteria for a better position.

If you want to switch companies or even careers (or break into the job market for the first time), you can search online job boards, like Monster.com (www.monster.com), shown in Figure 16-5, JobOptions (www.espan.com), or CareerSite (www.careersite.com) to find jobs for which your distance education has qualified you.

Figure 16-5: Monster.com is one of the more active job search/job listing services on the Internet.

You can also submit your updated resume to recruitment agencies, fondly known as *headhunters*. You don't have to go to the jungle to find headhunters; just search the Internet with the keyword "recruitment." Headhunters tend to specialize in certain career areas, such as those that require highly technical backgrounds or manufacturing experience. You can also find recruitment agencies that specialize in specific countries, like the one shown in Figure 16-6 for Scotland. If you want to make a move to another country in addition to making a career move, these can be a good place to start.

Figure 16-6: Geographic job-search sites like www. recruitment. scotland. net can help you find a job in a distant land.

Don't forget about the growing field of home-based careers. Through distance learning, you develop the skills needed to work on your own, manage your own time, and communicate remotely. Maybe starting a home-based business or finding a telecommuting job is a good way to transfer those skills to a new career direction. Check out listings at HomeEmployment (www.home-employment. com/simpson).

Whatever method you choose for shopping your new credentials around, just remember that you have something to be very proud of when you get an education via distance learning. Taking your courses online shows that you're open to new experiences, technologically bold, and able to take charge of your learning and your life. Don't be shy about letting others know about it!

Distance Learning
Online Directory

The 5th Wave   By Rich Tennant

"IT'S AMAZING HOW MUCH MORE SOME PEOPLE CAN GET OUT OF A PC THAN OTHERS."

In this directory . . .

When I began to do my homework for writing this book, I discovered one thing very quickly: A lot is going on out there in distance learning, and a great many new players are coming on the scene. Although this directory can't possibly be comprehensive in this ever-changing field, it does give you some great starting points in planning for your online education and getting what you need to succeed, from financing your eduction to buying your textbooks.

Look to this directory for resources in the following areas:

- ✔ Colleges and universities
- ✔ Distance-learning information sites
- ✔ Distance-learning organizations
- ✔ Financing
- ✔ Online study tools
- ✔ Personal development courses
- ✔ Publications
- ✔ Resources for learners with disabilities
- ✔ Software download sites
- ✔ Technical and professional schools
- ✔ Testing services
- ✔ Textbooks
- ✔ Training providers

About This Directory

Trust me, you'll have enough research to do when you start your distance learning, so I've saved you some work by compiling this handy directory of resources. To use this directory, just find a category that's of interest, browse through it, read the descriptions that appeal to you, and then visit those sites.

To help you judge at a glance whether a site may be what you're looking for, this directory includes some handy miniature icons (otherwise known as *micons*). Here's an explanation of what each micon means:

This resource is a book.

You can download software or other files at this site.

★★ ★★ This site is truly worthy of a four-star rating. It's a particularly valuable resource due to the strong distance-learning efforts of its authoring institution, its content, links, free software, or all of the above.

This site has free stuff, available for the taking.

This site can help with your school work, through research or other nifty study tools.

This site addresses international issues.

This site has particularly good hyperlinks, which can be very useful for research.

You can use this site to take care of some of your shopping needs.

☺ This site has information or resources for people with special needs.

This site includes an online database.

Colleges and Universities

You can find entire books dedicated to providing detailed listings of hundreds of colleges and universities offering distance learning. Some of those books are listed under the "Publications" section of this directory. I won't attempt to provide such a comprehensive listing of schools in the space available here. However, several schools have been at the forefront of distance learning. This section includes a description of these schools along with their contact information.

Athabasca
www.athabascau.ca

One of Canada's leading providers of distance education since 1970: Athabasca serves 20,000 students and offers 48 programs, including more than 450 courses that lead to degrees or certificates. Programs leading to a bachelor's degree include Arts, General Studies, Science, Administrative Studies, Commerce, and Nursing. Master's programs include Business Administration, Distance Education, and Health Studies. Distance-learning courses are delivered via a combination of videoconferencing, teleconferencing, and computer.

Address: 1 University Drive, Athabasca, Alberta, Canada T95 3A3

Phone: 800-788-9041 or 780-675-6100

Cardean University

www.cardean.com

★★
★★

Start-up university: Cardean University, a part of UNext.com, was just starting up in mid-2000; however, this group has some interesting credentials, because they develop course materials working with the likes of Stanford, Columbia Business School, and The London School of Economics in the distance-learning format. Currently, their offerings are confined to those that lead to an MBA. They are accredited by the Distance Education and Training Council (DETC) and the State of Illinois.

Address: 500 Lake Cook Road, Suite 150, Deerfield, IL 60015

Phone: 847-405-5000

Charles Sturt University

www.csu.edu.au/de

★★ 🌐
★★

Australian university with strong distance-learning emphasis: This school, with five locations servicing some 30,000 students, has a heavy focus on distance learning. It includes six areas of study: Arts, Commerce, Education, Health Studies, Science & Agriculture, and the Australian Graduate School of Police Management. Altogether, this school offers over 300 courses online.

Address: Panorama Avenue, Bathurst, NSW 2795 Australia

Phone: (02) 6338-4000

Indiana University

www.indiana.edu/~iude

Flexible degree programs: Through its Office of Distributed Education, IU offers video and online courses in areas such as science, information technology, and business management. You can also opt for a Bachelor of General Studies, which allows you to orchestrate several areas of study. The school serves over 18,000 distance-learning students around the world, in addition to the 65,000 students enrolled in its eight campuses around the state of Indiana.

Address: Continuing Studies, IUPUI, 620 Union Drive, Room 142, Indianapolis, IN 46202

Phone: 317-274-4501

Indira Gandhi National Open University

www.india.edu

★★ 🌐
★★

Driving the distance learning initiative in India: Although its use of technology may be a few years behind some other schools, IGNOU is in the process of building a distance-learning infrastructure that can respond to the demands of one of the most populous countries in the world. In addition to the Internet, IGNOU uses nationwide television broadcast of some materials, as well as both teleconferencing and phone-in radio counseling services for students.

Address: Centre for Extension Education, Maidan Garhi, New Delhi, India 110068

Phone: 6865923-32

Jones International University

www.jonesinternational.edu

★ ★
★ ★

Entirely virtual university: Jones may not have the quality of courses of, say, a Berkeley, but it is worth mentioning here because it was the first completely virtual university with accreditation. This school is accredited by the North Central Association of Colleges and Schools (NCAS). It also has certification from the Global Alliance for Transnational Education, which is an organization that deals with quality assurance for educational programs across nations. Courses of study include a BA or MA in Business Communications, a MA in Business Administration, or certificate programs in topics such as PR and Marketing, The Internet in Education, and Leadership and Communication.

Address: 9697 E. Mineral Avenue, Englewood, CO 80112

Phone: 800-811-5663 or 303-784-8045

The Open University

www.open.ac.uk

British institution with strong distance-learning roots: The Open University is one of the most seasoned and respected distance-learning organizations in the world today, with a network of schools throughout the United Kingdom. The OU still clings to some low-tech delivery methods such as books and audiotapes, but it is gradually exploring online activities and videoconferencing. The OU offers a wide variety of courses and degree programs, some with online content, including programs in the arts, law, math and science, social sciences, technology, education, and business.

Address: Walton Hall, Milton Keynes, UK MK7 6AA

Phone: 44 1908 274066

Penn State

www.worldcampus.psu.edu

★ ★
★ ★

Intriguing degree mix from a school at the forefront of distance learning: Through its World Campus division, Penn State offers some intriguing courses and degree programs online, including Turfgrass Management, Chemical Dependency Counselor, and Noise Control Engineering, as well as many more mainstream areas of study. Check out the Masters Degree in Adult Education, a Bachelor's Degree in Letters, Arts and Sciences, a Masters in Engineering Acoustics, and a Master of Education in Elementary of Education. Penn State also offers Associate Degree and Certificate programs.

Address: 207 Mitchell Building, University Park, PA 16802

Phone: 800-252-3592 or 814-865-5403

Rochester Institute of Technology

www.distancelearning.rit.edu

★ ★
★ ★

Distance learning from a respected university with a technology bent: RIT offers five graduate degrees, three undergraduate degrees, and twelve certificate programs through its distance learning program. RIT serves 2,000 students with 200 distance-learning courses. In fact, RIT has been ranked as the number-3 provider of distance learning in the United States by *Inside Technology Training* magazine. Programs include interesting technology choices such as the Digital Imaging and Publishing concentration and a BS in Electrical/Mechanical Engineering Technology.

Address: 91 Lomb Memorial Drive, Rochester, New York 14623

Phone: 800-225-5748

San Diego State University

www.ces.sdsu.edu

Strong distance learning with solid technology support: The College of Extended Studies at San Diego State offers an interesting mix of standard academic courses and some non-traditional courses focused on adult learners. Five divisions offer courses: Special Sessions, American Language, Professional Development, International Training Center, and Administrative Services. Technologies utilized include video, cable television, computer, and satellite and are supported by the Telecommunications and Information Technology division of SDSU.

Address: 5250 Campanile Drive, San Diego, CA 92182

Phone: 619-594-5821

University of California at Berkeley

www-cmil.unex.Berkeley.edu

★ ★
★ ★

Progressive California university with heavy distance-learning leanings: UC Extension Online is the department of Berkeley that specializes in distance learning. Certificate programs include Hazardous Materials Management and Computer Information Systems. This school offers literally hundreds of courses in a wide variety of disciplines.

Address: Center for Media and Independent Learning, 2000 Center Street, Suite 4, Berkeley, CA 94704

Phone: 510-642-4124

University of Maryland

www.umuc.edu/distance

State university with good variety in its distance-learning offerings: The University of Maryland offers distance learning through its Virtual University. You can get a bachelor's degree in one of 14 areas, such as accounting, behavioral sciences, communications, computer science, English, fire science, and information systems management. You can also earn a master's degree in ten programs including business, international management, computer science, environmental management, and software engineering. This school has a strong commitment to providing resources for people conducting research on distance learning, such as an online assessment center and information on online copyright issues.

Address: 3501 University Blvd. East, Adelphi, MD 20783

Phone: 301-985-7000

University of Phoenix Online

online.uophx.edu

One of the pioneers of full-blown distance-learning degrees: The University of Phoenix was a very aggressive entrant into university degree distance learning, offering MBAs remotely in the 1980s. Since then, it has become one of the most active schools in providing online education. It offers bachelor's and master's degrees as well as certificate programs online in a wide variety of subject areas such as foreign languages, human resource management, purchasing, business, healthcare, and education.

Address: 3157 E. Elwood St., Phoenix, AZ 85034

Phone: 800-765-4922 or 480-921-8014

University of South Africa

www.unisa.ac.za

★★
★★

A self-described mega distance-learning center: UNISA provides degree programs — bachelor's through Ph.D. — in arts, law, education, science, theology, and management sciences to students worldwide. The school, founded in 1873 as the University of the Cape of Good Hope, started exploring distance learning in 1946. The school now serves 120,000 students from all over the world.

Address: P.O. Box 392, Unisa, 0003, South Africa

Phone: +27 12 429-3111

University of Washington

www.outreach.washington.edu

★★
★★

Team of on-staff distance-learning designers: The University of Washington considers itself one of the four top distance-learning schools in the United States. With staff dedicated to designing and delivering quality course material in the distance-learning format, it has created a broad grouping of undergraduate courses and graduate courses in areas such as public health, library media, educational technology, and more.

Address: UW Educational Outreach, 5001 Twenty-fifth Avenue NE, Seattle, WA 98105-4190

Phone: 206-543-2320

University of Wisconsin

learn.Wisconsin.edu

★★
★★

One of the oldest distance-learning organizations in the United States: The University of Wisconsin was one of the first universities in the United States to offer distance learning, back in the 1800s. Engineering gets strong emphasis among the degree programs. The University of Wisconsin system offers a variety of distance-learning courses through its 13 campuses, located throughout the state, including degree programs in Public Administration, Education, Business, and Sociology.

Address: 432 North Lake Street, Madison, WI 53706

Phone: 608-262-3980

Western Governor's University

www.wgu.edu

Associate's degrees and certificates: Using the distance-learning format, this school (which is actually a consortium of schools in several states) deals in associate's or certificate programs in electronic manufacturing technology, software applications, and network administration. It awards degrees based on demonstrated competencies, allowing students to get credit for what they've learned outside of school.

Address: 9136 E. Tenth Place, Denver, CO 80230

Phone: 877-435-7948

Other Sites to Check Out

Lesley College
www.lesley.edu/online_courses.html

National Technological University
www.ntu.edu

New York Institute of Technology
www.nyit.edu/olc

Oklahoma State University
www.osuokc.edu/t&d.htm

Purdue University
www.purdue.edu/distance

University of Calgary
www.ucalgary.ca/cted

University of Colorado
www.colorado.edu/CATECS/distance.html

University of London
www.lon.ac.uk/external

Distance-Learning Information Sites

Many Web sites out there today gather tons of information and links about the topic of distance learning in one place. They are a good starting point for researching your own distance-learning choice, because they gather so many useful links in one place.

Distance-Educator.com

www.distance-educator.com

 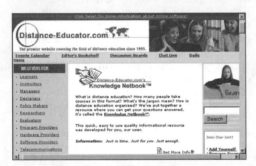

The latest scoop on what's going on in distance learning: This is a wonderful site for both learners and designers of distance learning programs. The Learner section has informational articles and links about topics such as Is Distance Learning for Me?, Getting Your Money's Worth from Distance Education, and an Online Guide to Videoconferencing. One feature spotlights books on distance learning.

Embark

www.embark.com

Clearinghouse for testing, applications, scholarship info, and more: This handy site helps you in the planning phases of your distance learning. Check out their School

Search or a feature called School Matchmaker to find the school for you. This site also has areas with information about test preparation and financial aid. And check out the Apply Online feature for quick applications to schools.

International Centre for Distance Learning

www-icdl.open.ac.uk/icdl

Part of Britain's Open University: The ICDL maintains an online database of resources in distance learning around the world, including courses, teaching organizations, journal articles, conferences, and book abstracts.

LifeLongLearning.com

www.lifelonglearning.com

Online database: This site offers information on distance-learning courses that are available, as well as student resources such as financing for distance learning.

The World Lecture Hall

www.utexas.edu/world/lecture

Extensive listings of international distance-learning providers: This site, run by the University of Texas, has an exhaustive listing of links to pages created by faculty using distance learning worldwide. It also includes special link sections on courses in languages other than English.

Videoconference.com

www.videoconference.com

Everything you ever wanted to know about videoconferencing: This site holds a collection of forums and articles for people interested in videoconferencing. There is no manufacturer alliance going on here, so information is generally objective. Also included are links to related sites and a glossary of videoconferencing terminology.

Videoconferencing for Learning

www.kn.pacbell.com/wired/vidconf/home.html

Connecting videoconferencing with applications in education: A helpful site for understanding the role of videoconferencing in the classroom, including sections on working with compressed video, ideas and examples of how schools are using videoconferencing, and multipoint videoconferencing.

Other Sites to Check Out:

www.dlcoursefinder.com
www.hec.ohio-state.edu/bradshaw/distance.htm
uwex.edu/disted/compvid.html
www.wested.org/tie/dlrn

Distance-Learning Organizations

To find out more about distance learning and what various countries are doing in this area, log onto any of the following Web sites. Many of these sites also have links of related sites that may help you in researching your own distance-learning options.

American Society for Training and Development (ASTD)

www.astd.org

Where the trainers go to learn: This member association caters to professional trainers and those developing training and courseware. Browsing ASTD's different publications and forums gives you a good idea of what those who are delivering distance learning are thinking and talking about.

Phone: 800-628-2783

Distance Education & Training Council

www.detc.org

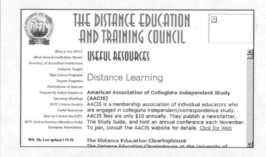

One of the foremost councils overseeing distance-learning activities: The Distance Education and Training Council was formerly known as the National Home Study Council. The association, founded in 1926 as a joint effort of the Carnegie Corporation and the National Better Business Bureau, functions as a clearinghouse for information on remote learning. DETC also sponsors an accrediting agency of its own called, logically enough, the Accrediting Commission of the Distance Education and Training Council.

Phone: 202-234-5100

The Open and Distance Learning Association of Australia (ODLAA)

www.odlaa.org

Based in Australia, but with information of international scope: ODLAA is basically an association of member organizations and individuals who are interested in following what's going on in distance learning. Australia is a country at the forefront of distance learning today, and ODLAA's membership tends to come mainly from the Pacific Rim. The goal of this association is to advance distance learning in Australia and foster communication among distance educators worldwide.

Phone: (02) 6338 4391

Canadian Association of Distance Education (CADE)

www.cade-aced.ca

Help for finding a distance-learning provider in Canada: This organization works to promote the advancement of distance learning in Canada, and publishes the *Journal of Distance Learning.* Probably the most useful aspect of this site to the potential distance learner is the listing and links area where you can see which Canadian schools are involved in distance learning.

Phone: 613-241-0018

Other Sites to Check Out

British Association for Open Learning Ltd.
www.baol.co.uk

European Distance Education Network
www.eden.bme.hu

International Council for Distance Education
www.icde.org

Open and Distance Learning Quality Control
www.odlqc.org.uk/odlqc

Pacific Islands Regional Assocation for Distance Education
www.col.org/pirade

South African Institute of Distance Education (SAIDE)
www.saide.org.za

Financing

Some organizations have sprung up that specialize in financing distance learning. If you think that you'll need some help finding funds when the tuition comes due, you may want to contact these organizations to see what they have to offer.

eStudentLoan

www.estudentloan.com

Loan research and application site: The Loan Finder feature of this site helps you research and compare available loans quickly. After you find the loan that meets your needs, you can also complete applications online.

Key Education Resources

www.key.com/educate

Online lending institution: This part of Key Bank specializes in educational loans, providing both federal and private financing packages. Key CareerLoan is tailored for part-time students of distance learning.

Distance Learning Calculator

sln.suny.edu/admin/sln/original.nsf/
40e29b6d09ba77a88525642d004a0bb4
?OpenForm

Handy financial research tool: Yes, it is worth typing in all the characters in this Web site's address if you want a calculator to help you figure out how much money you can save taking a distance-learning course over a face-to-face course. This tool is also handy for corporate-training folks trying to prove the value of distance learning to their management.

Online Study Tools

If you think the Internet is just one big search engine, think again. The Internet also offers many tools to students, including full-text encyclopedias, searchable dictionaries, and help to improve your writing.

Berkeley Digital Library SunSITE

sunsite.berkeley.edu

Digital library online: This site, created jointly by Sun Microsystems and Berkeley, offers extensive text and image collections, search tools, databases, and lists of teaching and training resources.

Britannica Online

www.Britannica.com

The online version of a venerable publication: With this great resource for online study, you get hot news stories, magazines, and books to browse, as well as a searchable Merriam Webster Dictionary and the entire Encyclopedia Britannica online.

Considering the printed version costs $1,250 and weighs more than a Chevy, this site is a bargain.

Information Please

www.infoplease.com

Centralized research help: Infoplease.com — brought to you by Information Please, a division of Family Education Company — is a great place to access all kinds of research links, databases, and tools. Almanacs, history information, biographies, and current-events stories are available here. This makes a great home page for the avid researcher.

Merriam Webster Dictionary

www.m-w.com/dictionary.htm

Classic dictionary online: You can search for word definitions, play word games, and use features to improve your vocabulary from this site.

MindEdge

www.mindedge.com

Online education directory: This site offers useful tools for students, such as a free e-mail account, search engine for online courses and degree programs, financial aid information, and links for buying textbooks. It also has a useful research section.

ResearchPaper.com

www.researchpaper.com

A great resource for online research: This site includes a writing center with tips for effective writing and an idea directory to help you focus your assignments. The Research Center provides tips and tools for researching online, as well as several pages of searches by topic.

Roget's Thesaurus

www.thesaurus.com

Online thesaurus and more: Word games, an instant text translator, and word of the day — this is not your father's thesaurus! Of course, you can search alphabetically for synonyms for any word you want. But you can also look at words in categories like abstract relations, space, and matter.

StudentOnline

www.studentonline.com

One-stop help for students: This site was just getting underway at the time of writing this book, but it may be worth taking a look at. It offers a personal organizer that can be automatically updated to reflect your classes and other activities. You can access the service remotely with an Internet-ready cell phone or portable organizer device. When a school is signed onto the service (few are, at this point in time), this organizer is automatically updated to reflect the participating school's calendar information.

Personal Development Courses

A great way to get your feet wet with distance learning is to take a course that's strictly for fun or personal enrichment. For one thing, many of these courses are free or very low cost. For another, they give you a glimpse of what to expect of course content and how to communicate in an online classroom setting, preparing you for more serious distance-learning endeavors down the road. Here are a few online training companies to check into.

Virtual University

www.vu.org

Entertaining classes on a variety of topics: Virtual University offers courses in four categories: Internet; Writing and the Arts; Mind, Body, and Soul; and Global Village.

Dear Myrtle

www.ancestry.aol.com/lessons/beginners/ beginners.htm

Online genealogy lessons: Dear Myrtle offers lessons in genealogy techniques, as well as links to many genealogy related articles and sites. A great place for the beginning family-tree researcher to start. And it's all free!

iUniverse

www.iuniverse.com

Writer's University online: iUniverse is a great resource for people who write. Its Writer's University has courses for a wide variety of writing genres as well as information about how to get published.

Metastudies University

www.metastudies.com/

Taking care of your spirit: This online university offers classes in topics such as handwriting analysis, tarot, and astrology. Not your typical university, but the courses are robust and informative and the topics are intriguing.

Dr. Barbara Denny George's Online Instructional Site

www.bdgonline.com/couinpro.htm

Hobbies and educational and family topics: This site is great for family learning, with courses geared towards kids, seniors, and everybody in between.

Gardening & Horticulture

www.acs.edu.au/hort/

Australian gardening tips: Get the latest on herbs, perennials, and more on this Australian-based distance-learning site. It even has some impressive accreditation for its courses, so if you're serious about gardening, this site is for you. Check out the free guide to gardening.

Other Sites to Check Out

Interior Design Classes
 www.met-design.com

Courses for K-12 Teachers
 www.hol.edu

Web Design Classes
 www.webacademy.com

Publications

Several of the books on distance learning are directed at distance learners themselves, as opposed to those developing distance-learning courses. Most of these books consist of detailed directories of distance-learning providers. In addition to books, this section includes some journals dealing with the topic of distance learning, in the event that you who want to read more about what's going on in this area.

Barron's Guide to Distance Learning

Comprehensive school listing: This 530+ page directory updated in 1999 gives a good overview of distance learning, including information about skills needed to succeed, accreditation and transferring credits, and financing. The bulk of the book, however, consists of detailed listings of colleges and universities (most in the United States, but a few overseas) offering courses online. It also provides detailed contact information for schools, as well as information about courses and degree programs available, financial aid, and admission requirements.

Publisher: Barron's Educational Series

Author: Pat Criscito

The Best Distance Learning Graduate Schools

A selection of the best schools for the graduate student: The focus here is on graduate schools. In it's 320 or so pages, this book offers advice on getting admitted to the school of your choice, information about studying abroad, tips on avoiding scams and rip-offs, and a chapter on corporate-sponsored distance learning. Like Barron's book, this is mainly a directory listing programs, admissions policies, and tuition and fee information for 195 accredited schools.

Publisher: The Princeton Review

Authors: Vicky Phillips and Cindy Yager

College Degrees by Mail & Internet

Directory to schools includes international entries: In a compact 205-page book, the authors have profiled 100 schools that offer degrees by home study (which can be a combination of mail, video, teleconference, or online study). A thorough listing of accrediting agencies at the front of the book covers every state in the United States as well as international agencies. Each school listing provides information about fields of study, how to contact the school, year established, and a cost index to give you a general idea of how pricey each school is.

Publisher: 10 Speed Press

Authors: John Bear and Mariah Bear

DEOSNEWS

listserve@psuvm.psu.edu

Free online journal: DEOSNEWS offers the most current take on what's going on in university-level distance learning. To subscribe, send an e-mail to `listserve @psuvm.psu.edu` and include in the subject the phrase **subscribe DEOSNEWS [first name, last name]**.

Publisher: American Center for the Study of Distance Education of Pennsylvania State University

Inside Technology Training

www.trainingsupersite.com/ittrain

Print and online magazine: This magazine offers intriguing articles on what's going on in distance learning with a focus on technology. You can get a free subscription for six months, or read articles online.

Publisher: Bill Communications

The Unofficial Guide to Distance Learning

Insider insights on distance learning providers: Part of Arco's Unofficial Guide series, this book offers a bit more critical look at those providing distance learning courses. The directory of schools included here helps you find a school alphabetically, by location, or by subject. This book also includes advice on choosing the right school and dealing with accreditation and required exams.

Publisher: Arco

Author: Shannon Turlington

Other Publications to Check Out

Videoconferencing: The Whole Picture, Telecom Books
Peterson's 2 Year Colleges 2000, Peterson's Guides
The College Board College International Student Handbook, College Board

Resources for Learners with Disabilities

If you want to take advantage of distance-learning methods to get an education and you has a visual, hearing, movement, or other disability, check into some of these resources. Several offer assistive technology such as speech recognition software or special keyboards. Others are gathering places for people with disabilities and those working to improve their access to education.

Trace Center, University of Wisconsin

www.trace.wisc.edu

Research department of a major university: Part of the School of Engineering at the University of Wisconsin, the Trace Center focuses on developing ways for people with disabilities to access education. Take a look at the discussion forums, product information, and links to other sites of interest.

Computer to Help People, Inc.

www.execpc.com/~chpi

Assistive Technology Center and more: private, nonprofit organization's site dedicated to finding ways to make computers accessible to those with disabilities. This site addresses a wide variety of disabilities with information about computer adaptations that make learning and other activities possible.

Learning Independence Through Computers

www.linc.org

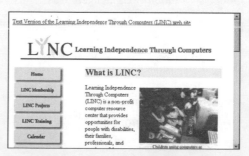

Nonprofit resource center: LINC is a centralized place to get information about how computers are connecting people with disabilities to learning opportunities. Look on this site for information on special projects for learning and disabilities to give you ideas about how people are using computers to overcome physical challenges.

Henter-Joyce, Inc.

www.hj.com

Software for learning: Henter-Joyce is the manufacturer of several of the leading software products for people who have visual impairments or are blind. Their products include Form-Mate, JAWS (Job Access With Speech), and WordScholar to speak and highlight words simultaneously.

Gus Communications, Inc.

www.gusinc.com

Products for mobility challenged: Gus Communications, Inc., gathers together information and products for those with mobility challenges such as people who have experienced a stroke or who have multiple sclerosis or aphasia.

Dragon Systems, Inc.

www.dragonsys.com

Most popular speech-recognition software: Dragon Systems was one of the first mainstream voice-recognition products on the market (as opposed to smaller programs

aimed only at the visually impaired). Dragon has created an easy-to-use product, and it's getting better all the time.

Family Village

www.familyvillage.wisc.edu

Great gathering place: Family Village is a Web community built through the University of Wisconsin for people with disabilities. This site includes areas for educational advocacy, discussion groups, and a library of information.

Other Sites to Check Out

AccessAbility
 www.4access.com

Associated Services for the Blind
 www.libertynet.org/asbinfo

DeafWorldWeb
 www.deafworldweb.org

IBM Accessibility Center
 www.ibm.com/sns

Software Download Sites

Throughout this book, I mention software products and plug-ins that work with other products that you're liable to encounter while learning online. Here's how to find the software and download it online.

Flash

www.macromedia.com/software/flash

Animation-development tool: Many Web developers use Flash (from Macromedia) to produce animation, sounds effects, and interfaces on their Web sites. The Flash Player is available separately and for free so you can view sites created with Flash.

NetMeeting

www.microsoft.com/windows/netmeeting

A free synchronous meeting software product with whiteboard and video capabilities: Microsoft NetMeeting is often built into Windows-based PCs that you buy new, or you can download it from this site.

RealPlayer

www.real.com

Free video and audio player: You can download the bare-bones version of this product from RealNetworks and use it to play most formats of video and audio files.

Stuffit

www.aladdinsys.com

Compression software for Macintosh: In addition to compressing files, Stuffit (from Aladdin Systems) also decodes and converts file formats. The Deluxe version sells for $79.95, but you can download a free demo version for free from this site.

Winzip

www.winzip.com

Compression software for Windows: Winzip, from Niko Mak Computing, costs $29 for an individual copy. However, you can download a trial version for free from this site.

Tucows

www.tucows.com

Grandaddy of shareware sites: This is the site of preference for many computer-savvy people. Tucows has great shareware in many categories and on-target rankings of what's good and what's not. Check the What's Moo section for the latest in shareware.

Other Sites to Check Out

www.download.com
www.lights.com/publisher/freeware/
www.supershareware.com

Technical and Professional Schools

Many schools target training in certain industries or professions, including technical, healthcare, and finance. The schools listed in this section offer programs in the distance-learning format and are accredited by the Distance Education and Training Council (DETC).

American College of Prehospital Medicine

www.acpm.edu

Focus on emergency medical services: If ambulance sirens make your heart go pitter-pat, check out this school. Here you can earn a certificate, associate's degree, or bachelor's degree in emergency medical services.

American Institute for Computer Sciences

www.aics.edu

Technology training online: This school offers courses in computer technology, culminating in either a bachelor's or master's in computer science or a bachelor's in information systems.

California College for Health Sciences

www.cchs.edu

Online studies in health topics: This school offers almost a dozen associate's degrees in topics ranging from Early Childhood Education to EEG Technology and Medical Transcription.

College for Financial Planning

www.fp.edu

Online training for financial wizards: Get your Master of Science with a focus on financial planning from this Colorado-based school.

Hospitality Training Center

www.htcfuturecareers.com

Focus on travel: Take courses that focus on motel management, medical-office computer skills, and home-based travel agencies.

Minneapolis Community and Technical College

www.mctc.mnscu.edu

Online courses with a technical edge: You can take courses online from this school in topics such as biology, chemistry, physics, and pharmacology.

Other Sites to Check Out

Cleveland Institute of Electronics
www.cie-wc.edu

Community College of Philadelphia
www.ccp.cc.pa.us

Florence-Darlington Technical College
www.flo.tec.sc.us

Ivy Tech State College
ivytech7.cc.in.us/distance-education

Testing Services

This section includes some of the organizations that administer standard college-entry tests such as ACT and GRE. You can register for most of these tests online through these Web sites.

American College Testing Program (ACT)

www.act.org

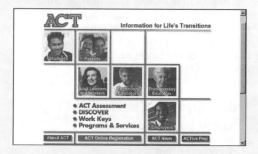

Organization that administers the ACT: The ACT college entrance exam tests in four skill areas: English, mathematics, reading,

and science. You can register for the test on this site and request score reports. The site even includes sample test questions to help you prepare.

Phone: 319-337-1270

College Entrance Examination Board

www.collegeboard.org/clep

Organization that administers the CLEP: The College Level Examination Program (CLEP), enables you to obtain college credit by testing for knowledge you already possess. Visit this site to find out more information about how the program works or to locate a testing center near you.

Phone: 609-771-7865

Educational Testing Service (ETS)

www.ets.org

Organization that administers the GRE: The Graduate Record Examination (GRE) is required by some schools for admission to graduate programs. GRE tests include a General Aptitude Test and Subject Tests that focus on specific areas of study. Count on spending between three and four hours on any GRE test you undertake.

Phone: 609-734-5410

Test of English as a Foreign Language (TOEFL)

www.toefl.org

English-proficiency testing services for international students: If you're a foreign student applying to study in the United States or other English-speaking country, you may be required to prove your English-language competency by taking this test, developed by the Educational Testing Service (ETS). Contact the TOEFL to find out about testing sites and dates worldwide.

Other Sites to Check Out

www.collegeboard.org
www.gocollege.com
www.review.com
www.testprep.com
testing.byu.edu

Textbooks

If you're studying online, you may also want to shop online. Both save time, and sometimes money. Here are some leading bookstores and textbook sites to explore.

Amazon.com

www.amazon.com

Virtual bookstore: One of the first and still one of the best online bookstores, Amazon is strictly virtual. The focus here is on treating customers well, and services such as express ordering and suggested titles of interest based on a customer's buying habits make this a good online buying experience.

B&N.com

www.bn.com

Online bookstore: This is the online counterpart of the bricks-and-mortar bookstores, Barnes and Noble. Except for the cappuccino and comfy armchairs, you can find everything here that the offline stores offers, and more, because everything is in-stock most of the time.

Classbook.com

www.classbook.com

Online textbook store: Classbook.com offers both new and used books, along with a buy-back policy. They claim to have over 555,000 titles (pity the fellow who had to count them). A recent deal offered a 60-minute phone card if you sell them $50 or more worth of books.

efollett.com

www.efollett.com

Online textbook superstore: The focus at efollett.com is on textbooks, both new and used. This site has a special area for medical textbooks. One big advantage to this site is that you can search for a book by the course at your school, in addition to searching by title, author, or ISBN.

Textbooksatcost.com

www.textbooksatcost.com

Textbooks at discount: One unique thing about this site is the book-swap feature that lets you deal directly with other students to find the title you need. Links here lead you to hardware and software specials, as well.

Other Sites to Check Out

bigwords.com
www.ecampus.com
www.etext.net
www.studentadvantage.com
www.textbooksource.net
www.textbooks.com
www.1800student.com

Training Providers

Much of the action today in distance learning doesn't originate behind the walls of university campuses. If you are looking for skills-based training provided online, one of these organizations might fit the bill. Many of these companies teach courses in topics that relate to an exam and certification process, such as those granted by Oracle, PeopleSoft, Novell, and Microsoft.

Click2Learn

www.click2learn.com

Learning portal to various publishers' courses: This site is great for business professionals who want to hone their computer, management, or entrepreneurial skills. Courses are offered online as well as through CD-ROM, video, audio, and books. IT folks can take certification courses including MCSE, Novell, and Oracle. This site even has a section for occupational health and safety courses.

Digital Think

www.digitalthink.com

Online training company focused on technology: DigitalThink has a strong focus on technical computer courses, including programming and networking topics. You can take a free course to experience their product before putting your money down.

Fatbrain.com

www1.fatbrain.com/training/

Online bookstore that also offers courses: Fatbrain.com is a popular online technical bookstore (they also run a lot of bookstores at computer trade shows). Fatbrain.com has stepped into the training arena by offering courses in topics like Java, Novell Netware, and Visual InterDev from Microsoft. You can get the latest on technical certification in the Certification Watch feature on this Web site.

GeoLearning

www.geolearning.com

Online computer training company: GeoLearning has a focus on technical computer courses, as well as safety courses to bring you into OSHA compliance. If you think your company should get into distance learning, check out GeoLearning's Custom Online University, which will "design and host a customized university with your logo and colors" for free. You do pay $50 per user when you access any of their 58 courses, but it's still a pretty good deal.

Headlight

www.headlight.com

A clearinghouse of courses from various publishers: At this site, you can tour a sample class and take advantage of a free skills-assessment feature to help you choose the course that's right for you. Courses include general business topics, desktop computer applications, and IT and network certification.

HungryMinds

www.hungryminds.com

A site that gathers various offerings in one portal: This site claims to offer "a way to learn anything, anytime." What HungryMinds does is sift through what's available and guide you to courses, books, and Web sites that you are likely to find useful.

These folks partner with companies and colleges they consider to be providing good content and lead you to them for free.

Learn2.com

www.learn2.com

Online training company that offers course outlines for review: A little broader than some of the computer-skills focused sites, Learn2.com also has courses for children and soft-skills training. Delivery formats include Web, CD-ROM, and video. Course outlines are available on the Web site for review.

National College

www.nationalcollegeonline.com

Online training company: More of a technical training company than a college, National College offers computer courses with discounts for corporate users. This school has been providing distance-learning solutions for 36 years, but it's keeping up with changes in technology admirably.

Netskills (U.K.)

www.netskills.ac.uk

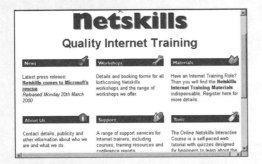

Bringing education to Newcastle: Based out of the University of Newcastle in England, Netskills offers face-to-face courses in Web design and communication at several schools around the U.K.; however, it does

have an online interactive self-paced tutorial on the Web to help those new to the Internet learn how to get around. If you're getting acquainted with the Web while considering distance learning, running through their free tutorial online is a good way to start.

SmartPlanet

www.smartplanet.com

Low-cost online training: SmartPlanet offers low-cost ($9.95 to $19.95) courses in categories such as Body and Mind, Career and Business, Hobbies and Recreation, Finance and Investing, and Science and Technology (everything seems to come in twos on this site!). You can also go the membership route, in which case you pay $15.95 a month or $89.95 a year for unlimited access to what they call standard courses.

THINQ

www.thinq.com

Bringing together business and technology courses from many providers: THINQ (formerly called TraningNet) represents more than 1,200 providers of online courses. It offers audio, video, and CD-ROM courses, as well. The focus here is on business skills and technology, with additional courses in engineering and legal topics.

youachieve.com

www.youachieve.com

Online training company: youachieve.com is in the soft-skills arena, with topics such as negotiating, team building, and presentation skills topping the list of 372 online classes. It offers subscriptions for access to multiple courses, as well as a pay-as-you-go model to learn a course at a time.

University Access

www.universityaccess.com

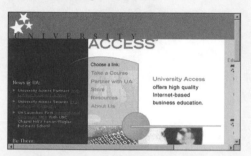

Business courses online: You can take classes in business communications, macroeconomics, marketing, and entrepreneurship at this online business school.

Other Sites to Check Out

online-training.pharoservices.net
www.computraining.co.uk
www.i-training.com
www.msofficeonlinetraining.com
www.pbs.org/als
www.oltraining.com
www.train-online.com

Part VII
The Part of Tens

The 5th Wave   By Rich Tennant

©RICHTENNANT

"Ronnie made the body from what he learned in Metal Shop, Sissy and Darlene's Home Ec. class helped them in fixing up the inside, and then all that anti-gravity stuff we picked up off the Web."

In this part . . .

Condensing the wisdom of the world into ten pithy ideas isn't easy, so I cheated: I created three sets of ten here, which gave me 30 pithy ideas to throw out. In this part, you get a list of ten of the best distance-learning providers and what makes them so special. You also get ten tips for taking distance-learning courses from a school outside your own country. And, finally, you get ten gems of wisdom about how to get along with the other kids in your classes.

So prepare yourself for 30 — count 'em, 30 — of my best ideas, all summed up in easy-to-digest sets of ten.

Chapter 17

Ten Schools to Watch

In This Chapter

▶ Reviewing some of the hottest distance-learning schools

▶ Understanding some trends in distance learning around the world

*1*dentifying ten schools that are doing interesting things in the race to con-quer distance learning is as difficult as choosing the next Kentucky Derby winner. With that in mind, I will tell you my criteria for the choices I've made here.

I don't claim that these are the ten "best" distance-learning schools in the world. Some are simply the best schools in their own country and, therefore, performing an important role in promoting distance learning in one part of the world. Others have an impressive volume of distance-learning courses available. Some schools have intensive research institutes for the develop-ment of distance-learning technology, or have created unique partnerships with businesses that can benefit students. Several schools are here simply because of the high quality of their course materials. In short, each is explor-ing distance learning in a unique and committed way.

By visiting these school's Web sites, you can start to develop a sense of what's available and what well-done distance learning looks like.

For complete contact information and more details about courses of study offered by each of these schools, see the Online Directory section of this book.

University of California at Berkeley

```
www-cmil.unex.Berkeley.eduUC
```

Extension Online (shown in Figure 17-1) is the department of Berkeley that specializes in distance learning. UC Extension online was born in 1996 as a collaboration between Berkeley and the Center for Media and Independent Learning,
which is a distance-learning organization started over 80 years ago. The sheer
breadth of distance-learning offerings here is impressive: 15,000 courses taken
by 400,000 students. Berkeley also has an impressive faculty by any standards:
17 of them have a Nobel Prize collecting dust on their bookshelves.

Figure 17-1:
Try taking
the tour
listed on this
site
(learn.
Berkeley.
edu) to see
how
Berkeley
handles
distance
learning.

University of Wisconsin

```
www1.uwex.edu
```

The University of Wisconsin was one of the first universities in the United
States to offer distance learning back in the 1800s through mail-order courses
created for a land-grant program for farmers. Today, it offers 500 courses

through its Independent Learning Extension (shown in Figure 17-2). You can even obtain a high-school diploma through this division. Engineering seems to get strong emphasis among the degree programs. The University of Wisconsin System offers a variety of distance-learning courses through its 13 campuses, located throughout the state.

Figure 17-2: UW Extension's home page is the place to go to learn more about programs and policies.

Rochester Institute of Technology

distancelearning.rit.edu

Rochester Institute of Technology (RIT) is very dedicated to distance learning, and its research arm has been involved in helping to launch some interesting online-learning technology. RIT has been ranked as the third largest distance-learning degree provider in the United States, with seven graduate degrees, three graduate certificates, and thirteen certificates programs, with an emphasis on science and technology topics. RIT differentiates its approach to learning as having an emphasis on practical application of educational concepts for career technology professionals. Try the mini-course in distance learning, shown in Figure 17-3, to get an idea of how RIT does distance.

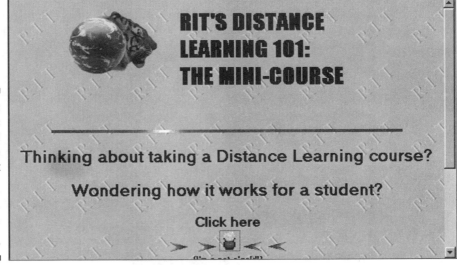

Figure 17-3:
RIT offers
this useful
mini-course
at
www.rit.
edu/
%7E609www/
dl101/
_private.

Charles Sturt University

www.csu.edu.au/de

Charles Sturt University promotes itself as Australia's largest distance-education institution. One of its strengths is a strong student support system; the school makes remote access to the library system, bookstore, and student services available. The university works with the corporate world to create what it calls "industry aligned" curricula, offering professional accreditation in several areas. Almost all of its 2,000 courses are available through distance learning. Charles Sturt University is also committed to continually improving the technology needed to provide cutting-edge distance learning to students worldwide.

Jones International University

www.jonesinternational.edu

Jones International University may not have the same quality of courses as a Berkeley, but it is worth mentioning here because it was the first completely virtual university to gain accreditation. The term *virtual university* means that it has no campus — anywhere. This school has no student union building and no football team. Instead, it is a totally distance-learning focused organization accredited by the North Central Association of Colleges and Schools (NCA), one of six accreditation-granting organizations for colleges in the United States. Jones also has certification from the Global Alliance for Transnational Education, which is an organization that deals with quality assurance for educational programs across nations. This is one university that is setting itself up to be truly global, with a current focus on business-oriented degrees and courses.

UNext/Cardean University

www.cardean.com

This choice was a bit of a stretch, because at the time of the writing of this book, the Cardean University portion of UNext (shown in Figure 17-4) was just starting up. However, this group has some interesting credentials, because they work with academics from the likes of Stanford, Columbia Business School, and The London School of Economics to create virtual college-level courses in the distance-learning format. Courses are both self-paced and interactive, using threaded discussion, e-mail, chat, and student/faculty interaction.

The underlying pedagogy here is to focus on projects, with students solving problem scenarios to learn. According to Michael Moe, an expert on distance learning from Merrill Lynch, UNext is positioned to be "the truly leading Internet university." If money means anything, the $1 million per course that UNext is investing ought to make for some very good learning experiences.

Figure 17-4: UNext offers online courses, and has just started up a subsidiary, Cardean University, which will offer degrees online.

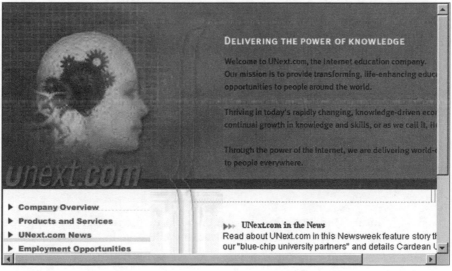

University of Washington

www.outreach.Washington.edu/dl

The University of Washington, which has offered distance learning in various forms since 1912, considers itself one of the top four providers of distance learning in the United States. UW has over 6,500 distance-learning students enrolled, and offers over 270 online courses through UW Online (see Figure 17-5). It has 10 degree programs and 17 certificate programs at the time of this writing, with many more to come in the near future. Through a partnership with the technology-company-down-the-road, Microsoft, UW has created a sophisticated course interface and prides itself on the scope of its library and student support. UW has the largest on-staff team of course designers in the country on tap to convert course material into online material, and consequently the quality of its courses tends to be quite good.

Figure 17-5: This page (outreach. Washington. edu/online) is the main screen for students accessing distance-learning classes and support services at the University of Washington.

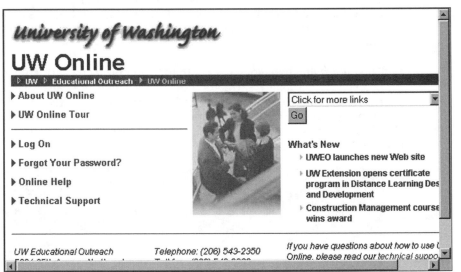

Indira Gandhi National Open University

www.india.edu

Indira Gandhi National Open University, whose Web page appears in Figure 17-6, is driving the distance-learning initiative in India. Although its use of technology may be a few years behind some other schools, IGNOU is in the process of building a distance learning infrastructure that can respond to the demands of one of the most populous countries in the world. In addition to the Internet, IGNOU uses nationwide television broadcast of some materials, as well as both teleconferencing and phone-in-radio counseling services for students. The school focuses on helping the population transition careers as demands for new skills increase, with a modular approach to coursework that adds flexibility in degree concentration.

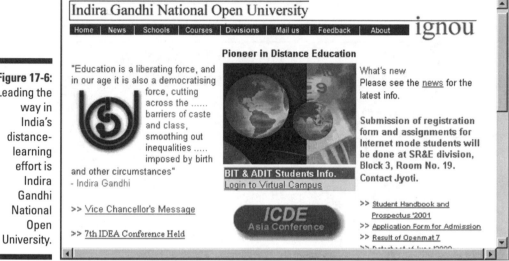

Figure 17-6:
Leading the way in India's distance-learning effort is Indira Gandhi National Open University.

Penn State

`www.outreach.psu.edu`

Penn State works closely with industry to offer distance learning to employees in corporate facilities. Courses in topics such as supply-chain management and engineering acoustics reflect this business focus. Through a grant from AT&T Foundation, Penn State created a major initiative called Innovations in Distance Education to support faculty in exploring advances in distance learning. Penn State's faculty are leading the way in establishing principles and practices for remote learning in conjunction with other distance-learning institutions worldwide.

University of South Africa

www.unisa.ac.za

The University of South Africa calls itself a "mega distance-teaching university." (See Figure 17-7.) In fact, it boasts five learning centers and five provincial centers around South Africa, as well as connections with 450 exam centers around the world to support remote students. The school's involvement in helping to restructure a society in transition in South Africa through its distance-learning efforts makes it an interesting place to study.

Figure 17-7:
The University of South Africa reaches out globally through 450 exam centers worldwide.

Chapter 18

Ten Tips for International Students

. . . .

In This Chapter

▶ Understanding special requirements for foreign students

▶ Dealing with issues of accreditation and credits

▶ Coping with language, customs, and time zones

. . . .

Are you intrigued by foreign locales and exotic accents? Do you find yourself wandering over to the Web sites of universities in Bora Bora, Belize, or Belgium as you consider which alma mater is right for you? Let's face it, distance learning is by definition perfect for studying across borders, because there's no classroom to get to except the one in cyberspace.

If you're contemplating taking courses from a school in a country other than the one in which you reside, you're in for some interesting and challenging situations. The rewards of studying at a foreign school can be great, broadening your outlook towards other cultures at the same time that you earn a degree. But to avoid the problems that can befall a stranger in a strange land, read through these words of wisdom for the international student.

Watch Your Language

The one thing you pretty much have to have to take a course from a foreign school is a command of the language in which the course is taught. Don't kid yourself into thinking that because you seldom, if ever, have to converse with someone in person during an online course, you can get by with makeshift sentences pieced together from a language dictionary. First, you won't have time for that kind of translation exercise, and second, you're likely to come across as an idiot to your instructor and fellow students.

Of course, to some degree, you can think through how you want to phrase something and edit and revise your online communications much more easily than you can on the spot in a regular classroom. But be sure that you have solid proficiency in the language before jumping in. Schools in the United States may require you to take the Test of English as a Foreign Language

(TOEFL, shown in Figure 18-1) to qualify for acceptance to their programs. Other countries use similar language testing before admitting a foreign student whose native language isn't their own. Check with your school to see what they require for language proficiency. See Chapter 11 for advice about dealing with communication challenges in distance learning.

Figure 18-1: Take advantage of tutorials and practice questions offered at the TOEFL Web site (www.toefl.org).

Observe Cultural Differences

A little study on the customs and habits of the country where your school is located can save you grief down the road. You may call your instructor by his first name in California, but don't take that same informality for granted in Japan. You may be encouraged to share personal stories online with fellow students in France, but posting that same personal information may be considered rude in more formal countries.

Travel books often give advice about local customs that you may find useful in your online interactions. Your school may also have an office that supports foreign students (often within the Student Services section of the site) and can give you some tips. Learning about what makes another culture tick is one of the added benefits of foreign study, so attack it with a positive and open-minded outlook.

Plan for and Budget an In-Person Visit

Many distance-learning programs require at least one face-to-face meeting, and that requirement often extends to students from other countries. Be sure to plan for the time and cost involved in such a visit when you create your educational budget (see Chapter 3). Even if a visit is not a requirement, you may want to make the trip anyway. Going to your school once to meet your instructors and some fellow students can help you feel more attuned to your school's country and its language and customs.

If your country provides a tax break for the cost of education, the cost of your trip can probably count towards that credit. Look for travel bargains and ask your foreign-student support office or your school's housing office if you might be able to get inexpensive on-campus accommodation during your stay to save money.

Find Out What Distance Learning Means Overseas

Distance learning programs in the United States place strong emphasis on online work. In England and other countries where phone-access charges are higher and the spread of high-tech equipment is slower, video, audio, and print make up a larger part of the course of study.

Ask questions of the school you're considering to understand the media and methods of learning they depend on most and be sure that's the delivery mechanism that fits your learning style. In most cases, if the school has the content you want, the delivery method is secondary; still, knowledge is power, so ask the right questions before you sign up and end up listening to six years of audiotapes.

Make Allowances for Time Differences

I figured out after the first few months of a distance-learning program I was taking that teleconference meetings always took place at 10 p.m. my time, no matter how often I reminded people that I was three hours ahead and would appreciate making the next meeting at 7 p.m. my time. Nobody on the other coast was home from work at 4 p.m. their time, so my minority vote went ignored.

This inconvenience may just be a reality of distance learning, and you'll probably survive the hassle. But if your country is eight hours ahead of your school, it becomes nearly impossible to find convenient times for live online chats and video or teleconferencing. If the school you're thinking of uses a great deal of real-time interaction in its courses, that may compound the potential problem. Discuss this issue with your instructor before class starts if you have concerns.

Accreditation Is Not Always Equal

Each country has its own system of accreditation, and they're not always compatible. If you take one degree in Country A and then decide to take an advanced degree in Country B, you may have difficulties if Country B doesn't recognize accreditation from Country A.

All you can do here is research the prospective school and make sure that it has solid accreditation in its own country. Look for information about accreditation on the school's Web site or in its catalog. When you find the name of the accrediting agency, locate that agency's Web site and see whether it has any additional information about exchange of credits with other countries.

If you know in advance that you will be seeking your next degree from a school in another country, compare the two countries' accreditation systems up front. Also remember that employers may look with disdain at degrees from poorly accredited schools. For more about accreditation, see Chapter 3.

Prerequisites Aren't All Alike

In the United States, you are quite often required to have a BA before you can take courses towards an MA. In England and Canada, that's not always the case. One country may require extensive testing to enter a program, another may not ask for any testing at all. Bottom line: You may be able to use the differences in prerequisites to get into a program in another country that you didn't think you could qualify for in your own country.

On the other hand, you may be from the country that requires little to get into a school and you're looking at a school in a country that mandates tests, degrees, and a note from the King to get in. Research prerequisites thoroughly and make sure that you can meet the requirements before going to the cost of paying an application fee.

Being a Student Doesn't Make You a Citizen

Many people make the mistake of thinking that if they are studying through a school in a foreign country, they are entitled to stay in that country at some point. Although schools usually help foreign students who are studying on campus to obtain a student visa, distance-learning students don't enjoy the same status. If you're accepted by a foreign school as a distance-learning student, you have no more rights in that country than the average tourist.

Look into Credit Transferability

When is an hour not an hour? When it's a credit hour earned in one country that doesn't have the same value as a credit hour from another. You can find organizations, such as Regents College Credit Bank Service shown in Figure 18-2, that will research credit equivalency for you and provide a transcript that takes into account these differences. These reports summarize all the credit you've earned, whether through testing, job or military training, or taking classes. This transcript is an invaluable tool to provide to prospective employers, especially if you've studied overseas. You can find other such organizations by checking with accrediting agencies in your country.

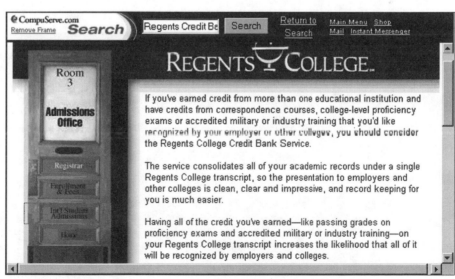

Figure 18-2: Regents College (www.regents.edu) consolidates your learning credit and converts the value of a credit in one country to the currency of another.

Take Advantage of the Experience

Don't let the frustrations you might encounter from functioning in a different language, time differences, or accreditation issues keep you from taking full advantage of the rich experience that studying in another culture can provide:

- ✔ Use the student chat area to ask other students about their lives outside of the online classroom.

- ✔ Form friendships that cross borders and provide contacts for future travel in other countries.

- ✔ Consider the wonderful benefit of improving your foreign language writing skills with all the e-mail you'll be writing.

- ✔ Share your own culture and help your fellow students to benefit from the global nature of distance learning as you do.

Chapter 19

Ten Ways to Get Along Online

. . . .

In This Chapter

▶ Avoiding e-mail abuse

▶ Showing respect in distance learning communications

▶ Steering clear of the illegal and immoral when studying online

. . . .

*W*hen you were just a little tyke, you learned how to behave in a classroom. You were taught to raise your hand if you wanted to speak or leave the room. You were told to share things with your classmates. You learned early on not to interrupt people when they speak and not to throw temper tantrums when you don't get your way.

Well, the online classroom has its own set of rules, rules that govern many of the same kinds of behavior — cyberstyle. In place of body language to give you clues about how those you're communicating with are reacting to your behavior, you can use these ten guidelines for communicating in the distance-learning world.

Don't Flame

Flaming is the equivalent of throwing a hissy fit in third grade. *Flaming* is simply attacking someone with an angry communication, whether that communication is in the form of e-mail or a response in a chat session. Flaming is a rude, destructive, and ineffective way of communicating online. It often involves SHOUTING, which is the practice of using all capital letters in the words you type to add emphasis.

So, am I saying that you can't be honest if you're upset about something that goes on in class? No, I'm not. Building an effective learning community online depends on the members being honest with each other. But there's a difference between the abusive tirade sent in the heat of the moment and a well-thought-out expression of concern, frustration, or even anger.

Whenever you find yourself writing an emotion-packed online communication, step back and disconnect from the Net for a while. Come back later, when you're calmer and more in control. If you're participating in a chat and can't leave at that moment, make a note of your point of contention and deal with it in a later posting or send an e-mail directly to the person who is upsetting you.

Don't Spam

For our purposes, spam isn't a luncheon meat, or the tool of shady Internet companies trying to sell you Austin Powers paraphernalia. I'm extending the meaning of *spam* to mean an unwelcome barrage of irrelevant communications towards your fellow students.

Because your online learning community could include several dozen people, sending that entire group an ad for your business services, a chain letter, or anything else that has nothing to do with class is an abuse of distance-learning communication. If you can't stop yourself from communicating about things not relevant to the course, or if, in the interests of community building, you feel some personal topic might be of interest to your fellow students, consider posting a message in a student lounge area of your course site. That way, you leave it up to your classmates to read the posting or not.

Respect Others' Time

Everybody's busy, and the people you encounter in a distance-learning setting are even busier. Here's a checklist of things you can do to show respect for your classmates' and instructor's time:

- ✔ **Be on time:** If your class is having a chat session or videoconference at a specific time, be prompt.
- ✔ **Be brief:** Always keep your communications concise and to the point.
- ✔ **Submit assignments on time:** Many online assignments require that other students review your comments and post a response. If you're two days late, you quite simply screw up their schedules.
- ✔ **Be alert to time zone differences:** Don't set a discussion with a study group at eight o'clock at night if some people live in a time zone three hours ahead of you.

Think Before You "Speak"

Keeping your temper in check and not flaming are important, but remember that not all inappropriate communication is angry. You have to be just as careful not to embarrass people, not to make inappropriate sexual innuendos to others, and not to hurt people's feelings with thoughtless or discriminatory remarks. Remember, you can't see your classmates, but there are likely to be people of many races, backgrounds, and levels of ability or disability in your class. Behave accordingly.

The wonderful thing about e-mail is that you can go back and edit it a few times before you send it. Always take a moment before you hit that Send button to be sure you feel comfortable with what you've written.

Don't Monopolize the Airwaves

In a face-to-face classroom, you always have some people who never raise a hand and a few who never stop making bids for the instructor's attention. The same is true online, except that a bell doesn't ring after an hour, mercifully sending everybody home. In many distance-learning settings, you are required to read everybody else's postings, and that can take a lot of time. If you see your own name popping up more than most other people's, try to consolidate some of your comments into fewer e-mails, or wait a bit and let somebody else make the point this time. Walk the fine line between participating enough to contribute and get a good grade, and monopolizing every discussion.

Watch e-breviations

Unlike your usual circle of friends, members of an online class can be very diverse. They may come from different cultures, different generations, and have different levels of Internet savvy. If you're used to using Internet shorthand, sometimes called *emoticons,* to express yourself, consider leaving them out of your distance-learning communications.

Just in case you're not sure what an emoticon or online abbreviation is, here are a few examples:

:)	Smile
:(	Frown
;-)	Wink
:o	Mouth open in amazement
:{)	Smile by someone with a moustache
LOL	Laughing out loud
BTW	By the way
IMHO	In my humble opinion

Instead of relying these techie conventions, become more adept at expressing your feelings by working at becoming a better writer. And don't worry that that's too much effort for one little class: Good writing is a skill you'll use in every walk of life. After all, Shakespeare didn't have smiley faces, but when you read his plays, you realize that his mastery of language made him the master of emotion.

Plagiarism: The Dark Side of Cut-and-Paste

Because cutting and pasting text from online articles or even other people's e-mails is so simple, stepping into the realm of plagiarism is all too easy online. The practice of citing sources and giving credit to others' ideas that comes into play when writing a term paper extends to online words. If you copy something from another person's e-mail and include that material in an e-mail of your own, use brackets (<< >>) to indicate that this text is from another person, as in the e-mail shown in Figure 19-1.

Always provide proper credit when you pass an online article that you have saved on to others or when you cut and past material from an article into an e-mail or discussion group. Include such information as the author's name, the publication or site the article appeared in, and the date.

Remember that a paragraph passed on in an e-mail may not land you in jail; but if a fellow student decides to quote what you represented as your comment in an article a year later and the original author sees it, you could be in trouble. Bottom line: You never know where an online communication will end up, so behave accordingly.

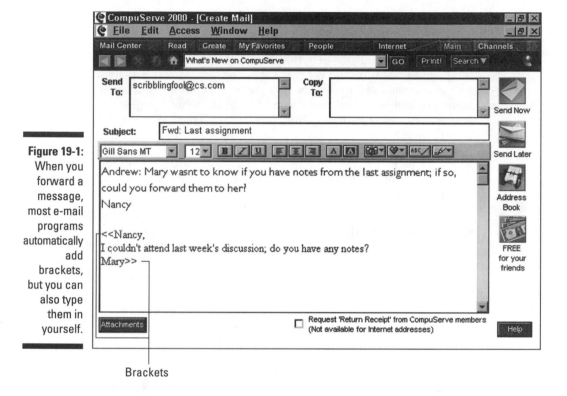

Figure 19-1:
When you forward a message, most e-mail programs automatically add brackets, but you can also type them in yourself.

Brackets

Don't Cheat

Many educators worry that distance learning is just an open invitation to cheating. Students can have other people do their work and even participate in online discussions for them with no one the wiser. Tests are always take-home (and you know how much your high-school teachers thought of that practice!).

Cheating is disrespectful to your instructor, but it's also disrespectful to your classmates who aren't cheating. Because distance learning tends to be so student-driven, and interaction among students is so important to its success, misrepresenting yourself in that interaction is like lying to a friend. And, if you don't do the work, you don't learn. So, who are you cheating but yourself?

Make What You Write Easy to Read

If you're forwarding an e-mail that's already made the rounds, save your recipients some time and get rid of the long header that lists every pit stop on the Information Superhighway. If you're responding to a particular comment, cut and paste just that comment, not the whole, long-winded e-mail, and place it below your response, in brackets. Try these other tips for easy-to-read e-mail:

✔ Consider checking the font your email uses and set it up to use a cleaner looking font, and perhaps a slightly larger type size. Just compare the readability in Figures 19-2 and 19-3. 'Nuff said.

✔ Choose a sans-serif font for readability. Serifs are those little flags you see coming off the top of letters like "l" and "P" in a font like Times New Roman. They are useful in longer documents like books and reports to speed the reader's eye along, but they are a bit busier than sans-serif fonts such as Arial. For short communications like e-mails, sans serif may be easier to read.

✔ Avoid obscure fonts that another person's e-mail program may not be able to read, such as Marigold or Perpetua Titling MT. Times New Roman, Helvetica, and Arial are dependable old standbys.

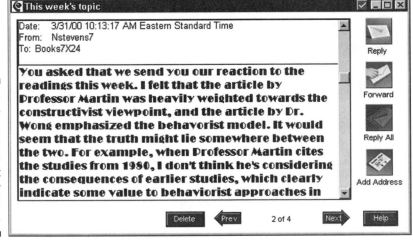

Figure 19-2: Broadway may be a great white way, but it's also a font that's really hard to read in e-mail.

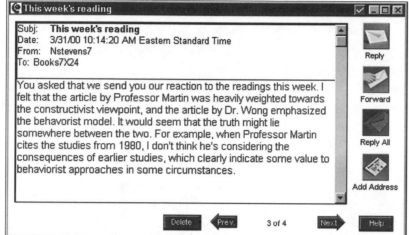

Figure 19-3:
Arial is a simple, easy-to-read font.

✓ Avoid script fonts, which can be difficult to read on screen.

✓ Avoid use of colored text except for emphasis.

✓ Don't make e-mail too lengthy; a couple of pages is absolutely the max for this medium. If you have to communicate something lengthier, create and attach a word-processed document.

Be Patient

Online time isn't always the same as offline time. Just because you send an e-mail or made a posting to an online discussion today doesn't mean that you'll have an answer first thing tomorrow. Give people a little time to respond, and if you need to nudge them for a reply, do it nicely.

Glossary

● ●

academic adviser: Member of a school's faculty who works with a student to plan a degree program.

academic year: Time period that constitutes a year of study at a college, usually consisting of two or three semesters and occurring within a one year period. In the United States, for example, the academic year usually runs from late August through July, including a summer session.

accreditation: Recognition by an agency that an institution meets a set of educational standards. Accreditation is typically standardized across different agencies so that recognized academic credits from a school accredited by one agency will be recognized by schools accredited by another agency.

accrediting agency: A private organization that regulates an established set of standards and recognizes educational institutions as meeting those standards. Accrediting agencies may or may not be recognized by an official body, such as the U.S. Department of Education.

adaptive technology: Technology that has been adapted for use by people with disabilities. A browser with screen-reading technology added is an example of an adaptive technology.

American College Testing (ACT): An organization that administers standardized college admission tests given to students at the high-school level in the United States.

American Council on Education: A private organization that analyzes college-level credit equivalencies for corporate and military education.

assistive technology: A technology used to assist people with disabilities, such as screen magnifier software for visually impaired computer users.

associate's degree: A college-level degree typically granted by a community, technical, or junior college upon completion of approximately 64 credit hours.

asynchronous: Events occurring at different times. In distance education, asynchronous communication occurs when one student posts a message on a bulletin board and another student or instructor responds to that message at a later time.

audit: To take a college-level course without receiving any credit.

bachelor's degree: A degree granted by a college or university when a student has completed approximately 128 semester hours, usually consisting of a four-year course of study.

bandwidth: The capacity of a computer to handle a volume of transmission. The greater the bandwidth, the faster information can be downloaded from a Web site to a computer.

broadband: High-speed transmission of data (such as transmission over a T1 line).

browser: A software program used to navigate the Internet and display Web pages. Internet Explorer and Netscape Navigator are examples of browsers.

bulletin board: An online message board where users can post a message and respond to others' messages asynchronously.

captioning: Words placed at the bottom of a computer or television screen to enable people with impaired hearing to understand the contents of the audio portion of a show or presentation. Formats for captioning include CAN, CART, closed, digital, and real-time.

certificate: Credential awarded on completion of a program of courses that does not result in a degree, but educates students in a specific area of study. Completion of such a program typically carries with it CEUs (continuing education units).

certification: A professional credential awarded as the result of passing an examination in a topic, such as computer networking. Someone who obtains certification is considered certified in that topic.

chat: A synchronous (real-time) method of communication over the Internet, an intranet, or LAN. People chat by typing messages to each other and reading those messages in a *chat room.*

chat room: A location on a Web site which people can access and communicate with each other in real time.

College Level Examination Program (CLEP): A testing program for knowledge gained outside the classroom. Colleges and universities grant college-equivalency credits based on an individual's test scores.

comprehensive exam: In the United Kingdom, schools give this exam as the culmination of a degree program.

compressed file: A file in which data is encoded in a way that causes it to take up less space.

computer-based training (CBT): a training program stored on and accessed from a CD-ROM.

Continuing Education Unit (CEU): Recognition given for completion of non-credit college courses. Most corporations, schools, and military organizations recognize CEUs as evidence of educational accomplishment. One CEU equals approximately ten hours of study.

credential equivalency: Recognition of credits taken at one institution as being equal to credit from some other institution, especially from one country to another.

credit: A unit that represents completion of a college course. Colleges usually grant credit in increments ranging from one credit to five credits.

curriculum: The set of courses you must take in order to meet the requirements of a particular degree program.

diploma: A certificate awarded for the completion of a degree program.

discussion: Distance learners may hold a discussion through a chat, bulletin board, group-meeting software, or teleconference; using text messages or voice; and in asynchronous or synchronous mode.

dissertation: A substantive written, research-based report on a topic usually prepared for a college-level doctorate program.

Distance Education and Training Council (DETC): A national agency in the United States that accredits distance-learning courses and programs.

distance learning: Learning in which the student and instructor are remote from each other. Distance learning can include one or more of the following media: correspondence courses by mail, audio and videotapes, teleconferencing, videoconferencing, faxing, and use of the Internet to disseminate and exchange information.

doctorate: An advanced degree granted for post-graduate university study. Doctorates include PhD, Ed.D, J.D., M.D. and so on.

download: To transmit files from an online source to the hard drive of a computer or other storage medium (such as a floppy disk).

elective: Courses that aren't required, but which you may take towards the total credit required to obtain a degree.

face-to-face: Traditional classroom setting where students and the instructor are in the same room.

file format: The structure of a file related to the software program it was created or saved in.

grade-point average: The average of all grades of classes that a student takes in a course of study.

Graduate Management Aptitude Test (GMAT): A college proficiency exam typically taken to get into an MBA program.

Graduate Record Examination (GRE): A standardized test of math and verbal aptitude, which many institutions require for admission to graduate level study.

graduate study: College level courses for students who have already obtained an undergraduate degree.

grant: A form of financial aid in which a student is not expected to repay the grantor.

independent study: A course of study customized for a student which is largely student-driven. Independent-study students are not typically required to complete courses on a semester basis.

Internet Service Provider (ISP): A company or organization that provides access to the Internet.

lab fee: A fee paid by a student for access to a computer or other technology facility of a university.

learning contract: An agreement between a learning institution and a student specifying a customized study program a student will follow and what credits and/or degree the institution will award upon successful completion of the work.

learning portal: An organization that provides access to multiple educational providers on its Web site.

liberal arts: A type of institution or degree program that provides a broad-based education in traditional topics such as literature, art, mathematics, and science.

Lifetime Learning Credit: A provision of the United States tax code that allows adult learners to claim a tax deduction for a percentage of tuition.

low-residency: Study at the university level which takes place primarily from a remote location, but does require some face-to-face classroom interaction.

major: The main focus of study in a degree-granting program at the university level.

master's degree: A degree that students with a bachelor's degree can obtain upon completion of a program of study typically lasting from one to three years.

mentor: A member of the faculty who works with a student to provide guidance and instruction in the topic of focus. Also a person in a work setting who provides guidance and training to another.

minor: A secondary area of concentration incorporated in the design of a degree major.

noncredit: A course taken without formal credit being awarded. Noncredit courses often carry continuing education units (CEUs), which signify to employers that you have completed coursework.

nonresident: A student at a university who does not live on campus.

open admission: A system of admission to a university that is not constrained to the semester timeline; with open admission, a student can begin a program at any time during the year.

orientation: An initial class or program meeting to provide general information about procedures and class work. In distance learning, attendance at an in-person orientation session is sometimes required.

pass/fail: The grading system for a course that offers no specific letter or number grade, but only the option of failing or passing the course based on a single level of acceptable performance. Pass/fail courses result in credit, but they are recorded as P/F on a student's transcript.

PDF (portable data format): The format of a file saved with document-exchange software from Abobe called Acrobat.

PhD: The highest level university degree. See also *doctorate.*

plug-in: A software program that works with another software program to add more functionality to it.

post: The term used for placing a message in an online communications area called a bulletin board or discussion group.

prerequisite: A course that a student must take before taking a more advanced course.

proctored exam: An exam setting where a student is monitored while taking the test. In distance learning, some organizations set up remote proctored exam scenarios to accommodate distance learners.

regional accrediting agency: One of several regional agencies in the United States that sets standards for educational quality and coordinates those standards with other regional agencies for consistency among schools.

registrar: The department in a university that handles student applications and enrollment. The term also refers to the person in charge of that department.

registration: The act of enrolling in a course or program, including the payment of any fees.

rolling admissions: An admissions system that allows students to register at any time during the calendar year. See also *open admissions*.

scholarship: A form of financial aid, often given based on merit, that the student does not have to repay.

screen-reader software: Any software product that converts text into spoken language to assist visually impaired computer users.

search engine: A program that enables you to search for information on the Internet. Yahoo! and Excite are well-known search engines.

semester: A period of time (usually approximately 16 weeks) during which college students take and complete courses. Most institutions have two semesters per academic year, and possibly a third summer semester.

standardized test: One of several tests, such as GMAT and ACT, given to evaluate a student's ability to handle college-level work required for admission to many colleges. These tests meet certain approved standards for educational testing.

Student Aptitude Test (SAT): A standardized test for college admissions, typically given to high-school students in the United States.

syllabus: An outline of all the lectures, exams, and assignments that make up a course.

synchronous: Communication that occurs in real time. In distance learning, chat would be an example of synchronous communication, because individuals are posting and replying to messages at one time.

teleconference: A phone meeting where several parties from different locations can participate at once, often by means of special speaker-phone units.

Test of English as a Foreign Language (TOEFL): A standardized test of competency in English that some colleges require for foreign-student applications.

thesis: A document that master's degree candidates produce as a final project for a graduate-level course.

transcript: The official record of a student's educational courses, credits, and grades.

transfer: In educational terms, students or course credits that are moved from one institution to another.

tuition: The fees you pay to take a course from an institution, which may include a course fee, lab fees, and fees for support services.

undergraduate: Study at the bachelor's degree level. Also refers to the student studying at this level.

upload: To copy a file to a Web site where others can access and read or download it.

videoconference: A communications session among people at remote locations utilizing video and audio technologies.

Web-based training (WBT): Training materials stored on a Web site that a student accesses and uses online.

whiteboard: A feature of online meeting software that enables participants in remote locations to draw or write on a "board" and have this work visible to all participants.

work-study: A form of financial assistance that allows a student to work part-time while studying. Often, this work takes place at the university itself, and the money students earn goes towards paying tuition.

zip: To compress the data in a file. Zipped files are smaller and therefore take less time to send as attachments over the Internet.

Index

• A •

academic calendar, 44, 46
academic performance, proof of, 253
accessibility aides, 93
accessibility features, setting up
    Windows', 94–96
accessibility standards, 91–92
accreditation, 44, 49
  accreditors, 51–53
  international students, 272
  overview, 50
  value of, 53–54
accreditors, 51–53
ACTs, 122
adaptive technology, 93
Adobe Acrobat Reader, 77
advisors, 183, 185
alumni connections, 251
Amazon, D-20
American College of Prehospital
    Medicine, D-18
American College Testing Program, D-20
American Institute for Computer
    Sciences, D-18
American Society for Training and
    Development, D-9
Apple QuickTime, 77
application and registration fees, 58
application essay, 128
application form, 126–128
applying to schools
  application essay, 128
  application form, completing, 126–128
  entrance tests, standardized, 122
  fees, 58
  overview, 121–122
  prior education, accounting for,
    124–125
  references, 126
assignments, 161, 170
  deadlines, 202–203
assistive technology, 93
asynchronous communication, 17, 157
Athabasca, D-3
audiotapes, 111–112
Australia, 13

• B •

bachelor's degree, foreign equivalents
    of, 125
back pain, computer-induced, 117
Barnes and Noble, D-20
Barron's Guide to Distance Learning
    (Criscito), 36, D-14
Berkeley Digital Library SunSITE, D-11
Best Distance Learning Graduate Schools
    (Phillips and Yager), 36, D-14
books online, 228
bookstore and textbook sites
  Amazon, D-20
  Barnes and Noble, D-20
  Classbook, D-21
  Click2Learn, D-21
  Digital Think, D-21
  efollett, D-21
  Fatbrain, D-22
  GeoLearning, D-22
  Headlight, D-22
  HungryMinds, D-22
  Learn2, D-22

bookstore and textbook sites *(continued)*
  National College, D-22
  Netskills, D-23
  SmartPlanet, D-23
  Textbooksatcost, D-21
  THINQ, D-23
  University Access, D-23
  youachieve, D-23
Britannica Online, D-11
browsers, 72, 83
budget
  application and registration fees, 58
  CEUs, 58
  extras, 59–60
  tuition, 57
built-in help systems, 237
bulletin boards. *See* discussion groups

• *C* •

cable modem, 75
California College for Health
    Sciences, D-19
Canada, 14
Canadian Association of Distance
    Education, D-10
Cardean University, 162, D-4, 265
career advancement, 256
career fairs, 251
career workshops, 251
catalogs, school, 41
CBT materials, 242
CD-ROM drive, 72
certificate programs, 14
certification training, 15, 33–34
CEUs, 54
  budget, 58
chairs, computer, 117
Charles Sturt University, D-4, 264

Charter Oak State College Credit
    Banking, 124
chat rooms, 157, 159
  overview, 176–177
  tips for, 177
chatting, 157, 159
cheating, 279
citizenship, international students not
    entitled to, 273
Classbook, D-21
CLEP, 46
Click2Learn, 14, D-21
College Degrees by Mail & Internet (Bear
    and Bear), 36, D-14
College Entrance Examination
    Board, D-20
College for Financial Planning, D-19
College Level Examination Program, 46
college-level courses, 28
  community colleges, 29
  four-year colleges and universities,
    28–29
  international schools, 30–31
college-level credit hours, 54
colleges and universities
  Athabasca, D-3
  Cardean University, D-4
  Charles Sturt University, D-4
  Indiana University, D-4
  Indira-Gandhi National Open
      University, D-4
  Jones International University, D-5
  Open University, D-5
  Penn State, D-5
  Rochester Institute of Technology, D-5
  San Diego State University, D-6
  University of California at Berkeley, D-6
  University of Maryland, D-6
  University of Phoenix Online, D-6
  University of South Africa, D-7
  University of Washington, D-7

University of Wisconsin, D-7
Western Governor's University, D-7
comments online, inappropriate, 277
communication skills
  evaluating, 191
  global community and, 193
  guidelines for, 192
  writing, 187–190
communication tools, 19, 20
company time, employer-provided
      training during, 246
computer labs, 244
computer system requirements
  browsers, 72
  CD-ROM drive, 72
  DVD-ROM drive, 72
  memory, 71
  modem, 71
  operating system, 71
  processor speed, 71
  RAM, 71
  recommendations for, 73
  ROM, 71
  sound card, 72
  video cards, 72
Computer to Help People, Inc., D-16
computer-mediated distance education.
      See distance learning
conflict resolution, 195
constructivist learning, 162
contacts, school, 143–144
cost of education, 44
course material, viewing, 165–166, 168
courses, 46–47
  adding, 132–133
  changing, 132–133
  choosing, 129–132
  dropping, 132–133
credentials, professional, 56
credit
  CEUs, 54
  college-level credit hours, 54

recognition of, 54
transferability, international students
      and, 273
criteria for choosing a school, 43
  academic calendar, 44, 46
  cost of education, 44
  courses, 46–47
  quality of education, 47–49
CTD, 116
cultural differences, international
      students observing, 270
cultural experiences, international
      students and, 274
Cumulative Trauma Disorders, 116
cybercasts, 180

• D •

database software, 80
Dear Myrtle, 16, D-13
degrees, earning, 12, 14
delivery method of information for
      international students, 271
DEOSNEWS, D-15
desktop videoconferencing, 178–180
Digital Think, D-21
directories, 36
disabled computer users
  accessibility features, setting up
      Windows', 94–96
  accessibility standards, 91–92
  Display settings, adjusting Windows', 97
  DO-IT program, 107
  hardware for, 102–106
  keyboards for, 102
  magnification software, 101
  mouse for, 103–104
  printed text, magnification of, 105–106
  printers for, 103
  school support for, 106
  screen reader programs, 100–101
  speech recognition software, 98–99
  TTY system, 104

disabled learners' resources
  Computer to Help People, Inc., D-16
  Dragon Systems, Inc., D-16
  Family Village, D-17
  Gus Communications, Inc., D-16
  Henter-Joyce, Inc., D-16
  Learning Independence Through
    Computers, D-16
  Trace Center, University of
    Wisconsin, D-15
discounts, student, 146–147
discussion board, 19
discussion groups
  composing messages, 175–176
  overview, 174
  sorting messages, 175
discussions, monopolizing, 277
Display settings, adjusting Windows', 97
distance education. *See* distance
    learning
Distance Education & Training Council,
    51, D-9
distance learning
  communication tools, 19–20
  defined, 11
  length of time for degree/certificate, 23
  overview, 17
  personality types and, 21–24
  self-directed learners, 23
  student-driven learning, 19
  technological advances and, 17, 19
  time commitment to, 21–22
Distance Learning Calculator, D-11
Distance-Educator, 28, D-8
distance-learning information sites
  Distance-Educator, 28
  Embark, D-8
  International Centre for Distance
    Learning, D-8
  LifeLongLearning, D-8

Videoconference, D-9
Videoconferencing for Learning, D-9
World Lecture Hall, D-8
distance-learning organizations
  American Society for Training and
    Development, D-9
  Canadian Association of Distance
    Education, D-10
  Distance Education & Training
    Council, D-9
  Open and Distance Learning
    Association of Australia, D-10
DO-IT program, 107
downloading files, 209
Dr. Barbara Denny George's Online
    Instructional Site, D-14
drag lock, 104
Dragon NaturallySpeaking, 99
Dragon Systems, Inc., D-16
DSL, 74–75
DVD-ROM drive, 72

• E •

e-mail, 85
  as supplies for class, 142
  overview, 172
  readability of, 280–281
  self-paced courses, help for, 237
  settings, 172, 174
  when to use, 159–160
Educational Testing Service, D-20
efollett, D-21
Embark, D-8
emoticons, 277–278
employer-provided training
  CBT materials, 242
  company time, during, 246
  computer labs, 244
  human resources department, 242

military organizations, 244
office hours, during, 246
overview, 241–242
third-party vendors, 245
training department, 242
WBT materials, 242
workgroups, 247
employers
  tuition reimbursement, 60–61
  view of distance education, 255
England, 13
entrance tests, standardized, 122
ergonomics, 115–117
essays
  application essay, 128
  tests, on, 224
eStudentLoan, D-10
etiquette, e-mail. *See* netiquette
etiquette, videoconferencing, 181–182
European Association for Distance
    Learning, 51
Excel, 80
extras, budgeting for, 59–60
eye strain, 116–117

• F •

face-to-face meetings, 135
facility-based videoconferencing, 178
Family Village, D-17
Fatbrain, D-22
fax equipment, 85
feedback, 183
fees, 58, 133
file formats, 213
files
  downloading, 209
  formats, 213
  zipping, 209–213
FilterKeys, 95

financial Web sites
  Distance Learning Calculator, D-11
  eStudentLoan, D-10
  Key Education Resources, D-10
FirstFlight, 16
flaming, 275–276
Flash, 77, D-17
flat-bed scanners, 86
four-year colleges and universities, 28–29
fraud, 55
  credentials, 56
  online training companies, 56–57
  university, attending, 55

• G •

games, 228
Gardening & Horticulture, D-14
GeoLearning, D-22
global community, communication skills
    and, 193
GMATs, 122
grants, 63–64
GREs, 122
group videoconferences, 180
guidance, 147
Gus Communications, Inc., D-16

• H •

hands, stress to, 116
headhunters, 256
Headlight, D-22
Henter-Joyce, Inc., D-16
Home Page Reader, 100
home setup, 109
  audiotapes, 111–112
  change, coping with, 114–115
  location, finding, 110
  phone use, 110–111

home setup *(continued)*
  support from family and friends, 113
  time constraints, 112–113
  videotapes, 111–112
home-based careers, 257
Hospitiality Training Center, D-19
HungryMinds, D-22

• *I* •

in-person visits for international
    students, 271
Indiana University, D-4
Indira-Gandhi National Open
    University, D-4
Information Please, D-11
Inside Technology Training, D-15
instructors, 162
  feedback, 183
  interaction with, 182
interaction, 171. *See also* chat rooms;
    discussion groups; e-mail;
    videoconferencing
  advisor, with, 183, 185
  feedback, 183
  instructors, with, 182
  questions, asking, 182
interactive courses, 228
International Centre for Distance
    Learning, D-8
international schools, 30–31
international students, tips for, 269–274
Internet connections, 73
  cable modem, 75
  DSL, 74–75
  ISDN, 74–75
  modem, 75
Internet Service Providers. *See* ISPs
ISDN, 74–75

ISPs, 81–83
iUniverse, D-13

• *J* •

JAWS for Windows Screen Reader, 100
Jones International University, 14, 245,
    D-5, 264–266

• *K* •

Key Education Resources, D-10
keyboards for disabled computer
    users, 102
keyword search, 205
keywords, 206–207

• *L* •

language proficiency for international
    students, 269–270
Learn2, D-22
learning communities
  conflict resolution, 195
  online citizen, becoming a better,
    194–195
  overview, 193
  workgroups, 195
learning hubs, 14
Learning Independence Through
    Computers, D-16
learning portals, 14
lecture information, 160
library, 145–146
life experience credit, 185
LifeLongLearning, D-8
Linux, 74
loans, 61–62

logging on, 152–155, 163–164
Lotus 1-2-3, 80
Lotus cc:mail, 85
LP-Deluxe Magnification, 101

• *M* •

Macintosh, PC compared, 74
MAGic, 101
magnification software, 101
marketing
  credentials, publicizing, 256–257
  school resources used for, 250–252
measured access, 83
memory, 71
Merriam Webster Dictionary, D-11
Metastudies University, 16, D-13
Microsoft Internet Explorer, 83
Microsoft Outlook, 85
Middle States Association of Colleges
    and Schools, 52
military distance education, 244
MindEdge, D-12
Minneapolis Community and Technical
    College, D-19
modem, 71, 75
motivation, 203–204, 216
mouse for disabled computer users,
    103–104
multimedia courses, 228
multiple choice questions, 223, 232

• *N* •

National College, D-22
natural language interface, 205
netiquette, 275–279, 281
NetMeeting, 17, 77, 180, D-17
Netscape Messenger, 85
Netscape Navigator, 83
Netskills, D-23

New England Association of Schools and
    Colleges, 52
North Central Association of Colleges
    and Schools, 52
Northwest Association of Schools and
    Colleges, 52

• *O* •

office hours, employer-provided training
    during, 246
on-campus orientation, 136
online access, steps for, 81–83, 85
online citizen, becoming a better,
    194–195
online classroom experiences
  assignments, 161, 170
  chatting, 157, 159
  course material, viewing, 165–166, 168
  e-mail, 159–160
  help, 168–169
  instructor and, 162
  lecture information, 160
  logging on, 152–155, 163–164
  online discussions, 156–157
  overview, 151–152
  posting messages, 160
  progress, checking your, 169–170
  resources, 168–169
  syllabus, viewing, 155–156
  threaded discussions, 156–157
online discussions, 156–157
online payment, 134
online research
  files, downloading, 209
  overview, 204
  search engines, 205–208
  searches for schools, 37–38
  Web navigation, 208
  zipping files, 209, 211–213
online rush hour, 201

online study habits. *See* study habits
online study tools
  Berkeley Digital Library SunSITE, D-11
  Britannica Online, D-11
  Information Please, D-11
  Merriam Webster Dictionary, D-11
  MindEdge, D-12
  ResearchPaper, D-12
  Roget's Thesaurus, D-12
  StudentOnline, D-12
online training companies, 32–33, 56–57
Open and Distance Learning Association
    of Australia, D-10
open education. *See* distance learning
Open University, D-5
operating system, 71
orientation
  face-to-face meetings, 135
  on-campus orientation, 136
  small group interaction, 136–137

• *P* •

paper-fed scanners, 86
passwords, 152–155
patience while online, 281
payment. *See* tuition
PC, Macintosh compared, 74
Penn State, D-5
personal development courses
  Dear Myrtle, D-13
  Dr. Barbara Denny George's Online
    Instructional Site, D-14
  Gardening & Horticulture, D-14
  iUniverse, D-13
  Metastudies University, D-13
  Virtual University, D-13
personality types, 21–24
Peterson's Guide to Distance Learning
    Programs 2000, 36
phone support, 237

plagiarism, 278
plug-ins, 76–78
poor test grades, 225
posting
  assignments, 161
  messages, 160
PowerPoint, 80
prerequisites for international
    students, 272
presentation software, 80
printed information, 138
printed text, magnification of, 105–106
printers for disabled computer
    users, 103
prior education, 124–125
procedures tests, 232
processor speed, 71
proctored exams, 219–220
publications
  Barron's Guide to Distance Learning
    (Criscito), D-14
  Best Distance Learning Graduate Schools
    (Phillips and Yager), D-14
  College Degrees by Mail & Internet
    (Bear and Bear), D-14
  DEOSNEWS, D-15
  Inside Technology Training, D-15
  Unofficial Guide to Distance Learning
    (Turlington), D-15

• *Q* •

quality of education, 47–49
questions, asking, 182

• *R* •

RAM, 71
rapid site switching, 182
RealPlayer, 77, D-17
recommendations, 254

references, 126
refunds, 134
Regents College Credit Bank, 124
registration, 129
  adding courses, 132–133
  changing courses, 132–133
  courses, choosing, 129–132
  dropping courses, 132–133
remote learning. *See* distance learning
reputation of school, 44
research, 35. *See also* online research
  directories, 36
  school catalogs, 41
  school sites, 40
ResearchPaper, D-12
resources for students, 168–169
respect for others' time online, 276
resume, 254, 256
Rochester Institute of Technology, D-5
Roget's Thesaurus, D-12
ROM, 71
rush hour, online, 201

• S •

San Diego State University, D-6
SATs, 122
scanner, 86
scholarships, 63–64
school contacts, 143–144
school fees, 133
school resources
  alumni connections, 251
  career fairs, 251
  career workshops, 251
  employer services, 251
  job search tools, 250
  Web sites, 251
school sites, 40
screen reader programs, 100–101

search engines, 205–208
self-assessment, 169–170
self-directed learners, 23
self-paced courses, 163–166, 168–170
  books online, 228
  built-in help system, 237
  e-mail support, 237
  exercises, 236
  games, 228
  help, 237
  interactive courses, 228
  matching items in tests, 233
  multimedia and, 234–235
  multimedia courses, 228
  multiple choice questions, 232
  navigation of, 229–231
  overview, 227, 229
  phone support, 237
  practicing, 236
  procedures tests, 232
  scoring tests, 234
  types of, 228
services
  discounts, student, 146–147
  guidance, 147
  library, 145–146
  overview, 145
  support services, 147
Shockwave, 77
ShowSounds, 95
small group interaction, 136–137
SmartPlanet, D-23
software as class supplies, 141–142
software download sites
  Flash, D-17
  NetMeeting, D-17
  RealPlayer, D-17
  Stuffit, D-18
  Tucows, D-18
  Winzip, D-18

software requirements, 78
  databases, 80
  presentation, 80
  spreadsheets, 80
  word processing, 78, 80
sound card, 72
SoundSentry, 95
South Africa, 13
Southern Association of Colleges and
    Schools, 52
spam, 276
speech recognition software, 98–99
spreadsheet software, 80
StickyKeys, 95
student-driven learning, 19
StudentOnline, D-12
study habits
  deadlines, assignment, 202–203
  time managment, 200
  weekly study plan, 201–202
Stuffit, D-18
supplies, 137
  checklist for, 144
  contact information, 143–144
  ordering, 144
  printed information, 138
  software, 141–142
  textbooks, 138–141
support services, 147
syllabus, viewing, 155–156
synchronous communication, 17, 157

• T •

tax credit for education, 65
technical and professional schools, 31
  American College of Prehospital
    Medicine, D-18
  American College Testing
    Program, D-20
  American Institute for Computer
    Sciences, D-18
  California College for Health Sciences,
    D-19
  College Entrance Examination
    Board, D-20
  College for Financial Planning, D-19
  Educational Testing Service, D-20
  Hospitality Training Center, D-19
  Minneapolis Community and Technical
    College, D-19
  Test of English as a Foreign
    Language, D-20
technical skills, 14
technical support, 87–89
technological advances, 17, 19
technology requirements, 70
Test of English as a Foreign Language,
    123, D-20
testing
  attitude and approach during, 223
  automated grading of tests, 216
  essay writing, 224
  grading tests, 218–219
  language clues, 224
  matching items in self-paced
    courses, 233
  motivation of learner and, 216
  multiple choice questions, 223
  overview, 215
  poor test grades, 225
  proctored exams, 219–220
  scoring for self-paced courses, 234
  techniques for taking tests, 221–222
  time limits for, 218
  tips for, 221–225
  types of, 216–217
Text Only file format, 213
textbooks, 138–141
Textbooksatcost, D-21
THINQ, D-23

third-party vendors, training with, 245
Thomas Edison State College Credit Bank, 124
threaded discussions, 156–157
time commitment, 21–22
time differences, international students observing, 271–272
time management, 200
time needed to complete degree/certificate, 23
ToggleKeys, 95
Trace Center, University of Wisconsin, D-15
transcripts, 253
TTY system, 104
Tucows, D-18
tuition, 57
  online payment, 134
  refunds, 134
  reimbursement by employers, 60–61
  school fees, 133
two-way audio and video, 181

• U •

UNext, 265
University Access, D-23
University of California at Berkeley, D-6, 262
University of London, 13
University of Maryland, D-6
University of Phoenix Online, D-6
University of South Africa, 13, D-7, 268
University of Washington, 152, D-7, 266
University of Wisconsin, D-7, 262
Unofficial Guide to Distance Learning (Turlington), 14, 36, 58, D-15

• V •

VCR, 86
ViaVoice, 99
video cards, 72
Videoconference, D-9
videoconferencing, 87, 177
  attending, 178–179
  cybercasts, 180
  desktop, 178–179
  etiquette, 181–182
  facility-based, 178
  group videoconferences, 180
  NetMeeting, 180
  point-to-point connections, 180
  two-way audio and video, 181
Videoconferencing for Learning, D-9
videotapes, 111–112
Virtual University, 16, D-13
VoiceXpress Professional, 99

• W •

WBT materials, 242
Web browsers, 72, 83
Web navigation, 208
Web-based learning. *See* distance learning
weekly study plan, 201–202
Western Association of Schools and Colleges, 52
Western Governor's University, D-7
Windows Media Player, 77
WinZip, 210–213, D-18
Word, 78
word processing software, 78, 80
word processor as class supplies, 142
WordPerfect, 78
WordPro, 78

work-study programs, 64
workgroups, 195, 247
World Lecture Hall, D-8
World Wide Web Consortium, 92
wrists, stress to, 116
writing, 187
  improving, 188
  mechanics, 188
  process for, 190
  style, 189

• •

youachieve, D-23

• Z •

zipping files, 209–213
ZoomText Xtra, 101

Notes

Notes

Notes

Notes

Notes

Notes

Notes

Notes

Discover Dummies Online!

The Dummies Web Site is your fun and friendly online resource for the latest information about *For Dummies*® books and your favorite topics. The Web site is the place to communicate with us, exchange ideas with other *For Dummies* readers, chat with authors, and have fun!

Ten Fun and Useful Things You Can Do at www.dummies.com

1. Win free *For Dummies* books and more!
2. Register your book and be entered in a prize drawing.
3. Meet your favorite authors through the IDG Books Worldwide Author Chat Series.
4. Exchange helpful information with other *For Dummies* readers.
5. Discover other great *For Dummies* books you must have!
6. Purchase Dummieswear® exclusively from our Web site.
7. Buy *For Dummies* books online.
8. Talk to us. Make comments, ask questions, get answers!
9. Download free software.
10. Find additional useful resources from authors.

Link directly to these ten fun and useful things at
http://www.dummies.com/10useful

For other technology titles from IDG Books Worldwide, go to
www.idgbooks.com

Not on the Web yet? It's easy to get started with *Dummies 101*®: *The Internet For Windows*® *98* or *The Internet For Dummies*® at local retailers everywhere.

Find other *For Dummies* books on these topics:
Business • Career • Databases • Food & Beverage • Games • Gardening • Graphics • Hardware
Health & Fitness • Internet and the World Wide Web • Networking • Office Suites
Operating Systems • Personal Finance • Pets • Programming • Recreation • Sports
Spreadsheets • Teacher Resources • Test Prep • Word Processing

IDG BOOKS WORLDWIDE BOOK REGISTRATION

Register This Book and Win!

We want to hear from you!

Visit **http://my2cents.dummies.com** to register this book and tell us how you liked it!

- Get entered in our monthly prize giveaway.
- Give us feedback about this book — tell us what you like best, what you like least, or maybe what you'd like to ask the author and us to change!
- Let us know any other *For Dummies*® topics that interest you.

Your feedback helps us determine what books to publish, tells us what coverage to add as we revise our books, and lets us know whether we're meeting your needs as a *For Dummies* reader. You're our most valuable resource, and what you have to say is important to us!

Not on the Web yet? It's easy to get started with *Dummies 101*®: *The Internet For Windows*® *98* or *The Internet For Dummies*® at local retailers everywhere.

Or let us know what you think by sending us a letter at the following address:

For Dummies Book Registration
Dummies Press
10475 Crosspoint Blvd.
Indianapolis, IN 46256

™

FOR DUMMIES

BESTSELLING
BOOK SERIES